Teacher's Book

A RESOURCE FOR PLANNING AND TEACHING

Level 6 Quest

Introductory Selection: **Summer School**

Theme 1   **Survival!**

Theme 2   **In Search of the Real Me**

Theme 3   **Unwrapping Ancient Mysteries**

Theme 4   **Imagination at Work**

Theme 5   **Finding Common Ground**

Theme 6   **Ocean Quest**

Senior Authors

J. David Cooper
John J. Pikulski

Authors

Kathryn H. Au
Margarita Calderón
Jacqueline C. Comas
Marjorie Y. Lipson
J. Sabrina Mims
Susan E. Page
Sheila W. Valencia
MaryEllen Vogt

Consultants

Dolores Malcolm
Tina Saldivar
Shane Templeton

INVITATIONS TO LITERACY

Houghton Mifflin Company • Boston

Atlanta • Dallas • Geneva, Illinois • Palo Alto • Princeton

Literature Reviewers

Librarians: **Consuelo Harris,** Public Library of Cincinnati, Cincinnati, Ohio; **Sarah Jones,** Elko County Library, Elko, Nevada; **Maeve Visser Knoth,** Cambridge Public Library, Cambridge, Massachusetts; **Valerie Lennox,** Highlands Branch Library, Jacksonville, Florida; **Margaret Miles,** Central Library, Sacramento, California; **Danilta Nichols,** Fordham Library, New York, New York; **Patricia O'Malley,** Hartford Public Library, Hartford, Connecticut; **Rob Reid,** L.E. Phillips Memorial Public Library, Eau Claire, Wisconsin; **Mary Calletto Rife,** Kalamazoo Public Library, Kalamazoo, Michigan

Teachers: **Sylvia Brown,** Lawrence Middle School, Lawrence, New York; **Anya Cronin,** Virgil Middle School, Los Angeles, California; **Terry Hejl,** Orange Grove Elementary School, Gulfport, Mississippi; **Joseph Lavizzo,** Sbarbaro School, Chicago, Illinois; **R. Suzanne Mercer,** C.E. Williams Middle School, Charleston, South Carolina; **Jan L. Robertson,** Robert Gray Middle School, Tacoma, Washington; **Judy Rosenbloom,** Lawrence Middle School, Lawrence, New York

Program Reviewers

Anya Cronin, Virgil Middle School, Los Angeles, California; **Sherry Krause,** Riebli Elementary School, Santa Rosa, California; **Kay Lustgarten,** West Little River Elementary School, Miami, Florida; **Toby C. Malin,** Martha Washington School, Philadelphia, Pennsylvania; **R. Suzanne Mercer,** C.E. Williams Middle School, Charleston, South Carolina; **Patricia Olsen,** Memorial Middle School, Las Vegas, New Mexico; **Judy Rosenbloom,** Lawrence Middle School, Lawrence, New York; **Judy Velasquez,** Healdsburg Elementary School, Healdsburg, California

Be a Writer Feature

Special thanks to the following teachers whose students' compositions are included in the Be a Writer features in this level: **Julie Welch,** Kane School, Lawrence, Massachusetts; **Joyce Hansen,** Charles R. Drew Intermediate School 148, Bronx, New York; **Miki Hayes,** Kamehameha Schools, Honolulu, Hawaii; **Cathi Elsbree,** Gertrude Scott Smith School, Aurora, Illinois; **Jeanne Duell,** St. Luke School, Beavercreek, Ohio; **Deborah Broccoli,** Luis Muñoz Marín School, Bridgeport, Connecticut

Credits

Cover photography by Tony Scarpetta

Photography:

Tracey Wheeler Studio
p. 332D, 332G, 332H, 345K, 357J, 357K, 357L, 357M, 385K, 385M, 396L, 396M, 396N, 396O, 419K, 419N, 419M

Tony Scarpetta Studio
p. 345K, 385K

Banta Digital Group
p. 330A, 331A, 332A, 332B, 332C, 332D, 333A, 345K, 357K, 357L, 357M, 357N, 363A, 385K, 385M, 389A, 396M, 396N, 396O, 403A, 419L, 419M

Photo Courtesy of Norton Juster, p. 333A; Photo by Tara Turner. Courtesy of Little, Brown and Company, p. 363A; Photo Courtesy of Betsy Byars, p. 389A; Arthur Gloor/Animals Animals, p. 396N; Paul Freed/Animals Animals, p. 396N; Photo Courtesy of Holiday House, p. 403A

Acknowledgments

Special thanks to David E. Freeman and Yvonne S. Freeman for their contribution to the development of the instructional support for students acquiring English.

Printed in U.S.A.

ISBN: 0-395-79597-4

23456789-B-99 98 97

IMAGINATION
AT
WORK

An Iron Giant Rises

While it was under construction, the 984-foot-high tower designed by Gustave Eiffel for the 1889 Paris Universal Exposition inevitably attracted sightseers and artists, who recorded its progress with engravings such as these. For two years workmen labored to erect the colossus, planting masonry piers 40 feet into the earth and joining 12,000 iron girders with two and a half million rivets. It was the world's tallest structure until 1930 when New York's 1,046-foot Chrysler Building superseded it.

Sightseers inspect one of the tower's half-finished foundations of big stone blocks.

The unfinished bulk of the structure looms above men building exhibition halls.

The completed tower proudly flies the f

Table of Contents

THEME: Imagination at Work

Bibliography
Books for Independent Reading

 ⭐ Multicultural

 🎵 Science/Health

 📦 Math

 🌐 Social Studies

 🎸 Music

 🎨 Art

VERY EASY

The Wonderful Towers of Watts
by Patricia Zelver
Tambourine 1994 (32p)
Simon Rodia created three towering monuments in a Los Angeles neighborhood.

Beethoven Lives Upstairs
by Barbara Nichol
Orchard 1994 (48p)
Ten-year-old Christoph writes to his uncle about the "madman" who has moved into their house.

Catwings
by Ursula Le Guin
Orchard 1988 (48p) Scholastic 1992 paper
Four young cats with wings leave their home in search of safety and kind humans.

Linnea in Monet's Garden
by Christina Björk
Farrar 1987 (56p)
Linnea explores Impressionism and the works of Monet and Manet.

Great Black Heroes: Five Outstanding Inventors
by Wade Hudson
Scholastic 1995 (48p)
Stories about Garrett Morgan, Elijah McCoy, Jan Matzeliger, Madame C. J. Walker, and Granville Woods.

Diego
by Jeanette and Jonah Winter
Knopf 1994 (40p) also paper
The life and work of muralist Diego Rivera. **Text in English and Spanish.**

EASY

Talking with Artists
by Pat Cummings
Bradbury 1992 (96p)
The author/artist interviews other children's book illustrators.

The Wizard of Oz
by L. Frank Baum
Puffin 1983 (192p) other editions
Dorothy tries to make her way back to Kansas from the Land of Oz.
Available in Spanish as El mago de Oz.

Oh, the Places He Went: A Story about Dr. Seuss
by Maryann N. Weidt
Carolrhoda 1994 (64p)
The life story of the author of some of literature's most memorable books and characters.

The Librarian Who Measured the Earth
by Kathryn Lasky
Little 1994 (48p)
The story of Eratosthenes, a curious boy who grew up to write the first geography book.

Starting Home: The Story of Horace Pippin, Painter
by Mary E. Lyons
Macmillan 1993 (48p)
The life story of a self-taught African American folk artist.

The Picture History of Great Inventors
by Gillian Clements
Knopf 1994 (80p)
A decade-by-decade look at the world's great inventors and their inventions.

The Master Violin Maker
by Paul Fleisher
Houghton 1993 (32p)
Artisan John Larrimore creates a violin using tools and methods hundreds of years old.

AVERAGE

The Will and the Way: Paul R. Williams, Architect
by Karen E. Hudson
Rizzoli 1994 (64p)
The author's grandfather designed over 3000 buildings around the world, including homes of Beverly Hills movie stars.

Incredible Cross-Sections
by Richard Platt
Knopf 1992 (32p)
Cross-section drawings of some of the world's most fascinating and ingenious structures. **Available in Spanish as Del interior de las cosas.**

Bill Peet: An Autobiography
by Bill Peet
Houghton 1989 (192p)
The author's life story, including his years with the Disney Studio.

Forest
by Janet Taylor Lisle
Orchard 1993 (160p)
Twelve-year-old Amber tries to make peace between an intelligent community of squirrels and human society.

Frank Lloyd Wright for Kids
by Kathleen Thorne-Thomsen
Independent Publishers 1994 (144p)
The life and work of the famed architect and designer.

The Ink-Keeper's Apprentice
by Allen Say
Houghton 1994 (192p)
The author writes about his early life as an apprentice to a famous cartoonist.

Invention
by Lionel Bender
Knopf 1991 (64p)
The evolution of tools devised by humans, from the abacus to the silicon chip. **Available in Spanish as Los inventos.**

The Bellmaker
by Brian Jacques
Philomel 1995 (352p)
In the latest of the Redwall series, Joseph the Bellmaker is concerned for the safety of his daughter Mariel.

Georgia O'Keeffe
by Robyn Montana Turner
Little 1991 (32p) also paper
The life of artist Georgia O'Keeffe, famous for her paintings of the Southwest.

The Neverending Story
by Michael Ende
Puffin 1993 (448p) paper
Bastian Balthazar Bux becomes a hero in the enchanted world of Fantasia. **Available in Spanish as La historia interminable**

Patrick DesJarlait: Conversations with a Native American Artist
as recorded by Neva Williams
Runestone 1995 (56p)
The author's recorded interviews with the late Chippewa artist.

The Mennyms
by Sylvia Waugh
Greenwillow 1994 (216p)
The Mennym family have a good reason to remain aloof from their neighbors.

Afternoon of the Elves
by Janet Taylor Lisle
Orchard 1989 (128p) Apple 1991 paper
Sarah-Kate's new friend Hillary thinks she has found an elf village in her backyard.

Dorothea Lange
by Robyn Montana Turner
Little 1994 (32p)
The story of the photographer famous for her Depression-era photographs.

Tom's Midnight Garden
by Philippa Pearce
Harper 1959 (240p) also paper
In this classic, Tom slips into the midnight garden when the clock strikes thirteen.

Jazz, My Music, My People
by Morgan Monceaux
Knopf 1994 (64p)
Through his paintings, the author celebrates the men and women of jazz.

Flying Machines
by Andrew Nahun
Knopf 1990 (64p)
Our determination to fly, from Icarus to Leonardo to modern jets.
Available in Spanish as Máquinas voladoras.

Starting from Home: A Writer's Beginnings
by Milton Meltzer
Puffin 1991 (160p)
The children's author discusses his life and writing.

Lives of the Musicians: Good Times, Bad Times (and What the Neighbors Thought)
by Kathleen Krull
Harcourt 1993 (96p)
Informative and amusing insights into the lives of several musicians, including Beethoven and Mozart.

The Willows in Winter
by William Horwood
St. Martin's 1994 (304p)
The author takes Grahame's characters from *The Wind in the Willows* on new adventures.

A Wrinkle in Time
by Madeline L'Engle
Farrar 1962 (224p) Dell 1976 paper
Charles and Meg's search for their father leads them to the planet of Camazotz. **Available in Spanish as Una arruga en el tiempo.**

Bridge to Terabithia
by Katherine Paterson
Harper 1977 (144p) also paper
In this classic, two lonely children become friends before tragedy strikes. **Available in Spanish as Un puento hasta Terabithia.**

The Westing Game
by Ellen Raskin
Dutton 1978 (192p) Puffin 1992 paper
An eccentric millionaire leaves a puzzling will in this perennial children's favorite.

Books for Teacher Read Aloud

The Wind in the Willows
by Kenneth Grahame
Scribner's 1983 (256p) many paper editions
The humorous adventures of Water Rat, Mole, Toad, and Badger.
Available in Spanish as El viento en los sauces.

The Voyage of the *Dawn Treader*
by C. S. Lewis
Macmillan 1988 (224p) also paper
Through a painting, Edmund and Lucy and their cousin Eustace enter the kingdom of Narnia. **Available in Spanish as El viaje del Amanecer.**

The Twenty-One Balloons
by William Pène du Bois
Viking 1947 (192p) many paper editions
Professor Sherman leaves San Francisco in a balloon in 1883, hoping to be the first man to cross the Pacific. **Available in Spanish as Los 21 globos.**

Technology Resources

Software

Great Start™ Macintosh or Windows CD-ROM software. Includes story summaries, background building, and vocabulary support for each selection in the theme. Houghton Mifflin Company.

Student Writing Center™ Macintosh or Windows software. The Learning Company®.

Channel R.E.A.D. Videodiscs "The Ordinary Princess," "The Case of the Missing Mystery Writer," and "Heroes of the Marsh." Houghton Mifflin Company.

Internet See the Houghton Mifflin Internet resources for additional bibliographic entries and theme-related activities.

Teacher's Resource Disk Macintosh or Windows software. Houghton Mifflin Company.

Video Cassettes

Bill Peet in His Studio Houghton

The Phantom Tollbooth by Norton Juster. MGM/UA Home Video

The Secret Garden by Frances Hodgson Burnett. Listening Library

Diego by Jeanette and Jonah Winter. Media Basics Available also in Spanish.

The Neverending Story by Michael Ende. Listening Library

Audio Cassettes

A Wrinkle in Time by Madeline L'Engle. Listening Library

The Twenty-One Balloons by William Pène du Bois. Live Oak Media

Tom's Midnight Garden by Philippa Pearce. Listening Library

Audio Tapes for Imagination at Work. Houghton Mifflin Company.

AV addresses are on page H9–H10.

Theme at a Glance

Selections	Reading		Writing and Language Arts	
	Comprehension Skills and Strategies	Word Skills and Strategies	Responding	Writing
The Phantom Tollbooth	Making Judgments, 337 Genre: Fantasy, 339 ✔ Fantasy/Realism, 343, 357A–357B Reading Strategies, 336, 342, 344, 348, 350	✔ Homophones, 357E; Decoding Longer Words, 357F	Personal Response, 356 Literature Discussion, 356 Selection Connections, 356 Home Connection, 357	Word Play, 353 Writing Instructions, 357C
Meet George Lucas: Setting the Scene for Adventure	Genre: Interview, 361		Discussion, 362	
Faith Ringgold	Making Inferences, 367 ✔ Noting Details, 369, 385A–385B Compare and Contrast, 371 Text Organization, 373 Genre: Biography, 379 Reading Strategies, 364, 366, 370, 374, 376	✔ Word Roots graph and ven, 385E; Dictionary: Word Forms, 385F	Personal Response, 384 Literature Discussion, 384 Selection Connections, 384 Home Connection, 385	Time and Sequence, 365 Writing a Biographical Sketch, 385C
A Gallery of Ideas				Journal, 387; Writing as Art; Poetry, 389
The Moon and I	Noting Details, 391 ✔ Author's Viewpoint, 393, 396B–396C Reading Strategies, 392, 394	✔ Word Roots scrib/script and port, 396F; Dictionary: Homographs, 396G	Personal Response, 396 Literature Discussion, 396A Selection Connections, 396 Home Connection, 396	How to Start, 395 ✔ Elaborating with Adjectives, 396D
Summer's Bounty	Concrete Poetry, 397		Poetry Response, 396P	
Reading-Writing Workshop Be a Writer: Imagination Changes My World			Discussing the Model, 399	Minilessons: Keeping the Focus, 399A; Using Examples, 399B; Openings and Closings, 399C
Savion Glover: Making the Rules				Writing, 403
The Wright Brothers	Making Judgments, 407 ✔ Text Organization, 411, 419A–419B Problem Solving/Decision Making, 413; Genre: Narrative Nonfiction, 415; Author's Viewpoint, 417 Reading Strategies, 406, 410, 414	✔ Absorbed Prefixes, 419E; Think About Words, 419F	Personal Response, 418 Literature Discussion, 418 Selection Connections, 418 Home Connection, 418	Using Primary Sources, 409 Answering an Essay Question, 419C
On Top				
The Way Things Work			Discussion, 422, 424	
The New Wave in Feature Animation				

✔ *Indicates Tested Skills.* See page 332F for assessment options.

Theme Concept

Imagination makes art and technology possible.

Pacing

This theme is designed to take 4 to 6 weeks, depending on your students' needs.

Multi-Age Classroom

Related theme from:
Grade 5–Journey to Adventure!

Cross-Curricular

Spelling	Grammar, Usage, and Mechanics	Listening and Speaking	Viewing	Study Skills	Content Area
✔ Plurals of Words Ending with *f*, 357H	✔ Principal Parts of Regular and Irregular Verbs, 357I Daily Language Practice, 357J	Reader's Theater, 357K Debate: The Watchdogs Versus the Lethargarians, 357K	Films, Fantasy, and Special Effects, 357L Make a Flip Book, 357L		**Science:** Biological Time, 357M **Social Studies:** The Time of Your Life, 357M; What Time Is It Where You Are?, 357N; Old Timers, 357N
		Interview, 363	Home Connection, 363		Technology, Music, Social Studies, 363
✔ Plurals of Words Ending with *o*, 385H	✔ Adjectives, 385I Daily Language Practice, 385J	Dialect, 385K Listening to Jazz and Blues, 385K	Ringgold's Books, 385L Looking at Quilts, 385L	✔ Index, 385N, H2	**Art:** Quilt Making, 385M **Social Studies:** The Harlem Renaissance, 385M **Math:** Symmetry, 385N **Careers:** Artists Everywhere!, 385N
					Math, Art, 389
✔ Prefixes *dis-*, *mis-*, and *ex-*, 396I	✔ Comparing with Adjectives, 396J Daily Language Practice, 396K	Visit from an Author, 396L How-to Writing Books, 396L	Symbols and Signs, 396M Snakes Alive!, 396M		**Science:** Snake Take, 396N; Why Moon?, 396N **Careers:** Books: Idea to Sale, 396O; Be a Publisher!, 396O
					Social Studies, Music/Dance, 403
✔ Prefixes *per-*, *pre-*, and *pro-*, 419H	✔ Avoiding Double Negatives, 419I Daily Language Practice, 419J	Invention Exposition, 419K Adventure in Air, 419K Breaking the News, 419K	Model Planes, 419L Video View, 419L Pictures and Information About Early Flight, 419L	K-W-L, 405, H3 Almanac, 419N, H4	**Science:** On Wings, 419M **Social Studies:** The First Flights, 419M; The Turn of the Century, 419N; Great Inventions, 419N
				Using Diagrams, 423, H5	Science, Social Studies, Music, Art, 425
		Home Connection, 429			Technology, Science, Drama, Art, 429

Meeting Individual Needs

Performance Standards

During this theme, all students will learn to

- recognize how imagination fuels art, technology
- write an essay about using the imagination
- apply effective reading strategies
- distinguish fantasy from reality
- analyze how writers use details and word play
- understand the components of author's viewpoint
- appreciate various ways authors organize text
- present information using diagrams
- exercise and stimulate their own imaginations

Key to Meeting Individual Needs

 Students Acquiring English

Activities and notes throughout the lesson plans offer strategies to help students understand the selections and lessons.

 Challenge

Challenge activities and notes throughout the lesson plans suggest additional activities to stimulate critical and creative thinking.

 **Extra Support**

Activities and notes throughout the lesson plans offer additional strategies to help students succeed in learning.

Managing Instruction

Independent Work: Free Writing

Encourage students to pursue independent writing activities. Begin by suggesting one reason to write, such as remembering an important event. Gradually introduce other reasons: describing a book, film, or piece of art; corresponding with friends; working out problems; making plans for the future. Free writing is not corrected, but samples can be dated and saved to show growth over time or as "seeds" for future full-length writing projects.

For further information on this and any other Managing Instruction topics, see the *Professional Development Handbook*.

Students Acquiring English	Challenge	Extra Support
• **Understand Key Concepts** Support in Advance suggestions draw on students' background to help them focus on each selection and relate to the key concepts in the theme "Imagination at Work."	• **Perform at Advanced Levels** Challenge activities provide ideas for research as well as creative ventures that students can pursue to exercise their imaginations.	• **Enhance Self-Confidence** Support in Advance activities prepare students to learn challenging content in the theme by validating what students already know about fantasy, artistic expression, symbols, and technological innovation.
• **Nonverbal Communication** This theme encourages and models a variety of nonverbal forms of expression: visual art, music, dance, film, technological invention.	• **Art/Technical Vocabulary** This theme offers many new words from the worlds of art and technology that will expand vocabulary and enhance understanding of word histories.	• **Increase Instructional Time** Extra Support suggestions within the selection increase instructional time and focus student learning or develop reading skills and vocabulary.
• **Multicultural Awareness** Encourage students to contribute their unique cultural perspectives to whole-class activities such as Inventors' Day in Celebrating the Theme.	• **Complex Thinking Skills** Activities in this theme require students to analyze or synthesize, make judgments and inferences, analyze and contrast authors' viewpoints, and compare and contrast.	• **Reading Competence** Suggestions for rereading, reading with a partner, oral reading, and dramatization will help students become competent.

Additional Resources

Language Support
Translations of selection summaries in Chinese, Hmong, Khmer, and Vietnamese. *Teacher's Booklet* provides instructional support in English.

Students Acquiring English Handbook
Provides general guidelines, as well as strategies and additional instruction for students acquiring English.

Extra Support Handbook
Includes additional theme, skill, and language support for literature in the program plus strategies for increasing reading fluency and self-selected reading and writing.

 Great Start CD-ROM Software
Extra support in English and Spanish.

Writing Software
The Learning Company's new elementary writing center software.

Channel R.E.A.D. Videodiscs
- "The Ordinary Princess"
- "The Case of the Missing Mystery Writer"
- "Heroes of the Marsh" For students requiring extra support.

Planning for Assessment

Informal Assessment

Informal Assessment Checklist

- Reading and Responding
- Fantasy/Realism, Noting Details, Author's Viewpoint, Text Organization
- Elaborating with Adjectives
- Word Skills and Strategies
- Grammar
- Listening and Speaking
- Attitudes and Habits

Literacy Activity Book

- Selection Connections, pp. 147–148
- Comprehension Check, pp. 150, 160, 171, 184
- Comprehension Skills, pp. 151, 161, 172, 185
- Writing Skills, pp. 152, 162, 173, 186
- Word Skills, pp. 153, 163, 174, 187

Reading-Writing Workshop

- Writing an Essay, pp. 398–399F
- Scoring Rubric, p. 399F

Performance Assessment

- Planning an Invention, p. 429A
- Scoring Rubric, p. 429A

Retellings—Oral/Written

- *Teacher's Assessment Handbook*

Formal Assessment

Integrated Theme Test

Test applies the following theme skills to a new reading selection:

- Reading Strategies
- Fantasy/Realism, Noting Details, Author's Viewpoint, Text Organization
- Word Skills and Strategies
- Writing Fluency
- Grammar and Spelling (optional)
- Self-Assessment

Theme Skills Test

- Fantasy/Realism, Noting Details, Author's Viewpoint, Text Organization
- Homophones, Word Roots *graph, ven, scrib/script, port*
- Writing Skills
- Study Skills
- Spelling
- Grammar

Benchmark Progress Test

- Give a Benchmark Progress Test two or three times a year to measure student growth in reading and writing.

Managing Assessment

Monitoring Independent Work

Question: How can I monitor student's independent reading and writing?
Answer: Try these tips:

- For monitoring reading, use a book log that includes a place for students to write the date, what they are reading, and a few comments. Have students use their logs to share favorite books or to do a class chart of types of books they are reading.

- Use book logs for a two-week period several times during the year rather than all year long. Also, have students design new book logs for each two-week period.

- Use students' writing folders, portfolios, or journals to monitor independent writing. Students may want to keep lists of their writing projects. Have them share their lists with classmates and bring them to their writing conferences with you.

- Focus on a few students each time you have independent reading and writing. Notice students who are able to stick with their reading and writing and those who need extra support. Record your observations on the Informal Assessment Checklist.

For more information on this and other topics, see the *Teacher's Assessment Handbook*.

Portfolio Opportunity

The portfolio icon signals portfolio opportunities throughout the theme.

Additional portfolio tips:

- Helping Students Make Selections for the Portfolio, p. 429B
- Evaluating Oral Language, p. 429B

Launching the Theme

Literacy Activity Book, p. 148

Imagination at Work

How does the imagination work? After reading each selection, fill in the chart to show what journeys and discoveries you can find in the imagination at work.

	The Moon and I	The Wright Brothers
How was the imagination at work here?		
What inspires the mind to be creative?		

Literacy Activity Book, p. 147

Imagination at Work

How does the imagination work? After reading each selection, fill in the chart below and on the next page to show what journeys and discoveries you can find in the imagination at work.

	The Phantom Tollbooth	Faith Ringgold
How was the imagination at work here?		
What inspires the mind to be creative?		
What sort of discovery or journey did the imagination bring about?		
What is the connection between creativity and invention?		

Imagination at Work 147

Selection Connections

Ask students to look at the chart on *Literacy Activity Book* pages 147–148. Note that students will return to this chart after reading each selection and after completing the theme.

See the Houghton Mifflin **Internet** resources for additional activities.

See the **Teacher's Resource Disk** for theme-related support material.

INTERACTIVE LEARNING

Theme Concept   Imagination makes art and technology possible.

Setting the Scene

Write these phrases on the board:

- a symphony
- a public sculpture
- an electric fly swatter
- a surgeon's laser scalpel
- a novel
- computer-generated cartoons

See if students can figure out what these things have in common. (If they have difficulty, pose questions such as, Where do they come from? How do they begin? What makes them possible?) Once they've agreed on a common idea, ask them to add at least six more items to the list. (Samples: the light bulb, an abstract painting, a ballet, a new TV series)

Interactive Bulletin Board

MEETING INDIVIDUAL NEEDS

Assemble a bulletin board or wall display of examples of how real people put their imaginations to work: writers, filmmakers, artists, inventors, innovators. Encourage students to bring in newspaper and magazine articles. Invite them to make original drawings and captions of people in history who have used their imaginations to create something new. From time to time, observe the items displayed and talk about similarities and differences.

Choices for Projects

Making Kites

Cooperative Learning

Have pairs of students imagine, create, and fly their own diamond-shaped kites. Suggest that they write words on their kites as well as use colors and designs. Have a kite-flying day in which students try out their creations and let their imaginations soar!

Materials

- wooden sticks or dowels: 1/8" in diameter
- glue
- paper
- acrylic paints
- string, cord, or fishing line

1 Help students cut two sticks or dowels 28" and 34". Have them join the sticks 8" from the top of the longer piece and in the middle of the shorter. Help them cut notches on each end to accommodate a string guideline.

2 Cut a piece of paper in the exact shape of the diamond frame but with a 1/2" margin all around. The margin will be folded over the string and glued down.

3 Paint the paper and then glue it around the frame with as few wrinkles as possible. Attach string to the intersection of the two pieces of frame.

Inventing Toys

Invite students to invent a new toy that will teach or stimulate children's imaginations. Suggest these categories:

- Toys About Colors
- Toys About Shapes
- Toys About Letters
- Toys About Animals
- Toys About Numbers
- Toys That Make Noise

Suggest using common items and soft, nontoxic materials such as paper, cloth, yarn, cardboard, or foam. They can present their inventions to the class, display them in your school library, or even donate them to a local day care facility or preschool.

Independent Reading and Writing

Plan time each day for independent reading and writing. For independent reading, provide books from the Bibliography on pages 332A–332B, or encourage students to read the Paperbacks Plus for this theme:

Easy reading: *A Young Painter: The Life and Painting of Wang Yani, China's Extraordinary Young Artist* by Zhensun Zheng and Alice Low

Average/challenging reading: *Tuck Everlasting* by Natalie Babbitt

For independent writing, encourage students to discover and develop their own activities. If they need help getting started, suggest activities on pages 357D, 385D, 396E, or 419D.

 See the Home/Community Connections Booklet for theme-related materials.

Portfolio Opportunity

- Save *Literacy Activity Book* pages 147–148 to show students' ability to compare and contrast selections.
- The Portfolio Opportunity icon highlights other portfolio opportunities throughout the theme.

SELECTION:

The Phantom Tollbooth

by Norton Juster

Other Books by the Author

Otter Nonsense

AS: A Surfeit of Similes

- **Best Books for Children**
- **George C. Stone Center for Children's Books Recognition of Merit**

Selection Summary

Milo is a boy who never knows what to do with himself. He finds life pointless and boring until the day he receives a mysterious package. The package contains a tollbooth, complete with a map and instructions. Milo assembles the tollbooth and sets off on a journey through an unfamiliar landscape. His first stop is at Expectations, "the place you must always go to before you get where you're going." Milo then takes a wrong turn and ends up in the Doldrums, where nothing ever happens and thinking is illegal. Luckily, a creature called the Watchdog explains that the way to get out of the Doldrums is to start thinking. The plan works, and Milo continues on his way.

Lesson Planning Guide

	Skill/Strategy Instruction	Meeting Individual Needs	Lesson Resources
1 **Introduce** *the* **Literature** *Pacing: 1 day*	**Preparing to Read and Write** Prior Knowledge/Building Background, 333C **Selection Vocabulary,** 333D • dejectedly • wistfully • expectations • procrastinating **Spelling Pretest,** 357H • leaves • puffs • roofs • loaves • lives • beliefs • halves • shelves • thieves • chiefs	**Support in Advance,** 333C **Other Choices for Building Background,** 333C **Students Acquiring English,** 333C **Spelling Challenge Words,** 357H • themselves • tariffs • kerchiefs • wharves • chefs	***Literacy Activity Book:*** Vocabulary, p. 149 **Transparencies:** Building Background, 4–1; Vocabulary, 4–2 **Great Start** CD-ROM software, "Imagination at Work" CD
2 **Interact** *with* **Literature** *Pacing: 1–3 days*	**Reading Strategies** Evaluate, 336, 342 Think About Words, 336, 344, 350 Predict/Infer, 336, 348 **Minilessons** Making Judgments, 337 Genre: Fantasy, 339 ✓ Fantasy/Realism, 343 Writer's Craft: Word Play, 353	**Choices for Reading,** 336 **Guided Reading,** 336, 340, 346, 354 **Students Acquiring English,** 336, 344, 347, 350, 352, 356 **Extra Support,** 339, 342, 345, 346, 349, 351, 353, 354 **Challenge,** 355	**Reading-Writing Workshop:** A Personal Essay, 398–399F ***Literacy Activity Book:*** Selection Connections, p. 147–148; Comprehension Check, p. 150 **Audio Tape** for Imagination at Work: *The Phantom Tollbooth* **Student Writing Center,** writing and publishing software
3 **Instruct** *and* **Integrate** *Pacing: 1–3 days*	✓ **Comprehension:** Fantasy/Realism, 357A **Writing:** Writing Instructions, 357C **Word Skills & Strategies** ✓ Homophones, 357E Decoding Longer Words, 357F **Building Vocabulary:** Vocabulary Activities, 357G ✓ **Spelling:** Plurals of Words Ending with *f,* 357H ✓ **Grammar:** Principal Parts of Regular and Irregular Verbs, 357I **Communication Activities:** Listening and Speaking, 357K; Viewing, 357L **Cross-Curricular Activities:** Science, Social Studies, 357M–357N	**Reteaching:** Fantasy/Realism, 357B **Activity Choices:** Write Instructions, Write a Post Card Home, Shared Writing: Write an Ad, 357D **Reteaching:** Homophones, 357F **Activity Choices:** Antonyms, Traffic Words, Prefixes *inter-, intro-, intra-,* 357G **Challenge Words Practice:** 357H **Reteaching:** Principal Parts of Verbs, Daily Language Practice, 357J **Activity Choices:** Listening and Speaking, 357K; Viewing, 357L **Activity Choices:** Science, Social Studies, 357M–357N	**Reading-Writing Workshop:** A Personal Essay, 398–399F **Transparencies:** Comprehension, 4–3, 4–4; Writing, 4–5; Grammar, 4–6 ***Literacy Activity Book:*** Comprehension, p. 151; Writing, p. 152; Word Skill, p. 153; Building Vocabulary, p. 154; Spelling, pp. 155–156; Grammar, pp. 157–158 **Audio Tape** for Imagination at Work: *The Phantom Tollbooth* **Channel R.E.A.D.** videodisc: "The Ordinary Princess" **Student Writing Center,** writing and publishing software

✓ *Indicates Tested Skills. See page 332F for assessment options.*

Introduce *the* Literature

Preparing to Read and Write

Support in Advance

Use this activity for students who need extra support before participating in the whole-class activity.

Picture the Pun Use the illustration of the watchdog on page 353 to define a play on words. Ask students what kind of story would have such a character. (*Fantasy* or *make-believe*).

Management Tip
Students can write in their journals about how they keep from being bored.

Students Acquiring English
Discuss the meaning of *phantom* and *tollbooth*.

INTERACTIVE LEARNING

Prior Knowledge/Building Background

Key Concept
Fantasy Versus Reality

First discuss the title *The Phantom Tollbooth* with the class. Then let students use word webs to brainstorm their definitions of *fantasy* and *reality*. Then display Transparency 4–1. Ask students to list fantasy stories that they have read, heard, or seen. Record their list on the transparency. Then have them develop another list that includes examples of realism, including realistic fiction, biography, and informational articles. For example, students might compare a *Star Trek* episode to a documentary on space flight.

Transparency 4–1

Get a Clue!

Story elements provide clues telling you if the story is a fantasy. You can identify a fantasy by the characters, setting, and events.

CHARACTERS
• traits are exaggerated
• possess unreal powers

SETTING
• may be futuristic
• may take place in another world
• may be in an imaginary land

EVENTS
• occur that would not be possible in real life

Think about stories you have read, heard, or seen. Are they based on fantasy or reality?

Fantasy	Reality

Great Start For students needing extra support with key concepts and vocabulary, use the "Imagination at Work" CD.

Other Choices for Building Background

Quick Writing

Challenge Ask students to imagine a land they might like to travel to. Give them five minutes to write a short fantasy, beginning with: *I knew we had arrived as soon as. . . .* Encourage students to write freestyle from the imagination. If there's time, have volunteers read their stories aloud.

Literary Circle

Extra Support Have students gather in small groups to share their favorite fairy tales and fantasy or science fiction stories, including comic books and cartoon shows. Invite students to describe the elements of fantasy that most interest them. Combine this discussion with a drawing activity. Students can re-create their stories in illustration or with sketches.

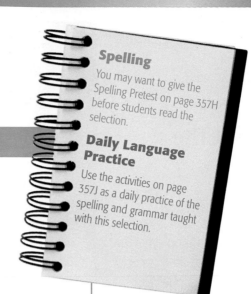

Spelling
You may want to give the Spelling Pretest on page 357H before students read the selection.

Daily Language Practice
Use the activities on page 357J as a daily practice of the spelling and grammar taught with this selection.

Selection Vocabulary

Key Words

dejectedly

wistfully

expectations

procrastinate

Display the top section of Transparency 4–2 and discuss the definitions of the vocabulary words. Ask volunteers to use the words in oral sentences. Then work with the class to complete the sentences on the rest of the transparency. Volunteers can write the appropriate vocabulary words in the blanks.

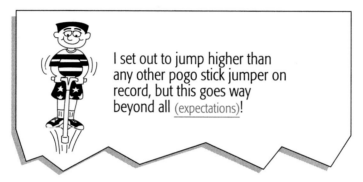

I set out to jump higher than any other pogo stick jumper on record, but this goes way beyond all (expectations)!

Vocabulary Practice Have students work independently or in pairs to complete page 149 of the *Literacy Activity Book.*

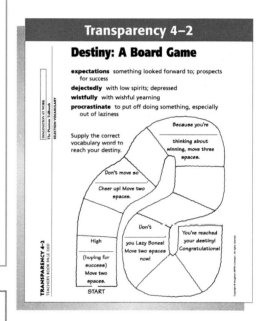

Transparency 4–2

Destiny: A Board Game

expectations something looked forward to; prospects for success

dejectedly with low spirits; depressed

wistfully with wishful yearning

procrastinate to put off doing something, especially out of laziness

Literature

Teacher FactFile

Mind Journey

Some students may be familiar with the journeys told in these books of fantasy:

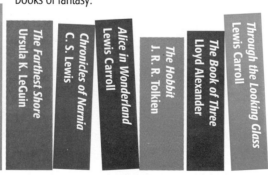

You might consider introducing your students to the most famous, certainly the oldest, fantasy quest, Homer's epic *Odyssey.*

Norton Juster is a master of puns and word play. You and your students might enjoy checking out *Otter Nonsense* (Morrow, 1994) and *As: A Surfeit of Similes* (Morrow, 1989).

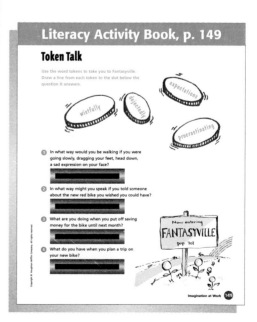

Literacy Activity Book, p. 149

Token Talk

Use the word token to take you to Fantasville. Draw a line from each token to the slot below the question it answers.

1. In what way would you be walking if you were going slowly, dragging your feet, head down, a sad expression on your face?

2. In what way might you speak if you told someone about the new red bike you wished you could have?

3. What are you doing when you put off saving money for the bike until next month?

4. What do you have when you plan a trip on your new bike?

Interact *with* **Literature**

More About the Author

Norton Juster

Norton Juster was born in Brooklyn, New York, in 1929. He trained as an architect and a city planner, and continues to practice architecture from his home in western Massachusetts. After publishing *The Phantom Tollbooth*, which made *The New York Times* Best Books list in 1961, Juster published several other children's books, including *The Dot and the Line* and *Alberic the Wise*. According to Juster, "Writing and architecture work well together; one acts like a relaxation from the other."

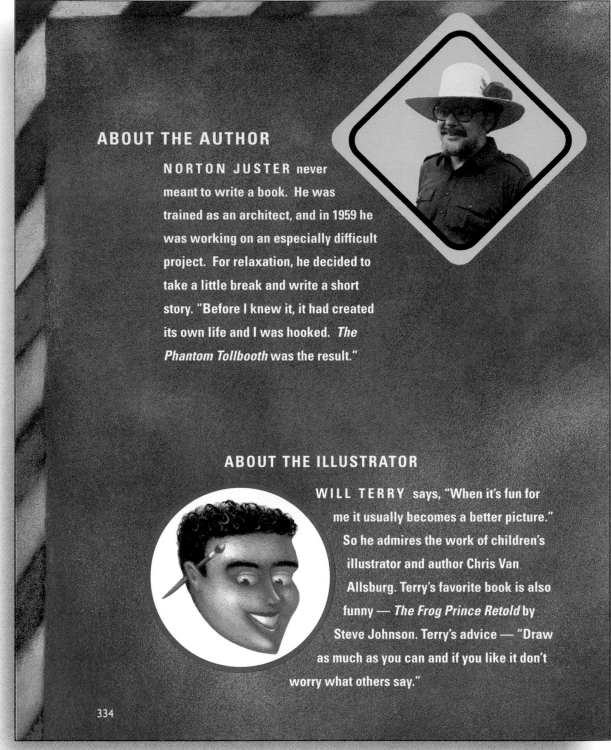

ABOUT THE AUTHOR

NORTON JUSTER never meant to write a book. He was trained as an architect, and in 1959 he was working on an especially difficult project. For relaxation, he decided to take a little break and write a short story. "Before I knew it, it had created its own life and I was hooked. *The Phantom Tollbooth* was the result."

ABOUT THE ILLUSTRATOR

WILL TERRY says, "When it's fun for me it usually becomes a better picture." So he admires the work of children's illustrator and author Chris Van Allsburg. Terry's favorite book is also funny — *The Frog Prince Retold* by Steve Johnson. Terry's advice — "Draw as much as you can and if you like it don't worry what others say."

334

The Phantom Tollbooth

MILO

BY NORTON JUSTER

There was once a boy named Milo who didn't know what to do with himself — not just sometimes, but always.

When he was in school he longed to be out, and when he was out he longed to be in. On the way he thought about coming home, and coming home he thought about going. Wherever he was he wished he were somewhere else, and when he got there he wondered why he'd bothered. Nothing really interested him — least of all the things that should have.

"It seems to me that almost everything is a waste of time," he remarked one day as he walked dejectedly home from school. "I can't see the point in learning to solve useless problems, or subtracting turnips from turnips, or knowing where Ethiopia is or how to spell February." And, since no one bothered to explain otherwise, he regarded the process of seeking knowledge as the greatest waste of time of all.

335

Interact *with* Literature

Reading Strategies

▶ **Evaluate**
Think About Words
Predict/Infer

Teacher Modeling Discuss how, as they read works of fantasy, strategic readers preview, predict, and pay attention to setting and events.

Think Aloud

What could a phantom tollbooth be used for? I will be sure to think about words as I read—are they silly or serious? Since this is a fantasy, I predict that extraordinary things are likely to happen. I'll have to monitor my reading to understand the events, and ask myself: Is it real, or is it fantasy?

Predicting/Purpose Setting

Ask students to predict what might happen to someone who travels through a phantom tollbooth.

Choices for Reading

Independent Reading	Cooperative Reading
Guided Reading	Teacher Read Aloud

Guided Reading

Have students read to the end of page 341. Use the questions on page 340 to check students' comprehension.

336

Quick REFERENCE

Students Acquiring English

Help students pronounce the *ph* sound. Compare the *ph* sound of the words *phantom* and *phonograph* (page 337) to the *p* sound in *punctuated*, *package*, and *opened*.

As he and his unhappy thoughts hurried along (for while he was never anxious to be where he was going, he liked to get there as quickly as possible) it seemed a great wonder that the world, which was so large, could sometimes feel so small and empty.

"And worst of all," he continued sadly, "there's nothing for me to do, nowhere I'd care to go, and hardly anything worth seeing." He punctuated this last thought with such a deep sigh that a house sparrow singing nearby stopped and rushed home to be with his family.

Without stopping or looking up, he rushed past the buildings and busy shops that lined the street and in a few minutes reached home — dashed through the lobby — hopped onto the elevator — two, three, four, five, six, seven, eight, and off again — opened the apartment door — rushed into his room — flopped dejectedly into a chair, and grumbled softly, "Another long afternoon."

He looked glumly at all the things he owned. The books that were too much trouble to read, the tools he'd never learned to use, the small electric automobile he hadn't driven in months — or was it years? — and the hundreds of other games and toys, and bats and balls, and bits and pieces scattered around him. And then, to one side of the room, just next to the phonograph, he noticed something he had certainly never seen before.

Who could possibly have left such an enormous package and such a strange one? For, while it was not quite square, it was definitely not round, and for its size it was larger than almost any other big package of smaller dimension that he'd ever seen.

Attached to one side was a bright-blue envelope which said simply:

"FOR MILO, WHO HAS PLENTY OF TIME."

337

M I N I L E S S O N

Making Judgments

REVIEW & MAINTAIN

Teach/Model

Encourage students to relate to the story by paying attention to and making judgments about what Milo says and does.

Think Aloud

This Milo character is really bored, but I think he might be boring too. After all, it seems to me that he doesn't put too much effort into doing anything to make his life more enjoyable—he doesn't take an active interest.

Practice/Apply

Have students think about Milo's statement on page 335, "It seems to me that almost everything is a waste of time." Ask them to make a judgment about Milo: What do they think of his attitude? Do they agree or disagree? Encourage students to tell how their own experiences shaped their judgment of Milo.

SKILL FINDER

| Full lesson/Reteaching, Theme 5 |
| Minilessons, p. 407; Theme 5 |

Interact
with
Literature

Of course, if you've ever gotten a surprise package, you can imagine how puzzled and excited Milo was; and if you've never gotten one, pay close attention, because someday you might.

"I don't think it's my birthday," he puzzled, "and Christmas must be months away, and I haven't been outstandingly good, or even good at all." (He had to admit this even to himself.) "Most probably I won't like it anyway, but since I don't know where it came from, I can't possibly send it back." He thought about it for quite a while and then opened the envelope, but just to be polite.

"ONE GENUINE TURNPIKE TOLLBOOTH," it stated — and then it went on:

"EASILY ASSEMBLED AT HOME, AND FOR USE BY THOSE WHO HAVE NEVER TRAVELED IN LANDS BEYOND."

"Beyond what?" thought Milo as he continued to read.

338

QuickREFERENCE

Social Studies Link

Cartography is the art of mapmaking. Humans have been making maps for over 2500 years. Ancient people created crude maps by carving into wood or bone, or assembling sticks and shells to represent geographical features. Invite interested students to research the history of maps.

"THIS PACKAGE CONTAINS THE FOLLOWING ITEMS:

"One (1) genuine turnpike tollbooth to be erected according to directions.

"Three (3) precautionary signs to be used in a precautionary fashion.

"Assorted coins for use in paying tolls.

"One (1) map, up to date and carefully drawn by master cartographers, depicting natural and man-made features.

"One (1) book of rules and traffic regulations, which may not be bent or broken."

And in smaller letters at the bottom it concluded: "Results are not guaranteed, but if not perfectly satisfied, your wasted time will be refunded."

Following the instructions, which told him to cut here, lift there, and fold back all around, he soon had the tollbooth unpacked and set up on its stand. He fitted the windows in place and attached the roof, which extended out on both sides and fastened on the coin box. It was very much like the tollbooths he'd seen many times on family trips, except of course it was much smaller and purple.

 Extra Support

Have students find examples of absurd notions, like the small print at the bottom of the tollbooth's instructions (page 339): *your wasted time will be refunded.* Ask students how they think that might happen.

Genre

Fantasy

Teach/Model

As a literary genre, fantasy deals with things that are not and cannot be. Story settings are strange, and characters are supernatural. Ask students what they think the difference is between fantasy and science fiction stories. (Science fiction takes place in a future world where technology makes events possible.) Discuss other elements and aspects of fantasy with the class:

- Wondrous, extraordinary events that cannot be explained occur.

- There are underlying themes: triumph of joy over despair; struggle between good and evil.

- The story can be mythlike.

Practice/Apply

Copy this chart on the board.

ELEMENT	EXAMPLE
strange setting	
inexplicable events	
bizarre characters or creatures	

Then have the class fill in the chart with examples from *The Phantom Tollbooth*.

Interact
with
Literature

 **Guided Reading**

Comprehension/Critical Thinking

1. Why doesn't Milo know what to do with himself? (He doesn't take an interest in anything; he considers everything a waste of time.)

2. Have you ever felt as Milo does about life? What are words that describe this feeling? (Sample: *bored, dull, listless, apathetic, flat, depressed*)

3. Which of the precautionary signs requires Milo to look at the map? ("Have Your Destination in Mind")

4. Do you think Milo could have come up with a destination without the map? (Answers will vary.)

Predicting/Purpose Setting

At this point students should know that the tollbooth exists for Milo to explore an imaginary land. Ask them if they want to revise their predictions, based on what they have read so far. Students using the Guided Reading option can read to the end of page 346. Use the questions on page 346 to check students' comprehension.

Informal Assessment

If students' responses indicate that they are understanding the selection, you may wish to have them finish reading it cooperatively or independently.

"What a strange present," he thought to himself. "The least they could have done was to send a highway with it, for it's terribly impractical without one." But since, at the time, there was nothing else he wanted to play with, he set up the three signs,

SLOW DOWN APPROACHING TOLLBOOTH

PLEASE HAVE YOUR FARE READY

HAVE YOUR DESTINATION IN MIND

and slowly unfolded the map.

As the announcement stated, it was a beautiful map, in many colors, showing principal roads, rivers and seas, towns and cities, mountains and valleys, intersections and detours, and sites of outstanding interest both beautiful and historic.

The only trouble was that Milo had never heard of any of the places it indicated, and even the names sounded most peculiar.

"I don't think there really is such a country," he concluded after studying it carefully. "Well, it doesn't matter anyway." And he closed his eyes and poked a finger at the map.

"Dictionopolis," read Milo slowly when he saw what his finger had chosen. "Oh, well, I might as well go there as anywhere."

He walked across the room and dusted the car off carefully. Then, taking the map and rule book with him, he hopped in and, for lack of anything better to do, drove slowly up to the tollbooth. As he deposited his coin and rolled past he remarked <u>wistfully</u>, "I do hope this is an interesting game, otherwise the afternoon will be so terribly dull."

340

Quick**REFERENCE**

Vocabulary

Analyze *Dictionopolis,* the invented word. (*polis* comes from the Greek word for *city; dict* is from the Latin verb *to say*) Students will recognize *dictionary* in the word. Ask students what they think a *word city* might be like and what Milo might find there.

 Journal

Encourage students to record their
reactions to *The Phantom Tollbooth*
in their journals. What do they think
of Milo? Do they identify with any of
the characters, however fantastic
they might be?

Interact
with
Literature

342

Reading Strategies

▶ **Evaluate**

Suggest to students that they evaluate the setting and events of the story to note what kind of changes take place. Are the events realistic or fantastic? Ask students to think about the sentence at the end of the first paragraph on page 342, *What had started as make-believe was now very real.* Have them consider whether Milo's room and the events that took place there were real or make-believe. Then consider the new setting. What has changed? In paragraph three, the description sounds almost too bright to be real. Ask students to evaluate Milo's outlook, or mood, now. How is it different? Have them explain their evaluations.

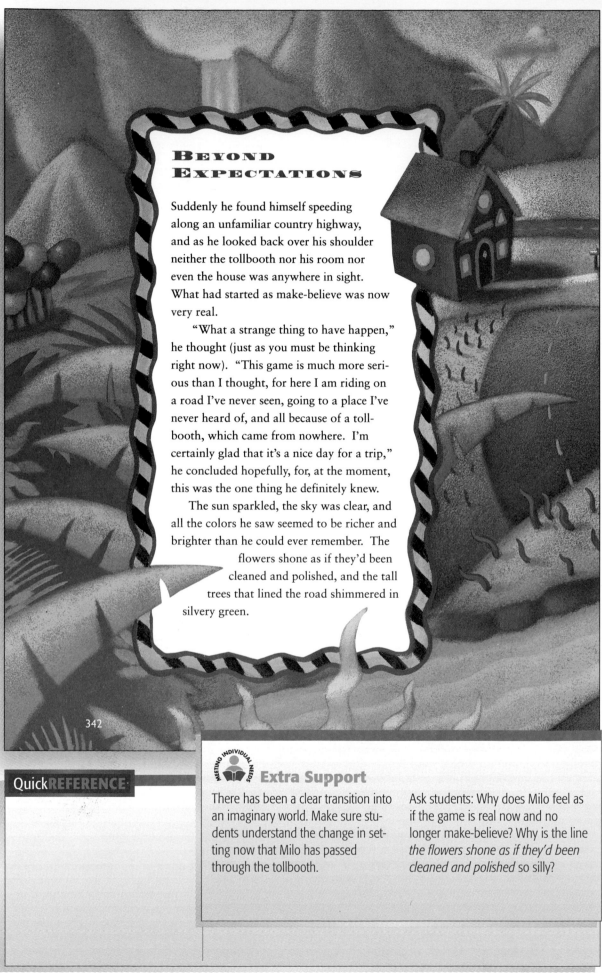

BEYOND EXPECTATIONS

Suddenly he found himself speeding along an unfamiliar country highway, and as he looked back over his shoulder neither the tollbooth nor his room nor even the house was anywhere in sight. What had started as make-believe was now very real.

"What a strange thing to have happen," he thought (just as you must be thinking right now). "This game is much more serious than I thought, for here I am riding on a road I've never seen, going to a place I've never heard of, and all because of a tollbooth, which came from nowhere. I'm certainly glad that it's a nice day for a trip," he concluded hopefully, for, at the moment, this was the one thing he definitely knew.

The sun sparkled, the sky was clear, and all the colors he saw seemed to be richer and brighter than he could ever remember. The flowers shone as if they'd been cleaned and polished, and the tall trees that lined the road shimmered in silvery green.

342

QuickREFERENCE·

Extra Support

There has been a clear transition into an imaginary world. Make sure students understand the change in setting now that Milo has passed through the tollbooth.

Ask students: Why does Milo feel as if the game is real now and no longer make-believe? Why is the line *the flowers shone as if they'd been cleaned and polished* so silly?

343

Fantasy/Realism

Teach/Model

TESTED SKILL

Many fantasy stories combine realistic and fantastic elements. There are events, settings, and characters that could be real, along with those that could not be real at all. Ask students if they think the story is completely real or completely make-believe.

Think Aloud

As I read, it helps me to know which things could happen in real life and which things could only happen in the writer's imagination. Milo acts very much like a real boy, and he could very well be reading a map and driving a little car. In real life, however, there's no way Milo could suddenly go from playing in his room to driving down a country road. This kind of thing only happens in fantasy.

Practice/Apply

Ask students to review the listed contents of Milo's surprise package as described on pages 338–339. Have them distinguish the realistic descriptions or items from the fantastic. Ask them to explain how they arrived at their assessments.

SKILL FINDER — Full lesson/Reteaching, pp. 357A–357B

Technology Link

Virtual reality combines video and computer technology. As more artists and writers use this modern medium, any one of us can share Milo's experience and pass through a "phantom tollbooth" to access new dimensions of the imagination.

Interact *with* Literature

Reading Strategies

▶ Think About Words

Discuss with students how Norton Juster uses descriptive words to build a fantasy land based on feelings and states of mind. Sometimes the language might even seem silly, absurd, or nonsensical. Ask students to focus on the word *Expectations*. Have them suggest words they associate with it and think about why the author chose this as a name for a town. As they read on, remind students to think about words that explain what kind of place *Expectations* is.

Help students make sense of the word *effusive*. Ask: What kind of greeting would make Milo react the way he does? Have a volunteer mimic the Whether Man's greeting. Help students see that *effusive* means "unrestrained or excessive in emotional display."

"**WELCOME TO EXPECTATIONS**," said a carefully lettered sign on a small house at the side of the road.

"**INFORMATION, PREDICTIONS, AND ADVICE CHEERFULLY OFFERED. PARK HERE AND BLOW HORN.**"

With the first sound from the horn a little man in a long coat came rushing from the house, speaking as fast as he could and repeating everything several times:

"My, my, my, my, my, welcome, welcome, welcome, welcome to the land of Expectations, to the land of Expectations, to the land of Expectations. We don't get many travelers these days; we certainly don't get many travelers these days. Now what can I do for you? I'm the Whether Man."

"Is this the right road for Dictionopolis?" asked Milo, a little bowled over by the effusive greeting.

"Well now, well now, well now," he began again, "I don't know of any wrong road to Dictionopolis, so if this road goes to Dictionopolis at all it must be the right road, and if it doesn't it must be the right road to somewhere else, because there are no wrong roads to anywhere. Do you think it will rain?"

"I thought you were the Weather Man," said Milo, very confused.

"Oh no," said the little man, "I'm the Whether Man, not the Weather Man, for after all it's more important to know whether there will be weather than what the weather will be." And with that he released a dozen balloons that sailed off into the sky. "Must see which way the wind is blowing," he said, chuckling over his little joke and watching them disappear in all directions.

"What kind of a place is Expectations?" inquired Milo, unable to see the humor and feeling very doubtful of the little man's sanity.

"Good question, good question," he exclaimed. "Expectations is the place you must always go to before you get to where you're going. Of course, some people never go beyond Expectations, but my job is to hurry them along whether they like it or not. Now what else can I do for you?" And before Milo could reply he rushed into the house and reappeared a moment later with a new coat and an umbrella.

"I think I can find my own way," said Milo, not at all sure that he could. But, since he didn't understand the little man at all, he decided that he might as well move on — at least until he met someone whose sentences didn't always sound as if they would make as much sense backwards as forwards.

Informal Assessment

Oral Reading On page 344 students can read aloud the dialogue for expression. Do they convey Milo's confusion or the Whether Man's absurdity?

Quick**REFERENCE**

Science Link

The Whether Man released balloons to see which way the wind was blowing. Have students research how meteorologists detect changes in wind patterns and predict how such shifts will affect the weather.

 Students Acquiring English

Pantomime the colloquialism *bowled over* (to be taken by surprise or overwhelmed) and what makes a greeting an *effusive* one (unrestrained emotion).

345

Interact
with
Literature

Guided Reading

Comprehension/Critical Thinking

1. Why does Milo say, on page 342, "This game is much more serious than I thought"? (because he wasn't expecting to find himself suddenly driving down a country road)

2. What do you think the Whether Man means when he says some people never go beyond Expectations? (Students' responses will vary. Sample: Some people are always planning or hoping and never actually doing or getting.)

3. How does the setting change by the end of page 346? Why do you think this happens? (The sky turns gray, and the color disappears. Milo wasn't paying attention and took the wrong turn.)

Predicting/Purpose Setting

Encourage students to evaluate and/or revise their predictions, based on what they have read so far. What do they expect will happen to Milo next?

Students using the Guided Reading option can read from page 347 to the end of the selection to check their predictions. Use the questions on page 354 to check students' comprehension.

"Splendid, splendid, splendid," exclaimed the Whether Man. "Whether or not you find your own way, you're bound to find some way. If you happen to find my way, please return it, as it was lost years ago. I imagine by now it's quite rusty. You did say it was going to rain, didn't you?" And with that he opened the umbrella and walked with Milo to the car.

"I'm glad you made your own decision. I do so hate to make up my mind about anything, whether it's good or bad, up or down, in or out, rain or shine. Expect everything, I always say, and the unexpected never happens. Now please drive carefully; good-by, good-by, good-by, good . . ." His last good-by was drowned out by an enormous clap of thunder, and as Milo drove down the road in the bright sunshine he could see the Whether Man standing in the middle of a fierce cloudburst that seemed to be raining only on him.

The road dipped now into a broad green valley and stretched toward the horizon. The little car bounced along with very little effort, and Milo had hardly to touch

the accelerator to go as fast as he wanted. He was glad to be on his way again.

"It's all very well to spend time in Expectations," he thought, "but talking to that strange man all day would certainly get me nowhere. He's the most peculiar person I've ever met," continued Milo — unaware of how many peculiar people he would shortly encounter.

As he drove along the peaceful highway he soon fell to daydreaming and paid less and less attention to where he was going. In a short time he wasn't paying any attention at all, and that is why, at a fork in the road, when a sign pointed to the left, Milo went to the right, along a route, which looked suspiciously like the wrong way.

Things began to change as soon as he left the main highway. The sky became quite gray and, along with it, the whole countryside seemed to lose its color and assume the same monotonous tone. Everything was quiet, and even the air hung heavily. The birds sang only gray songs and the road wound back and forth in an endless series of climbing curves.

Mile after
mile after
mile after
mile he drove, and now, gradually the car went slower and slower, until it was hardly moving at all.

346

QuickREFERENCE

Extra Support

Read aloud the first paragraph on page 346, the Whether Man passage beginning, "Splendid, splendid, splendid. . . ." Ask students to talk about what makes this passage so funny.

Does the Whether Man remind them of any person or character they know? What does he mean when he refers to "my way"? How could he have lost it? How could it go rusty?

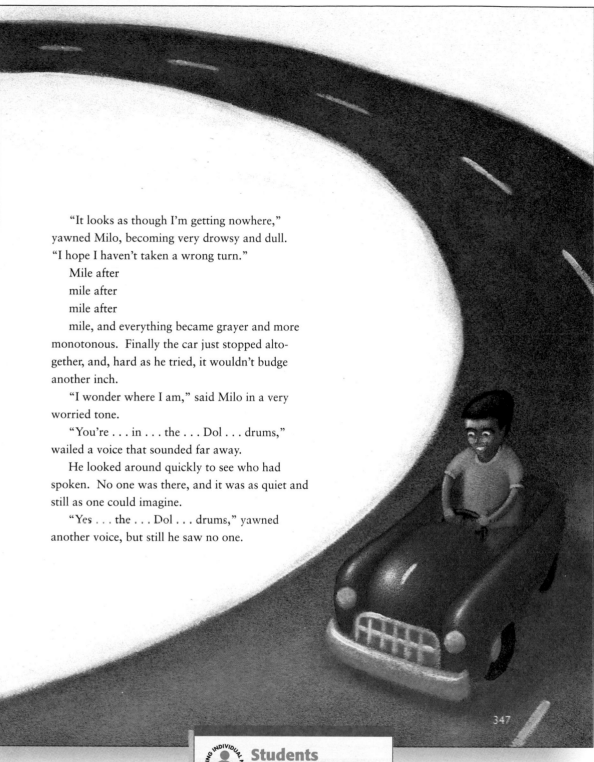

"It looks as though I'm getting nowhere," yawned Milo, becoming very drowsy and dull. "I hope I haven't taken a wrong turn."

Mile after

mile after

mile after

mile, and everything became grayer and more monotonous. Finally the car just stopped altogether, and, hard as he tried, it wouldn't budge another inch.

"I wonder where I am," said Milo in a very worried tone.

"You're . . . in . . . the . . . Dol . . . drums," wailed a voice that sounded far away.

He looked around quickly to see who had spoken. No one was there, and it was as quiet and still as one could imagine.

"Yes . . . the . . . Dol . . . drums," yawned another voice, but still he saw no one.

347

Vocabulary

Monotonous: repetitiously dull; never varied or enlivened. Help students use context clues and identify word parts to make sense of this word. (*mono*, single; *tonous*, tone)

Interact *with* Literature

Reading Strategies

▶ Predict

Have students give words that describe the current state of Milo's journey. *(monotonous, dull, drab, boring, slow)* Use a Think Aloud to model how you predicted a shift in setting and mood.

Think Aloud

I knew things would change as soon as Milo took the wrong turn: Everything lost its color, the birds sang "gray songs," the road went on and on without going anywhere, Milo was getting tired, and eventually the car just stopped. Now things have slowed way down. Because of the change in setting and mood, I predict that Milo is about to interact with characters who are very different from the hyperactive, fast-talking Whether Man.

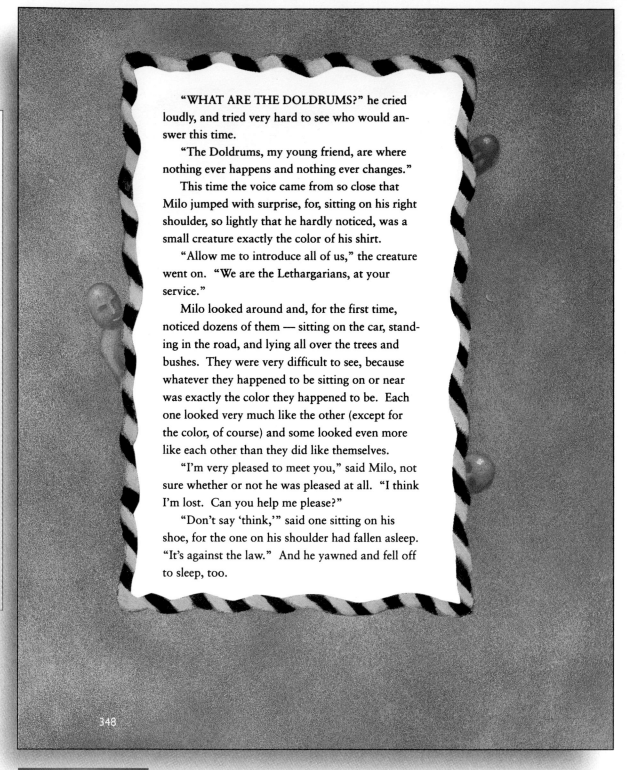

"WHAT ARE THE DOLDRUMS?" he cried loudly, and tried very hard to see who would answer this time.

"The Doldrums, my young friend, are where nothing ever happens and nothing ever changes."

This time the voice came from so close that Milo jumped with surprise, for, sitting on his right shoulder, so lightly that he hardly noticed, was a small creature exactly the color of his shirt.

"Allow me to introduce all of us," the creature went on. "We are the Lethargarians, at your service."

Milo looked around and, for the first time, noticed dozens of them — sitting on the car, standing in the road, and lying all over the trees and bushes. They were very difficult to see, because whatever they happened to be sitting on or near was exactly the color they happened to be. Each one looked very much like the other (except for the color, of course) and some looked even more like each other than they did like themselves.

"I'm very pleased to meet you," said Milo, not sure whether or not he was pleased at all. "I think I'm lost. Can you help me please?"

"Don't say 'think,'" said one sitting on his shoe, for the one on his shoulder had fallen asleep. "It's against the law." And he yawned and fell off to sleep, too.

348

QuickREFERENCE

Self-Assessment

Encourage students to reflect on how well they have understood the selection so far and how much they are enjoying it.

Social Studies Link

Doldrums 1. A period or condition of depression or inactivity. **2.** A region of the ocean near the equator where there is little or no wind. Have students locate the doldrums on a globe or map. Ask them what might happen to sailboats there.

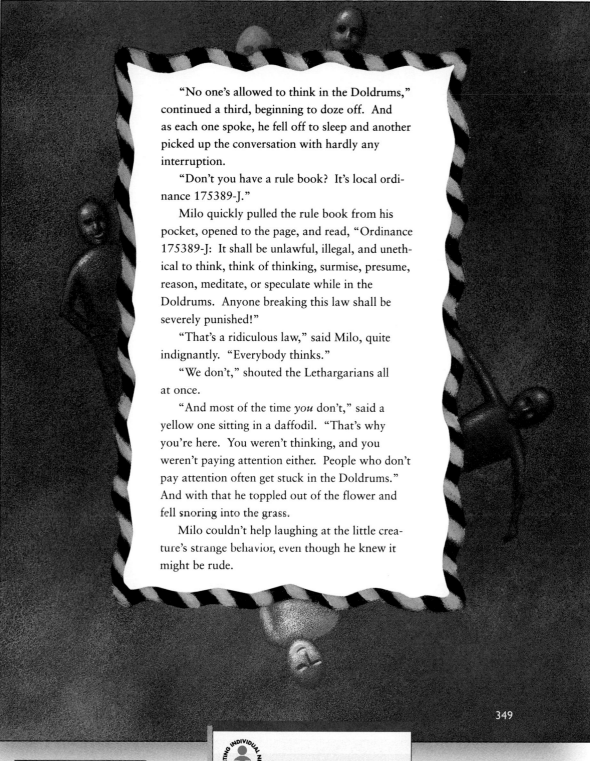

"No one's allowed to think in the Doldrums," continued a third, beginning to doze off. And as each one spoke, he fell off to sleep and another picked up the conversation with hardly any interruption.

"Don't you have a rule book? It's local ordinance 175389-J."

Milo quickly pulled the rule book from his pocket, opened to the page, and read, "Ordinance 175389-J: It shall be unlawful, illegal, and unethical to think, think of thinking, surmise, presume, reason, meditate, or speculate while in the Doldrums. Anyone breaking this law shall be severely punished!"

"That's a ridiculous law," said Milo, quite indignantly. "Everybody thinks."

"We don't," shouted the Lethargarians all at once.

"And most of the time *you* don't," said a yellow one sitting in a daffodil. "That's why you're here. You weren't thinking, and you weren't paying attention either. People who don't pay attention often get stuck in the Doldrums." And with that he toppled out of the flower and fell snoring into the grass.

Milo couldn't help laughing at the little creature's strange behavior, even though he knew it might be rude.

349

Interact *with* Literature

Reading Strategies

▶ **Think About Words**

Help students understand new vocabulary by exploring and appreciating the subtle shades of difference among synonyms. In the middle of page 349, for example, you might focus on *surmise, presume,* and *speculate.*

surmise: to conclude or infer something on slight evidence; to suppose

presume: to assume to be true in the absence of proof

speculate: to assume to be true without conclusive evidence

The Lethargarians' activity schedule on pages 350–351 provides another list of synonyms. Have students work together to find and record verbs for all the different ways to procrastinate.

"Stop that at once," ordered the plaid one clinging to his stocking. "Laughing is against the law. Don't you have a rule book? It's local ordinance 574381-W."

Opening the book again, Milo found Ordinance 574381-W: "In the Doldrums, laughter is frowned upon and smiling is permitted only on alternate Thursdays. Violators shall be dealt with most harshly."

"Well, if you can't laugh or think, what can you do?" asked Milo.

"Anything as long as it's nothing, and everything as long as it isn't anything," explained another. "There's lots to do; we have a very busy schedule —

"At 8 o'clock we get up, and then we spend

"From 8 to 9 daydreaming.

"From 9 to 9:30 we take our early midmorning nap.

"From 9:30 to 10:30 we dawdle and delay.

"From 10:30 to 11:30 we take our late early morning nap.

"From 11:00 to 12:00 we bide our time and then eat lunch.

"From 1:00 to 2:00 we linger and loiter.

350

Quick REFERENCE

Students Acquiring English

Have students work with proficient speakers of English to pantomime, define, and record these new verbs in their journals: *dawdle and delay, bide our time, linger and loiter, loaf and lounge,* and *dillydally.*

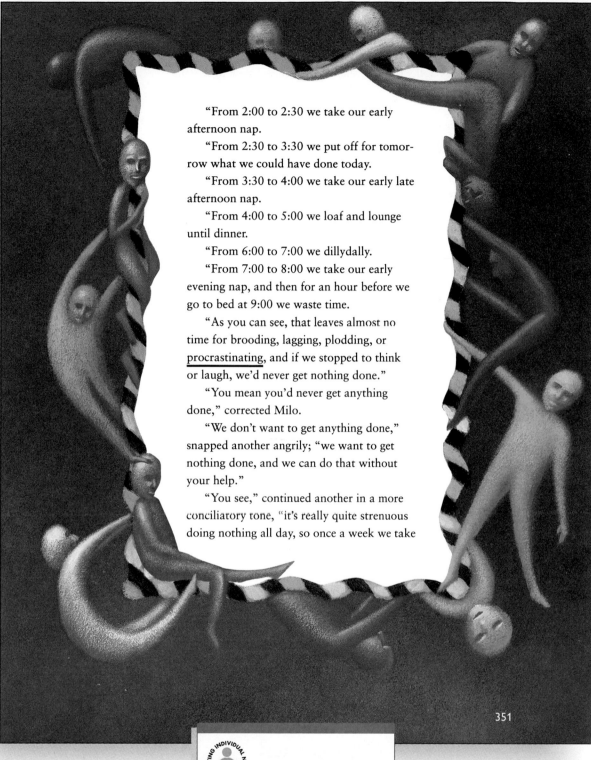

"From 2:00 to 2:30 we take our early afternoon nap.

"From 2:30 to 3:30 we put off for tomorrow what we could have done today.

"From 3:30 to 4:00 we take our early late afternoon nap.

"From 4:00 to 5:00 we loaf and lounge until dinner.

"From 6:00 to 7:00 we dillydally.

"From 7:00 to 8:00 we take our early evening nap, and then for an hour before we go to bed at 9:00 we waste time.

"As you can see, that leaves almost no time for brooding, lagging, plodding, or procrastinating, and if we stopped to think or laugh, we'd never get nothing done."

"You mean you'd never get anything done," corrected Milo.

"We don't want to get anything done," snapped another angrily; "we want to get nothing done, and we can do that without your help."

"You see," continued another in a more conciliatory tone, "it's really quite strenuous doing nothing all day, so once a week we take

351

Science Link

The Lethargarians' camouflage ability is similar to the chameleons'— tree lizards whose nervous system controls the pattern of color in skin pigmentation. Interested students can research and report on camouflage in other creatures.

Interact *with* Literature

a holiday and go nowhere, which was just where we were going when you came along. Would you care to join us?"

"I might as well," thought Milo; "that's where I seem to be going anyway."

"Tell me," he yawned, for he felt ready for a nap now himself, "does everyone here do nothing?"

"Everyone but the terrible watchdog," said two of them, shuddering in chorus. "He's always sniffing around to see that nobody wastes time. A most unpleasant character."

"The watchdog?" said Milo quizzically.

"THE WATCHDOG," shouted another, fainting from fright, for racing down the road barking furiously and kicking up a great cloud of dust was the very dog of whom they had been speaking.

"RUN!"

"WAKE UP!"

"RUN!"

"HERE HE COMES!"

"THE WATCHDOG!"

Great shouts filled the air as the Lethargarians scattered in all directions and soon disappeared entirely.

"R-R-R-G-H-R-O-R-R-H-F-F," exclaimed the watchdog as he dashed up to the car, loudly puffing and panting.

Milo's eyes opened wide, for there in front of him was a large dog with a perfectly normal head, four feet, and a tail — and the body of a loudly ticking alarm clock.

"What are you doing here?" growled the watchdog.

"Just killing time," replied Milo apologetically. "You see — "

"KILLING TIME!" roared the dog — so furiously that his alarm went off. "It's bad enough wasting time without killing it." And he shuddered at the thought. "Why are you in the Doldrums anyway — don't you have anywhere to go?"

"I was on my way to Dictionopolis when I got stuck here," explained Milo. "Can you help me?"

"Help you! You must help yourself," the dog replied, carefully winding himself with his left hind leg. "I suppose you know why you got stuck."

"I guess I just wasn't thinking," said Milo.

"PRECISELY," shouted the dog as his alarm went off again. "Now you know what you must do."

"I'm afraid I don't," admitted Milo, feeling quite stupid.

"Well," continued the watchdog impatiently, "since you got here by not thinking, it seems reasonable to expect that, in order to get out, you must start thinking." And with that he hopped into the car.

"Do you mind if I get in? I love automobile rides."

Milo began to think as hard as he could (which was very difficult, since he

353

Extra Support

Word play is confusing for any child acquiring language proficiency, and so students may miss some humorous context. Help them to appreciate Juster's wit. When you read something funny, share it with them.

Note, for example, how the author uses the opposite context, *laughter is frowned upon* (top, page 350). Encourage students to create word plays and share puns in their primary language.

Writer's Craft

Word Play

Teach/Model

In *The Phantom Tollbooth* the watchdog guards against the waste of time. Ask students what a *pun* is. (a play on words involving different senses of the same word, or the similar sense or sound of different words) Have them describe a typical watchdog. Then ask them to describe the watchdog character depicted here: He is part watch, part dog; he is watching (out for) time; he alarms the Lethargarians. Help students recognize and articulate that the word play is based on multiple meanings of *watch*:

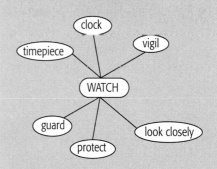

Practice/Apply

Invite students to look for and invent more puns and word plays.

SKILL FINDER

Writing Activities:
Write an Ad, p. 357D

Interact *with* Literature

 **Guided Reading**

Comprehension/Critical Thinking

1. How do you explain the sudden change in the Lethargarians' behavior when the watchdog appears? (Answers will vary.)

2. Why do you think the watchdog has an alarm clock? (He represents a wake-up call for lethargic people.)

3. Why doesn't it matter what Milo thinks about when he starts to think? (Because one thought leads to another, eventually to something interesting.)

4. Would you have wanted the watchdog to join you in the car? Why or why not? (Answers will vary.)

wasn't used to it). He thought of birds that swim and fish that fly. He thought of yesterday's lunch and tomorrow's dinner. He thought of words that begin with J and numbers that end in 3. And, as he thought, the wheels began to turn.

"We're moving, we're moving," he shouted happily.

"Keep thinking," scolded the watchdog.

The little car started to go faster and faster as Milo's brain whirled with activity, and down the road they went. In a few moments they were out of the Doldrums and back on the main highway. All the colors had returned to their original brightness, and as they raced along the road Milo continued to think of all sorts of things; of the many detours and wrong turns that were so easy to take, of how fine it was to be moving along, and, most of all, of how much could be accomplished with just a little thought. And the dog, his nose in the wind, just sat back, watchfully ticking.

354

Self-Assessment

Ask students if the predictions they made at the beginning of the selection helped them to follow or understand it better. Did it help to evaluate changes in characters and settings?

QuickREFERENCE

Extra Support

Rereading Some students may benefit from rereading all or part of the selection independently or in cooperative groups. Students may enjoy reading aloud for expression with a partner.

355

Interact
with
Literature

Responding Activities

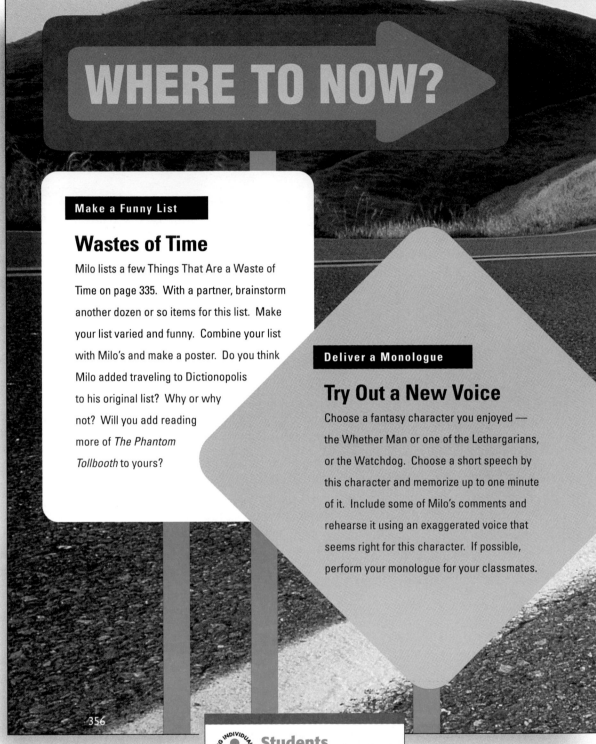

WHERE TO NOW?

Make a Funny List

Wastes of Time

Milo lists a few Things That Are a Waste of Time on page 335. With a partner, brainstorm another dozen or so items for this list. Make your list varied and funny. Combine your list with Milo's and make a poster. Do you think Milo added traveling to Dictionopolis to his original list? Why or why not? Will you add reading more of *The Phantom Tollbooth* to yours?

Deliver a Monologue

Try Out a New Voice

Choose a fantasy character you enjoyed — the Whether Man or one of the Lethargarians, or the Watchdog. Choose a short speech by this character and memorize up to one minute of it. Include some of Milo's comments and rehearse it using an exaggerated voice that seems right for this character. If possible, perform your monologue for your classmates.

Personal Response

Allow students to choose their own way of responding to the fantastic story elements or the use of word play in this selection.

Anthology Activities

Encourage students to choose an activity on Anthology pages 356–357.

Literature Discussion

Did any of the characters, situations, or places in *The Phantom Tollbooth* feel like real life to you? Explain.

Selection Connections

Have students complete the part of the chart on *Literacy Activity Book* pages 147–148 that refers to *The Phantom Tollbooth*.

Informal Assessment

Responses should indicate that students can differentiate fantasy from realism.

Additional Support:

Review the Fantasy/Realism minilesson on page 343.

Quick**REFERENCE**

Media Literacy

Invite students to listen to an abridged version of *The Phantom Tollbooth* on audio cassette as read by Pat Carroll (Caedmon). The selection is also available in an animated film version from MGM/UA Home Video or your local library.

Students Acquiring English

For the response activity Where Next? some students may prefer to write in their primary language. Then they can work with a partner who is proficient in English to summarize their chapter verbally.

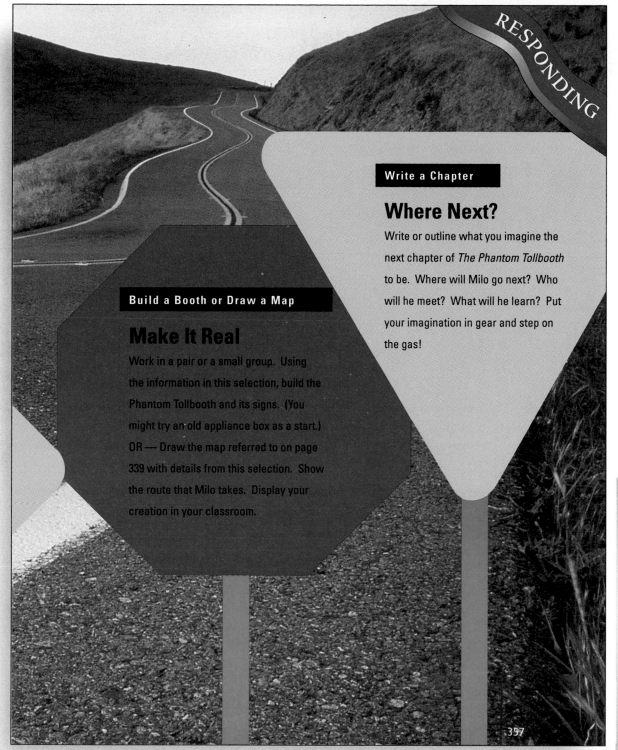

RESPONDING

Write a Chapter

Where Next?

Write or outline what you imagine the next chapter of *The Phantom Tollbooth* to be. Where will Milo go next? Who will he meet? What will he learn? Put your imagination in gear and step on the gas!

Build a Booth or Draw a Map

Make It Real

Work in a pair or a small group. Using the information in this selection, build the Phantom Tollbooth and its signs. (You might try an old appliance box as a start.) OR — Draw the map referred to on page 339 with details from this selection. Show the route that Milo takes. Display your creation in your classroom.

357

Comprehension Check

To check comprehension, use these questions or *Literacy Activity Book* page 150.

1. What do you think is the message of this story? (Answers will vary.)

2. Which story elements did you relate to the most? Which details helped you understand the author's message? (Answers will vary.)

3. Compare the Whether Man to the watchdog. Which one do you think had the most influence on Milo in his journey through the land beyond the phantom tollbooth? Explain.

Literacy Activity Book, p. 150

A Letter to the Editor

Suppose Milo wrote a letter to the editor about his journey. Fill in the spaces to help get his message across.

To the Editor

Perhaps your readers think that life is boring. Well, let me tell you something that happened to me the other day. I was hanging out in my room because nothing really _____ me. And I saw this huge package with a note on it that said _____. In it was a _____, which I quickly assembled. Also included were four other things: _____. I got into my electric car and headed for _____. I thought it was only a _____, but when I found myself on an actual _____, I knew this was _____. Suddenly, I was in _____, where I met _____. Then the bright countryside turned gray and I was in _____. And guess how I got out: by _____!

150 Imagination at Work

 Home Connection

Have students share the selection with their family. Ask them to find out if any of their family members know special puns or word plays. They might also share their unique experiences with or interpretations of *Expectations* and the *Doldrums*.

 Portfolio Opportunity

- Comprehension Check: Save *Literacy Activity Book* page 150.
- Save students' posters and written responses.
- Tape-record the monologues and save them in a class portfolio.

Instruct *and* Integrate

Comprehension

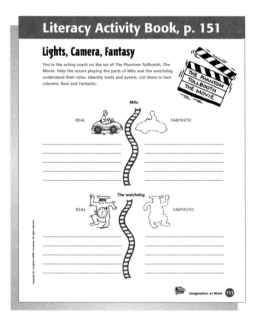
Literacy Activity Book, p. 151

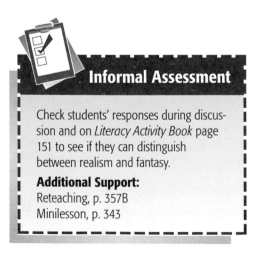

Lights, Camera, Fantasy

You're the acting coach on the set of *The Phantom Tollbooth, The Movie*. Help the actors playing the parts of Milo and the watchdog understand their roles. Identify traits and events. List them in two columns: Real and Fantastic.

Milo

REAL — FANTASTIC

The watchdog

REAL — FANTASTIC

Imagination at Work **151**

Informal Assessment

Check students' responses during discussion and on *Literacy Activity Book* page 151 to see if they can distinguish between realism and fantasy.

Additional Support:
Reteaching, p. 357B
Minilesson, p. 343

INTERACTIVE LEARNING

 **Fantasy/Realism**

LAB, p. 151

Teach/Model Ask students to identify a time when they found themselves daydreaming. Encourage them to determine why their mind wandered. Then ask them to suggest reasons why an author might combine fantasy and realism in literature. (to provide readers with variety, a different perspective, and sheer entertainment)

Display Transparency 4–3. Have students work with partners to determine three or four main events of the story and fill in the appropriate boxes in the left column of the chart. Then have them answer the questions for each event, filling in the rest of the chart. Have students identify whether the events are fantastic or real. Invite all students to share their observations and reasons to support each analysis.

What happened? (Event)	Has this ever happened to you?	Has this ever happened to anyone you know?	Could it really happen?	Is it fantasy or reality?

Practice/Apply
- Have students use *Literacy Activity Book* page 151 to analyze the characters in *The Phantom Tollbooth*.
- Divide the class into small discussion groups to focus on a story, movie, or television program of their choice. Ask them to discuss how the elements of fantasy combine with and are based on reality. Following their discussion, invite students to evaluate their understanding of fantasy and realism.

SKILL FINDER Minilesson, p. 343

Reteaching | Fantasy/Realism

MEETING INDIVIDUAL NEEDS

To help students recognize fantasy and reality, read aloud pages 340–342, which describe Milo as he sets off for Dictionopolis. Review with students these questions to help them differentiate between fantasy and reality.

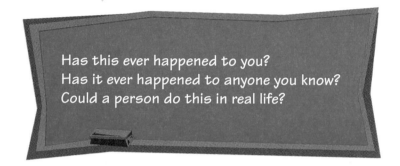

Has this ever happened to you?
Has it ever happened to anyone you know?
Could a person do this in real life?

Guide students to realize that if the answers to the questions are *no,* then the character or event is fantasy. Display Transparency 4–4, and discuss each event on the chart with the class. Have students write *R* for realism if the event is possible in real life, or *F* for fantasy if it is not. For example, in reality no manufacturer could create a game that would provide a highway, so for Milo to think that the tollbooth should have come with one is absurd and fantastic.

Students can use the **Channel R.E.A.D.** videodisc "The Ordinary Princess" for additional support with Fantasy/Realism.

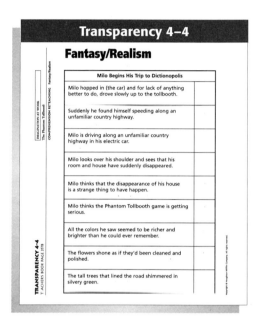

Transparency 4–4

Fantasy/Realism

Milo Begins His Trip to Dictionopolis	
Milo hopped in (the car) and for lack of anything better to do, drove slowly up to the tollbooth.	
Suddenly he found himself speeding along an unfamiliar country highway.	
Milo is driving along an unfamiliar country highway in his electric car.	
Milo looks over his shoulder and sees that his room and house have suddenly disappeared.	
Milo thinks that the disappearance of his house is a strange thing to have happen.	
Milo thinks the Phantom Tollbooth game is getting serious.	
All the colors he saw seemed to be richer and brighter than he could ever remember.	
The flowers shone as if they'd been cleaned and polished.	
The tall trees that lined the road shimmered in silvery green.	

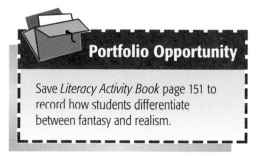

Portfolio Opportunity

Save *Literacy Activity Book* page 151 to record how students differentiate between fantasy and realism.

3

Instruct *and* **Integrate**

Writing Skills and Activities

Literacy Activity Book, p. 152

INTERACTIVE LEARNING

Writing Instructions

LAB, p. 152

Teach/Model

Encourage students to talk about how they have used instructions to make, do, or explain something. Ask volunteers if the directions were easy or difficult to follow and why. Good instructions:

- list the materials needed to complete a project

- specify the order of steps to follow

- include diagrams or pictures to help clarify the process

- give special advice or trouble-shooting tips

Display Transparency 4–5. Have students use the guidelines below to evaluate the instructions.

Guidelines for Writing Instructions

1. Think through the task you want to explain. Do the activity before writing the instructions.

2. Begin by stating what the instructions are for. If you have any warnings or words of advice, state those up front too.

3. Describe the kinds and amounts of materials needed to complete the task. You may need to tell where to find unusual materials.

4. Explain each step of the task clearly and completely, and present it in the order in which it should be performed. Use order words, such as *first, next, then, before, after,* and *finally*.

Practice/Apply

Assign the activity Write Instructions. Remind students to explain each step clearly and in the proper order.

Informal Assessment

Review students' instructions to make sure that they included the materials needed and that the steps are complete and in the proper order. You may want to have students try out each other's instructions to check for clarity and sense.

Writing Activities

Students can use the **Student Writing Center** software for all of their writing activities.

Write Instructions

Invite students to write instructions to share something they know how to do. The instructions might tell how to make a craft, such as a piñata; perform a science experiment; fix something, such as a flat tire on a bicycle; or do an activity or task, such as sew on a button. Encourage students to choose an activity that has about five or six steps and that can be clearly explained in writing. Have them use *Literacy Activity Book* page 152 for planning. Suggest that students write their final instructions on large file cards that other students can borrow. If possible, schedule a Demo Day when students can read and demonstrate their instructions.

Write a Post Card Home

Invite students to imagine that they are Milo and to create a post card that he would send home. What has he seen? Whom has he met? Tell students to draw a picture on one side of the post card and write a message in the appropriate place on the other side. Collect the post cards in a box, and have students draw them one at a time to show and read aloud.

The most amazing thing happened to me today.

The Lethargarians

Shared Writing: Write an Ad

Work with students to write a travel advertisement about one of the places Milo visits. Encourage them to incorporate some of the word play from the story. In order to do this, you may need to review the different kinds of word play used in the story. *(See the Writer's Craft Minilesson on page 353.)*

EXPECTATIONS

Purchase our Expectations travel package and you'll say: "Good Buy!"

Farewell Travel Agency, Inc.

Portfolio Opportunity

- Save *Literacy Activity Book* page 152 to show students' process of writing instructions.

- Save responses to activities on this page for writing samples.

Instruct *and* Integrate

Word Skills and Strategies

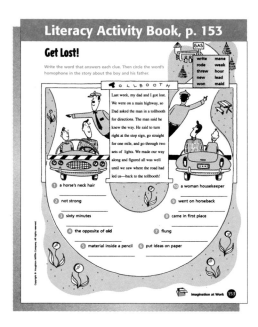

Homophones

LAB, p. 153

Teach/Model

Have students turn to page 344 in their anthologies and read along as you read aloud this sentence from *The Phantom Tollbooth*.

> "I'm the Whether Man, not the Weather Man, for after all it's more important to know whether there will be weather than what the weather will be."

Ask volunteers to identify each instance of *weather* or *whether* in the sentence and tell what each one means. Remind students that words that sound alike but have different spellings and meanings are called homophones. Remind them that readers and writers use context and spelling to match homophones with the right meaning.

Practice/Apply

Cooperative Learning Distribute the character descriptions listed below on pieces of folded paper. Then have students work in pairs to plan and perform a skit in which a Milo-like character has a brief and confusing conversation with one of these characters.

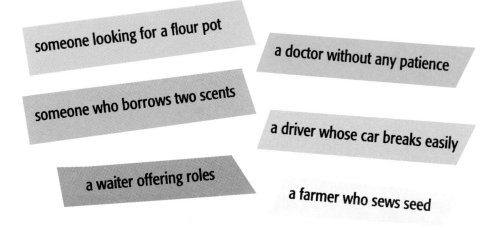

someone looking for a flour pot

a doctor without any patience

someone who borrows two scents

a driver whose car breaks easily

a waiter offering roles

a farmer who sews seed

Challenge the students watching each skit to try to guess the homophone being dramatized.

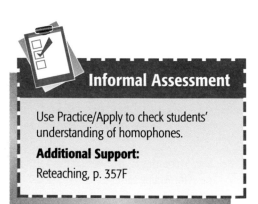

Informal Assessment

Use Practice/Apply to check students' understanding of homophones.

Additional Support:
Reteaching, p. 357F

SKILL FINDER Spelling, Theme 1

Reteaching | **Homophones**

Tell students that homophones are words that are pronounced the same way but are spelled differently and have different meanings. Write a pair of homophones from the list below on the board. Then ask a student to illustrate one word from the pair with an action. The other students should try to guess which word from the pair is being dramatized. Repeat with the other pairs.

write/right	wait/weight	heel/heal
sale/sail	mail/male	feet/feat
eight/ate	bored/board	pain/pane

> I see the prefix *pre-*, which I know means "before." The next two syllables look like *caution,* a word I know.

M I N I L E S S O N

Decoding Longer Words

precautionary

Teach/Model Remind students that when they come upon a long word, they can look at its parts for familiar base words, prefixes, and suffixes. Encourage them to try pronouncing each syllable and to try stressing different syllables until they find a pronunciation that sounds likely.

> This last part, *-ary,* must be a suffix. If I put the parts together I get *pre-caution-ary.* It must have something to do with being cautious before.

Practice/Apply Write the following words from *The Phantom Tollbooth* on the board. For each word, have students note familiar parts, compare and discuss possible pronunciations, and then pronounce the word.

accelerator	guaranteed	suspiciously
monotonous	destination	apologetically

Portfolio Opportunity

Save *Literacy Activity Book* page 153 to record students' understanding of homophones.

3

Instruct *and* Integrate

Building Vocabulary

Use this page to review Selection Vocabulary.

Vocabulary Activities

Antonyms

Direct students to page 346 of *The Phantom Tollbooth,* and have them read aloud the Whether Man's sentence beginning "I do so hate. . . ." Ask them to name the antonym pairs in that sentence. (*good/bad, up/down, in/out, rain/shine*) Then have students look through the rest of the paragraph for other words and suggest their antonyms. (*everything (nothing), unexpected (expected), never (always), carefully (recklessly), last (first), enormous (tiny), bright (dark), middle (edge),* and *fierce (gentle)*) Have students work in pairs or small groups to find as many words from the selection and their antonyms as they can.

Traffic Words

Students can collect words having to do with traffic, beginning with those in *The Phantom Tollbooth*. They then look at all their words, decide on major categories, and build a semantic map on the board.

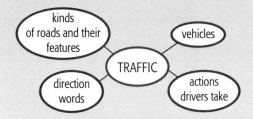

Selection words: *tollbooth, highway, turnpike, destination, fare, intersection, detour, park, drive, accelerator, fork, sign, left, right, route, automobile.*

Prefixes *inter-, intro-, intra-*

Use the selection word *intersection* to show students the prefix *inter-*. Tell students that the meaning of this prefix is "between or among." Explain that certain other prefixes resemble *inter-* but have different spellings and meanings. Offer this chart:

Prefix	Meaning	Example Words
inter-	"between or among"	intersection, interrupt, interview
intro-	"inward"	introduce, introverted, introspection
intra-	"inside or within"	intramural, intravenous, intrastate

Have students brainstorm in groups to name words with these three prefixes. When they run out of ideas, suggest they use a dictionary to find additional words.

Spelling

MINILESSON

Spelling Words

*leaves   beliefs
*puffs   halves
*roofs   shelves
*loaves   thieves
lives   chiefs

Challenge Words

*themselves
tariffs
kerchiefs
wharves
chefs

*Starred words or forms of the words appear in *The Phantom Tollbooth.*

Plurals of Words Ending with *f*

TESTED SKILL

- Write the following pairs of words on the board:

roof	leaf	puff	life
roofs	leaves	puffs	lives

- Ask how the plural of *roof* is formed. (-s is added.) Ask how the plural of *leaf* is formed. (The *f* is changed to *v*, and *-es* is added.) Tell students that the plural of a word ending with *f* is formed by adding *-s* or by changing the *f* to *v* and adding *-es*.

- Elicit that the plural of a word ending in *ff* is formed by adding *-s*. Elicit that the plural of a word ending in *fe* is formed by changing the *f* to *v* and adding *-s*.

- Write the Spelling Words on the board. Tell students that each Spelling Word is a plural form of a word ending with *f, ff,* or *fe.* Say the words and have students repeat them.

Spelling Assessment

Pretest

Say each underlined word, read the sentence, and then repeat the word. Have students write only the underlined words.

1. Tall trees wore brilliant, green <u>leaves</u>.
2. The dog <u>puffs</u> and pants in the heat.
3. The tollbooths have little pointed <u>roofs</u>.
4. I love eating fresh-baked <u>loaves</u> of bread.
5. My favorite character <u>lives</u> in town.
6. Your <u>beliefs</u> are different from mine.
7. Cory cut the oranges in <u>halves</u> to make juice.
8. Put your toys back onto the <u>shelves</u>.
9. Guards caught the <u>thieves</u> stealing jewels.
10. Two police <u>chiefs</u> spoke to us about safety.

Test

Spelling Words Use the Pretest sentences.

Challenge Words

11. Two players hurt <u>themselves</u> practicing.
12. You must pay <u>tariffs</u> to use the highway.
13. The dancers waved colorful <u>kerchiefs</u>.
14. Fishing boats unload at the <u>wharves</u>.
15. The <u>chefs</u> worked together in the hot kitchen.

SKILL FINDER

Daily Language Practice, p. 357J

Reading-Writing Workshop, pp. 398–399F

Literacy Activity Book, p. 155

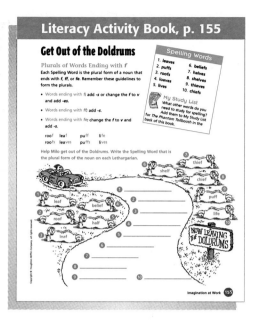

Literacy Activity Book, p. 156

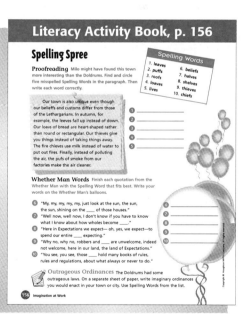

MEETING INDIVIDUAL NEEDS

Challenge

Challenge Words Practice Have students use the Challenge Words to offer Milo suggestions of ways to entertain himself when he's bored.

Instruct *and* Integrate

Grammar

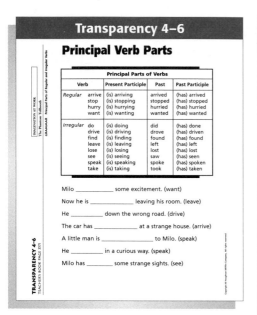
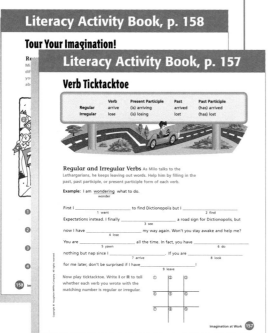
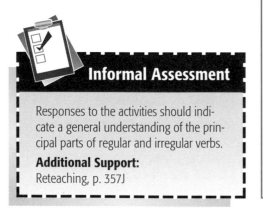
TESTED SKILL

Principal Parts of Regular and Irregular Verbs

LAB, pp. 157–158

- The **principal parts,** or basic forms, of a verb are the verb, the present participle, the past, and the past participle. All the verb tenses come from these four basic parts.
- A verb is **regular** when the past and past participle are formed by adding *-ed*. A verb is **irregular** when the past and past participle are formed in some other way.

Teach/Model On the chalkboard, write these two sentences without the underlines:

Milo walked across the room.

He thought about the present in the box.

Ask a volunteer to underline the verb in the first sentence. Elicit that it is a past tense verb formed by adding *-ed*. Then have a student underline the verb in the second sentence. Help students see that this verb also is in the past tense but is formed differently. Introduce and discuss the terms *regular* and *irregular verbs.* Encourage volunteers to provide several examples of both types of verbs.

Display Transparency 4–6. Introduce the term *principal parts*. Discuss the chart with students, pointing out the four principal parts, reviewing the spelling changes in the regular verbs, and eliciting the formation of the past and past participle of irregular verbs. Make sure students note that the present participle and the past participle are used with a helping verb.

Lead students to see why the principal parts of irregular verbs must be memorized. Then have volunteers write the correct verb form in each sentence and name the principal part after the sentence. Let students work in pairs to use the remaining verbs from the chart and their own verbs in sentences.

SKILL FINDER Reading-Writing Workshop, p. 399E

INTERACTIVE LEARNING (continued)

Practice/Apply

Literacy Activity Book Refer students to the Handbook at the back of the *Literacy Activity Book* for additional irregular verbs.

Cooperative Learning: Verb Comics Suggest that students work in small groups to create a cartoon or a comic strip about an unusual trip. Have them choose a regular verb and an irregular verb and write dialogue or captions using the past, the present participle, and the past participle forms of the verb.

Writing Application: Journal Entry Suggest that students write a journal entry describing what happened one day when they set out on an unexpected adventure. Have them use a variety of principal parts of both regular and irregular verbs in their entries.

Students' Writing Have students review their writing in process for correct verb forms. Suggest that they check principal parts in the dictionary.

Reteaching

Principal Parts of Verbs

MEETING INDIVIDUAL NEEDS

Prepare a set of 20 cards. Write an irregular verb *(be, blow, do, drive, find, have, leave, lose, make, ring, see, speak, swim, think, write)* or a regular verb *(worry, play, share, slip, travel)* on each one. Make one *is/are* and one *has/have* "necklace" with cards and string for each group of three students. Write the four principal part headings on the chalkboard. Remind students that they are the basic forms of a verb.

Have one member from each group choose a card while the others put on the "necklaces." Review with students how to decide whether the verb is regular or irregular and how to form the principal parts. Have the students wearing the necklaces write the present participle and past participle forms and the student choosing the card write the verb and the past tense. Suggest that members use their forms in an oral sentence.

Daily Language Practice

Focus Skills

Grammar: Principal Parts of Regular and Irregular Verbs

Spelling: Plurals of Words Ending with *f*

Each day write one sentence on the chalkboard. Have each student write the sentence correctly on a sheet of paper. Tell students to check for correct formation of regular and irregular verbs and for misspelled words. Have students correct their own paper as a volunteer corrects the sentence on the chalkboard.

1. Milo has receive a present unlike the other toys on his shelfs.
   Milo has **received** a present unlike the other toys on his **shelves**.

2. Milo driven through a pile of leves.
   Milo **drove/has driven** through a pile of **leaves**.

3. He seen pufs of clouds above the roofs of the houses.
   He **saw/has seen puffs** of clouds above the roofs of the houses.

4. Milo has find a place with unusual livs and beliefs.
   Milo has **found** a place with unusual **lives** and beliefs.

5. He thinked of warm lofs of bread and other kinds of food.
   He **thought** of warm **loaves** of bread and other kinds of food.

Communication Activities

Listening and Speaking

Reader's Theater

Divide the class into small groups to present dramatic interpretations of major events in *The Phantom Tollbooth*. Within the group, have students select characters to play, including that of narrator. Encourage students to be expressive as they play their parts. To give students more performance experience, you may want to have them read their roles in auditions and rehearsals for the Reader's Theater.

Debate: The Watchdogs Versus the Lethargarians

Have two teams debate "How Important Is Thinking?" Call on a volunteer to play Milo, the moderator. Encourage students to support their arguments and rebuttal statements with quotes from the selection. Invite questions from the audience, and allow panelists time to respond. Remind students that Lethargarians may have difficulty thinking through their arguments clearly and completely, so some waffling and whining is acceptable. The Watchdogs will most likely be jumpy, grumpy, and impatient, so expect some growling too.

Viewing

Films, Fantasy, and Special Effects

Discuss with students how special effects in movies can create fantastic conditions. Encourage them to think about the fantastic events depicted in movies they have seen: in comedies, *Home Alone;* animation, *Aladdin;* science fiction or futuristic movies, *Star Trek* or *Stargate.* Ask them if any of these films would be as imaginative if they didn't have the special effects? If possible, bring in a video with fantastic special effects for the class to view together.

Special Effects	
split-screen	allows actor to play twins or two different characters
mechanical puppets	creates realistic monsters, as in *Jaws* and *Jurassic Park*
computer graphics	creates state-of-the-art animation, as in *The Last Starfighter*

Make a Flip Book

Students can make their fantasies come to life by making flip books, simple examples of animation.

Materials
- paper
- markers
- black binder clips

1 Students should choose a "process" that they can illustrate in 12 to 20 steps on 5" x 5" pieces of paper.

2 Attach the pages with metal binder clips.

3 Encourage students to share their flip books with classmates, family, and friends.

Portfolio Opportunity

Make a videotape of the Reader's Theater or debate, and save it in a class portfolio.

3

Instruct and Integrate

Cross-Curricular Activities

Book List

Science

Time & Space
by John and Mary Gribben

The Super Science Book of Time
by Kay Davies and Wendy Oldfield

This Book Is About Time
by Marilyn Burns

Science

Biological Time

Living organisms have biological clocks that govern some aspects of their lives. Lead a discussion about some of the seasonal changes that occur in animals' behaviors and appearances. Have students develop a chart similar to the one shown here.

Animal	Season	Appearance/Behavior
mountain hare	summer	brown fur
	winter	white fur

Choices for Social Studies

The Time of Your Life

Some students may enjoy making personal time lines to record important events in their own lives.

2 Above the time line, they can list and/or sketch important things that happened to them.

1 Have them mark off long strips of tag board into equal segments, one for each year of their lives.

3 In the space below the time line, they can record historical events that occurred worldwide.

Materials

- tag board
- markers
- rulers

Choices for Social Studies *(continued)*

Old Timers

The ancient Babylonians created a calendar based on twelve lunar months, but extra days had to be added every few years.

The Egyptians based their calendar of twelve, thirty-day months on the first appearance over the horizon of the star Sirius—the brightest in the sky, about 8.7 light-years from Earth. That calendar, too, accumulated errors.

The Maya closely observed the sun, moon, and stars to arrive at a calendar year of 365 days.

Have students research other calendars in use today—Hebrew, Islamic, and Chinese calendars—and have them compute their birth dates in each.

What Time Is It Where You Are?

Explain that Earth is divided into 24 standard time zones. On a globe these divisions resemble the sections of an orange. Ask students to locate and mark the 0° and 180° meridians on a map and then mark each time zone at 15° intervals. Emphasize that 360° makes a complete circle of the globe.

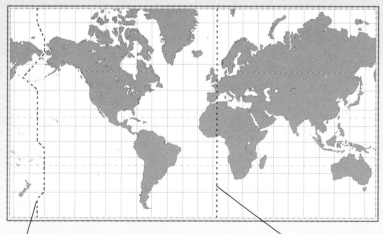

The meridian exactly opposite Greenwich, at 180°, is the International Date Line. There are some jogs in the line to accommodate political boundaries. Crossing the International Date Line from east to west adds one day.

The 0° meridian is an imaginary line circling Earth's surface through the North and South poles. It runs through Greenwich, England. Clocks to the east are set to a later hour, and clocks to the west to an earlier hour.

In the Chinese calendar, each month begins with the new moon. Years are designated in cycles of 60, and an animal name is assigned to each year.

To find the year in the Hebrew calendar, add 3,760 to the date in the Gregorian calendar, which is in use by most people in the Western world.

Building Background

Remind students that George Lucas imagined and created the films *Star Wars, The Empire Strikes Back*, and, with Steven Spielberg, *Raiders of the Lost Ark*. Then have students who have seen these films recall and describe them, prompted with questions such as these:

- What made these films interesting or enjoyable for you? (They were exciting adventures; they had amazing creatures and dazzling special effects.)

- Which characters do you remember most? Why? (Samples: Luke Skywalker, Han Solo, Princess Leia, and Indiana Jones, because they have wild adventures and survive all the dangers they face; Darth Vader, R2-D2, Yoda, because they're unique or unusual.)

MEET...GEORGE LUCAS

Join WORLD reporter Anthony Howard for an exclusive interview with the creator of *Star Wars* and Indiana Jones.

I never dreamed I'd be doing something like this!" says Junior Member Anthony Howard, 13. In the spring of 1992, Anthony, wearing a T-shirt in the photograph on page 360, found himself behind the scenes at a film studio near his home in Wilmington, North Carolina. He was on assignment for WORLD to talk to George Lucas, writer, director, and producer — sometimes all three — of such blockbuster films as *Star Wars, The Empire Strikes Back, Willow*, and *Raiders of the Lost Ark* and other Indiana Jones movies. Lucas was working on a TV series called *The Young Indiana Jones Chronicles*. It's about Indy's boyhood adventures traveling around the world from 1908 to 1918 and meeting famous people like President Teddy Roosevelt, inventor Thomas Edison, and Dr. Sigmund Freud.

On location in Africa. Ten-year-old actor Corey Carrier as Young Indiana Jones with a Masai on the set of *The Young Indiana Jones Chronicles.*

From October 1992 issue of *National Geographic World* magazine. Copyright ©1992 by *National Geographic World*. *World* is the official magazine for Junior Members of the National Geographic Society. Reprinted by permission.

358

SETTING THE SCENE FOR

ADVENTURE

On location. George Lucas operates a camera in Spain while filming *The Young Indiana Jones Chronicles*. This TV series was shot in 20 countries.

TAKE

Visual Literacy

Draw students' attention to the graphic representation of the photographs that represent actual frames from Lucas's films. The white pattern represents the holes on both sides of film that fit into sprockets on film projectors.

Students Acquiring English

- In the phrase *another car slammed into his two-seater* you might explain that *slammed* means "crashed."

- A sports car is called a *two-seater* because that's how many people can sit in it.

- On page 361, George Lucas claims that it wasn't until college that he *"took off."* Ask students what they think he means by that expression. (He started applying himself and worked hard to do what he really wanted to do.)

To prepare for the interview, Anthony read all he could about Lucas. He learned that as a teenager, Lucas loved photography and car racing more than school. He planned to be a race car driver. Then one day when he was 17, another car slammed into his two-seater, flipping it over and nearly killing him. After the accident Lucas turned from racing itself to photographing races. At one he met a Hollywood cameraman and racing fan who urged him to go to film school. That led him to his life's work.

Today Lucas is not just making movies. He is also using his *Star Wars* technology and dazzling special effects wizardry for education. He is creating exciting videos that make history, science, and other subjects come alive for kids in the classroom.

Anthony caught up with Lucas at the busy studio during a break in shooting the TV series. "It was kind of overwhelming to meet George Lucas," he says. "At first I didn't know what to say. But he's a real personal, nice kind of guy. He put me right at ease. Pretty soon we were talking."

Spaceships charge between canyon walls in the *Star Wars* epic.

Anthony Howard, WORLD reporter, talks with George Lucas for this interview.

Young George
at 10

Listen in on Anthony's interview:

Q Can you tell me a little about your background?

A Well, I come from Modesto, a small town in northern California. After high school I went to a junior college for two years and then to USC (University of Southern California) and became a film student. I found I really liked it.

Q What kind of student were you before college?

A I had a very difficult time in school. I found it kind of boring. And it was hard to concentrate. It wasn't until college that I really took off and became a good student.

Q What effect did your car accident have on you?

A It's a miracle I survived. The accident made me think about my life. It made me realize I needed to get more serious about school, to try to be a better student, and do something with myself. It made me more aware of my feelings. I began to trust my instincts.

Q What made you become a producer and writer?

A I started out as a cameraman in school. . . . I had to learn how to become a writer so I could become a director, basically so I could edit my own films without anybody telling me what to do.

Q What do you like best about what you do?

A I love what I do, especially film editing. I love writing and telling the stories, the screenplays. I also have directed and really done all the things involved. But post-production — the cutting together of all the pictures of the scenes — is very, very exciting to me.

The hero Luke Skywalker and his extra-terrestrial friends make contact in *Star Wars.*

361

Genre

Interview

Teach/Model

Have students analyze the interview with George Lucas. Make sure they understand how interesting questions elicit more personal and meaningful answers from the subject. Ask students:

- Which question did you think was most interesting? (Answers should include Lucas's more personal responses—for example, the effect of the car accident on his life.)

- Which question could Anthony have known the answer to without asking George Lucas? (The first interview question. This is the sort of biographical information he could have researched prior to the interview.)

- What would you ask George Lucas if you had the chance?

Practice/Apply

Students can work in pairs to prepare an interview. First have them prepare a background file on their subject. When this is complete, they can create a list of questions to ask their subject directly.

Discussion

Let students respond freely to the interview, or prompt them with questions such as these:

- How would you describe George Lucas's imagination to someone who hadn't read this article?

- What did you learn about Lucas that surprised you?

- Which part of Lucas's work is most interesting to you? Why?

- Do you agree with Lucas that film *"has an important place in our society . . . to tap in on values . . .?"* Why or why not?

- If you could put your imagination to work by making a film, what would it be about?

Q Do you plan to complete the *Star Wars* saga?

A Yes, I hope to do it in the next seven to eight years, after the TV series. The first ones were parts four, five, and six of *Star Wars*. Now I'll do parts one, two, and three.

Q What about Luke Skywalker? His name is Luke; yours is Lucas. Did you sort of identify with him?

A Yeah, that's pretty much what I did. Obviously, when you write a story, you identify with a character. Part of writing is pretending you're right in the story.

Q What are you doing now in your education projects?

A I'm working on a kind of experiment — to show teachers how film technology can work in the schools. I want to show what it could be like in the future.

Drama and adventure in *Return of the Jedi* **from the** *Star Wars* **trilogy**

Q What else do you like to do besides work?

A Well, I'm a father, and I'm raising two daughters. That's very important to me. And I like to have free time to read and play tennis and, you know, have fun.

Q What advice would you give kids who might want to get into filmmaking?

A Do as well as you can in school. Study things that will give you something to make movies about — like literature and history. Then get a film degree.

Q What would you say to kids to inspire them?

A I think film has an important place in our society . . . to tap in on values. It has a tremendous force for good or bad. . . . Making films is one way to help, in a small way, change the world and try to make things better.

Left, **Lucas supervises filming of his TV series.**

Right, **R2-D2 of** *Star Wars* **fame**

362

After the interview Anthony watched the actors in the cast of the TV series film a scene where young Indy solves a mystery in Thomas Edison's laboratory. "It was exciting to watch," says Anthony.

Anthony is looking forward to the next episode of his favorite Lucas story, *Star Wars* — set "a long time ago in a galaxy far away." What will Anthony do in *this* galaxy in the not too distant future? Would he be interested in making films? "Actually," he says, "after college, I want to play professional basketball. I know it will take a lot of work. But that's my dream."

Well, as Luke Skywalker might say, "Trust your instincts, Anthony. . . . And may the Force be with you."

by Judith E. Rinard

Below, Anthony meets Sean Patrick Flanery, who starred as 17-year-old Indiana Jones, and Robyn Lively, who played a girlfriend. "They were fun!" says Anthony.

NAME DROPPER The name of the little droid in *Star Wars* came from a note Lucas made while editing another film. His shorthand for "Reel two, Dialogue two" was R2-D2."

DOG DAYS While Lucas wrote *Star Wars*, his faithful dog, an Alaskan husky, kept him company each day. Later Lucas named a famous character after his pet. The dog's name? Indiana!

COASTER KING As a boy Lucas loved the thrilling rides of Disneyland. As an adult he created today's "Star Tours," one of Disneyland's most popular rides.

PUPIL POWER Lucas made his first major film in college — a science fiction movie called *THX–1138.* It won first prize at the 1967–68 National Student Film Festival.

MAIL CALL Lucas receives more than 20 fan letters a day, many from children.

🏠 Home Connection

Students and members of their families may enjoy watching a video of one of George Lucas's productions together. To learn more about the filmmaker, students and their families can write to: *Star Wars Insider Magazine*, P. O. Box 111000, Aurora, Colorado, 80042.

Technology

Encourage students to research and report on the special effects that were produced for *Star Wars*. Have students present their findings in visual format, such as a poster or bulletin board.

Speaking and Listening

Have pairs of students act out the interview, adding gestures and variations in volume, pitch, and tone. They might tape-record or video-tape these mock interviews to share with another class.

Music

Students may enjoy listening to a recording of the music John Williams composed for *Star Wars*. Encourage them to discuss how musical composition for film is another example of the imagination at work.

✏️ Social Studies

Have students imagine that they've been asked to make a new Indiana Jones film! What historical event would they choose as a jumping-off point? What new twists would they put on this adventure hero? Have them describe their ideas in a paragraph or essay.

SELECTION:
Faith Ringgold

by Robyn Montana Turner

Other Books by the Author

Rosa Bonheur

Mary Cassatt

Frida Kahlo

Georgia O'Keeffe

Dorothea Lange

 • **Notable Children's Trade Book in the Field of Social Studies**

Selection Summary

Early in her artistic career, Faith Ringgold began to question whether classic European art should be her model. Why not work in the media of the African American women who came before her: fabric, beads, storytelling, quilts? This selection—the second half of a full-length biography—shows how one artist's style, materials, subjects, and sense of self evolved through years of experimentation, struggle, and success. Through detailed studies of individual works of art, Robyn Montana Turner tells the story of a remarkable woman whose determination to be true to her heritage resulted in an entirely new art form.

Lesson Planning Guide

	Skill/Strategy Instruction	Meeting Individual Needs	Lesson Resources
1 **Introduce** *the* **Literature** *Pacing: 1 day*	**Preparing to Read and Write** Prior Knowledge/Building Background, 363C **Selection Vocabulary,** 363D • heritage • dimension • composition • media • abstract • convey • legacy **Spelling Pretest,** 385H • heroes • studios • radios • potatoes • mottoes • solos • pianos • echoes • stereos • volcanoes	**Support in Advance,** 363C **Other Choices for Building Background,** 363C **Students Acquiring English,** 363C **Spelling Challenge Words,** 385H • mementos • tuxedos • ghettos • avocados • vetoes	***Literacy Activity Book:*** Vocabulary, p. 159 **Transparencies:** Building Background, 4–7; Vocabulary 4–8 **Great Start** CD-ROM software, "Imagination at Work" CD
2 **Interact** *with* **Literature** *Pacing: 1–3 days*	**Reading Strategies** Predict/Infer, 364, 366 Summarize, 364, 370, 376 Evaluate, 364, 374 **Minilessons** Writer's Craft: Time and Sequence, 365 Making Inferences, 367 ✔ Noting Details, 369 Compare and Contrast, 371 Text Organization, 373 Genre: Biography, 379	**Choices for Reading,** 364 **Guided Reading,** 364, 368, 372, 378, 382 **Students Acquiring English,** 365, 371, 373, 377, 381, 384 **Extra Support,** 383 **Challenge,** 372	**Reading-Writing Workshop:** A Personal Essay, 398–399F ***Literacy Activity Book:*** Selection Connections, pp. 147–148; Comprehension Check, p. 160 **Audio Tape** for Imagination at Work: *Faith Ringgold* **Student Writing Center,** writing and publishing software
3 **Instruct** *and* **Integrate** *Pacing: 1–3 days*	✔ **Comprehension:** Noting Details, 385A **Writing:** Writing a Biographical Sketch, 385C ✔ **Word Skills and Strategies:** Word Roots *graph* and *ven*, 385E; Dictionary: Word Forms, 385F **Building Vocabulary:** Vocabulary Activities, 385G ✔ **Spelling:** Plurals of Words Ending with *o*, 385H ✔ **Grammar:** Adjectives, 385I **Communication Activities:** Listening and Speaking, 385K; Viewing, 385L **Cross-Curricular Activities:** Art, Social Studies, Math, Careers, 385M–385N	**Reteaching:** Noting Details, 385B **Activity Choices:** Biographical Sketch, Art Review, Create an Award, 385D **Reteaching:** Word Roots: *graph* and *ven*, 385F **Activity Choices:** Art Words, Number Prefixes, Imagination at Work, 385G **Challenge Words Practice:** 385H **Reteaching:** Adjectives, Daily Language Practice, 385J **Activity Choices:** Listening and Speaking, 385K; Viewing, 385L **Activity Choices:** Art, Social Studies, Math, Careers, 385M–385N	**Reading-Writing Workshop:** A Personal Essay, 398–399F **Transparencies:** Comprehension, 4–9; Writing, 4–10; Word Skills, 4–11; Grammar, 4–12 ***Literacy Activity Book:*** Comprehension, p. 161; Writing, p. 162; Word Skills, p. 163; Building Vocabulary, p. 165; Spelling, pp. 166–167; Grammar pp. 168–169 **Study Skills:** ✔ Index, 385N, H2 **Audio Tape** for Imagination at Work: *Faith Ringgold* **Channel R.E.A.D.** videodisc: "The Case of the Missing Mystery Writer" **Student Writing Center,** writing and publishing software

✔ *Indicates Tested Skills. See page 332F for assessment options.*

Introduce *the* Literature

Preparing to Read and Write

Support in Advance

Use this activity for students who need extra support before participating in the whole-class activity.

Art Talk Write the word *art* on the board and ask students to discuss what it means. Which are examples of art?

- a dance • a song • a blanket

Management Tip
Have other students write in their journals about kinds of art they like.

Students Acquiring English
Help students understand *art, artist,* and *artistic,* letting them use each word in sentences.

INTERACTIVE LEARNING

Prior Knowledge/Building Background

Key Concept
Artistic
Expression

Arrange to have a variety of art books in class for students to look through. Choose books that survey art from different time periods and different cultures. If your classroom has access to CD-ROM art software, include it in your survey. OR have students flip through their Anthologies to see various examples, styles, and types of art.

Ask small groups of students to brainstorm as many different kinds of art as they can and list them in a chart like the one on Transparency 4–7. Suggest that they include both visual art and aural art. Is there art that appeals to touch, smell, or taste? Ask a spokesperson from each group to share one or two of their best–or most unusual–examples with the whole class. As they do, note details on the transparency.

Transparency 4–7

Artistic Expression

Kind of Art	Materials Used	An Example	The Artist
painting	paint, paper or canvas, brushes, water	*Mona Lisa*	Leonardo da Vinci

---

Other Choices for Building Background

 Quick Writing

Ask students to write for five minutes about a piece of art that they have created or helped create: a painting, a dance recital, or a sculpture in art class. Suggest that they describe their creation in enough detail that someone might picture it from their description.

Inspiration

Challenge Direct students' attention to the word *inspiration* on page 364. In discussion have them use the word *inspire* in sentences about themselves, art, school, or other topics. Have them note examples of Faith Ringgold's inspiration as they read.

Great Start For students needing extra support with key concepts and vocabulary, use the "Imagination at Work" CD.

Selection Vocabulary

Key Words

heritage

media

dimension

abstract

convey

composition

legacy

This painting is *abstract*.

Display Transparency 4–8. Explain that each sentence uses one of the vocabulary words to describe one of the pictures. Have students identify and discuss the picture that each sentence describes. Then ask them to draw a line between the sentence and the picture.

Vocabulary Practice Have students work independently or in pairs to complete the description on page 159 of the *Literacy Activity Book*.

Spelling
You may want to give the Spelling Pretest on page 385H before students read the selection.

Daily Language Practice
Use the activities on page 385J as a daily practice of the spelling and grammar skills taught with this selection.

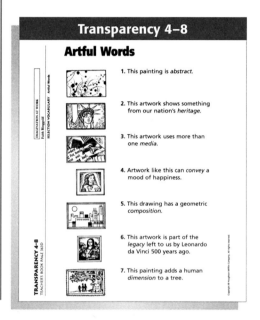

Transparency 4–8

Artful Words

1. This painting is *abstract*.
2. This artwork shows something from our nation's *heritage*.
3. This artwork uses more than one *media*.
4. Artwork like this can *convey* a mood of happiness.
5. This drawing has a geometric *composition*.
6. This artwork is part of the *legacy* left to us by Leonardo da Vinci 500 years ago.
7. This painting adds a human *dimension* to a tree.

Social Studies

Teacher FactFile
Quilting

Traditionally, quilts are bed covers made of two layers of fabric with a layer of cotton, wool, or down feathers in between, all stitched firmly together.

In a *pieced quilt,* many small pieces of fabric—often scraps of discarded clothing—are sewn together to form a pattern. A jumble of odd-shaped patches sewn together haphazardly is called a "crazy quilt."

Beautiful designs have been handed down from generation to generation, including the "Wedding Ring," the "Flower Garden," and the "Dresden Plate."

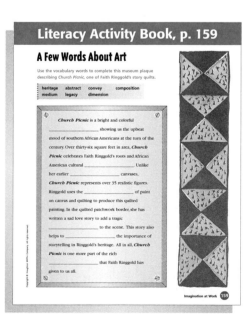

Literacy Activity Book, p. 159

A Few Words About Art

Use the vocabulary words to complete this museum plaque describing *Church Picnic*, one of Faith Ringgold's story quilts.

heritage	abstract	convey	composition
medium	legacy	dimension	

Church Picnic is a bright and colorful _____ showing us the upbeat mood of southern African Americans at the turn of the century. Over thirty-six square feet in area, *Church Picnic* celebrates Faith Ringgold's roots and African Americans cultural _____. Unlike her earlier _____ canvases, *Church Picnic* represents over 35 realistic figures. Ringgold uses the _____ of paint on canvas and quilting to produce this quilted painting. In the quilted patchwork border, she has written a sad love story to add a tragic _____ to the scene. This story also helps to _____ the importance of storytelling in Ringgold's heritage. All in all, *Church Picnic* is one more part of the rich _____ that Faith Ringgold has given to us all.

Imagination at Work **159**

Interact *with* Literature

Reading Strategies

▶ **Predict/Infer**
Summarize
Evaluate

Discussion Encourage students to discuss the importance of reading strategically, and ask them to choose strategies they might apply to this selection, such as

- using details and their own experience to predict what may happen next
- pausing to summarize events of Faith Ringgold's life
- evaluating examples of Faith Ringgold's art

Predicting/Purpose Setting

Have students make predictions before they begin to read. Encourage them to revise these predictions as they read the selection.

Choices for Reading

Independent Reading	**Cooperative Reading**
Guided Reading	**Teacher Read Aloud**

Guided Reading

Have students who are using the Guided Reading option read to page 368 to see if their predictions were confirmed.

by Robyn Montana Turner

FAITH RINGGOLD

. . . dreamed of becoming an artist since she was very young, but her art teachers didn't help her learn to express her African American heritage. Instead, Faith looked to her mother and her childhood as inspiration for her art. By experimenting with fabric, beads, sculpture, and quilts, Faith Ringgold created a new art form. Today she is a famous African American artist.

FAITH RINGGOLD
ROBYN MONTANA TURNER

364

QuickREFERENCE

Background: FYI

Bank Street College is a leading school of education in New York City. Early in her career, Ringgold was an art teacher in a public school. Today, she is a tenured professor at the University of California at San Diego.

Social Studies Link

Students might enjoy making a simple family tree to keep track of Ringgold's ancestors' names. (More details about them occur later in the selection.) Later, students can construct their own family trees, noting contributions of individual ancestors.

In 1972, something happened to take Faith Ringgold a step further toward expressing her true heritage. Teaching at Bank Street College in New York City, she was challenged by one of her students. Why did Ringgold encourage her students to create with fabric and beads — the media of African women — the student questioned, when her own artwork was made of paint on canvas?

At first Ringgold rejected the question even though she had sensed something distant and cold about the process she was using to paint. Soon she realized the worth of her student's words. Why *not* work with fabric and beads? After all, the women in her family had worked with these media for generations.

Suddenly Ringgold felt a link with her great-great-grandmother, Susie Shannon, a "house girl" who had been a slave on a plantation. Susie had taught Faith's great-grandmother, Betsy Bingham, to sew quilts. Betsy's granddaughter, Willi, had told Faith stories about watching Betsy boil and bleach flour sacks until they were as white as snow to line the quilts she made. Ringgold recalled the days when Willi, who operated powerful sewing machines in the garment district, had taught her to use the smaller sewing machines at home. Willi had taught her daughter everything about sewing. Now Ringgold knew she wanted to carry on the tradition of working with fabric and beads.

That summer, on another trip to Europe, Ringgold discovered *tankas*, cloth frames for sacred paintings from Tibet. When she returned home, she made some *tankas* for her paintings. The cloth border enhanced the images, and they could be easily rolled up and carried around. Ringgold knew she was onto something

Susie Shannon. *c. 1900.* Susie Shannon, Ringgold's great-great-grandmother, who was part Cherokee and a former slave, lived to be 110 years old.

365

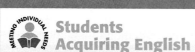
Students Acquiring English

Text Organization Encourage students to flip through the selection and notice the art. Explain that these works of art represent stages of development in Faith Ringgold's life as an artist, and they appear chronologically in the selection.

MINILESSON

Writer's Craft
Time and Sequence

Teach/Model

Ask a volunteer to describe why the phrase *In 1972* is a good way to begin this selection. (The words are time clues that help us begin to track the sequence, or order, of events in the selection.) Next, have students look at the second paragraph and find two time-clue words that begin sentences. (*At first, Soon*) Invite students to discuss how time clues often appear at the beginning of sentences and paragraphs to set the stage for the events that are about to be described.

Practice/Apply

Have students find the time-clue words in the third and fourth paragraphs on pages 365–366. (*Suddenly, Now; That summer; Soon*) Have them note time-clue words throughout the selection.

SKILL FINDER | Writing Activity: Biographical Sketch, p. 385D

Interact
with
Literature

Reading Strategies

▶ **Predict/Infer**

Ask students to discuss how early details—the student's question, Faith Ringgold's discovery of *tankas*, and her childhood in Harlem—helped them predict how her artwork would change. Ask them to infer the reasons for the change. Model this process with a Think Aloud.

Think Aloud

As I read these first two pages, I predicted that Faith Ringgold's art-work would change. But why? Some of her reasons are stated directly, but I also could "read between the lines" and think about other reasons. I guess I thought that Faith changed her art to make it more human (as it says in the selection) *and* to reflect more of her African American heritage.

wonderful. Soon she asked Willi to make *tankas* as frames for her other paintings.

As much as she liked the flat *tankas*, Ringgold wanted her art to have a more human <u>dimension</u>. So she reflected upon her childhood in Harlem, where people had been close to each other in a friendly and beautiful place. She remembered the faces and the souls of the people — everything about them. She began to form soft sculptures in the style of African masks. These pieces featured women who had been role models to her. All of those women had a sense of themselves. They were bold, not shy. They did not hold back. They did the best they could with what they had. The subjects of her soft sculptures, such as *Mrs. Jones and Family*, also came to include children, the elderly, and heroes such as Dr. Martin Luther King, Jr.

Faith Ringgold. **Mrs. Jones and Family.** *The Family of Woman Mask Series. 1973. Sewn fabric and embroidery. 60 x 12 x 16 inches.* Mrs. Jones and Family is a soft sculpture of Ringgold's family — Willi, Andrew, Barbara, and Faith. The mouths of the life-size mask figures are open to symbolize the rich storytelling tradition of Ringgold's culture.

366

QuickREFERENCE

Background: FYI
Willi Posey Jones, Faith's mother, was a sewing machine operator and later a clothing designer in New York City's garment district.

Visual Literacy
African masks were used largely in religious ceremonies, coronations, and royal funerals. Often made of wood, the imaginative sculptures influenced many modern artists such as Pablo Picasso and Georges Braque.

In the same year that she sculpted *Mrs. Jones and Family*, Ringgold gave up teaching to be a full-time artist. Willi, who had developed a busy career as a fashion designer, continued to help her daughter by sewing *tankas* and costumes for her soft sculptures. Ringgold was so resourceful that she packed her sculptures into trunks and sent them around to college campuses to be displayed. She also traveled to give art lectures and workshops. Without the help of gallery owners or dealers, Ringgold was getting her art before the eyes of the public.

During the next few years, Ringgold's art career thrived. She began doing theatrical performances to go with her art exhibits. In 1976, on her first trip to Africa, Ringgold observed the art and the people of Ghana and Nigeria, which gave her new ideas to weave into her own style.

Ringgold's daughters, Michele and Barbara, became women during the seventies. They both graduated from college. Barbara married. Michele published a book. Life for the Ringgold family could not have been better. In 1981, however, Ringgold was suddenly faced with the saddest event of her life — the death of her mother, who was seventy-nine years old. To express her grief, Ringgold turned to a friend and companion — her art.

Perhaps because she missed working with Willi, Ringgold changed her medium and style. She painted abstract images on canvas. No longer did her subjects look familiar. Instead, she painted irregular shapes moving about in bright colors. Each shape may have been taken from an idea or a memory.

Birdie, Barbara, and Michele were surprised to see this new means of expression. They could almost feel and listen to the shapes. Ringgold explained that the images came from deep within her soul. The mysterious nature of the paintings left them nameless until

Faith Ringgold Modeling in One of Her Mother's Fashion Shows. *1950.*
As a young woman, Ringgold sometimes modeled dresses that her mother had designed and sewn.

367

Background: FYI
Birdie is Burdette Ringgold, Faith's second husband. The couple married in 1962.

Background: FYI
Harlem is a community at the northern end of Manhattan Island and has long been a center for African American business and culture.

MINILESSON

Making Inferences

REVIEW & MAINTAIN

Teach/Model

Ask a volunteer if Faith Ringgold was *bold*. Then ask for details from the selection that prove that she was (or was not). Explain that writers often expect readers to "add up" details and their own experience to get more information than what the words actually express. It's "reading between the lines" to learn more than what is specifically stated.

Practice/Apply

Invite students to find details about Faith's mother, Willi, from pages 365–367. (told stories about grandmother, taught Faith to sew, made *tankas*, was successful fashion designer, her death changed Faith's life) **Based on these details—and their own experiences with mothers and daughters—ask them to draw an inference about the relationship between the two women.** (Faith was very close to her mother. Her mother was a source of knowledge and inspiration.)

SKILL FINDER

Full lesson/Reteaching, Themes 2, 5

Minilessons, Themes 1, 2, 5

Interact *with* Literature

 Guided Reading

Comprehension/Critical Thinking

1. After 1972, what major change did Faith Ringgold make in the materials she used for her art? (Ringgold decided to work with fabric and beads, materials that women in her family had used for generations.)

2. How would you describe Faith Ringgold's soft sculptures? (The soft sculptures are like cloth African masks; they feature Ringgold's role models.)

3. Why did Faith Ringgold begin painting abstract images? (The abstract images were her response to her mother's and sister's deaths; she seemed to be searching for a new means of expressing her innermost feelings.)

Predicting/Purpose Setting

Remind students to revise or add to their predictions. Have them continue to read to the end of page 373. Use the questions on page 372 to check students' comprehension.

Birdie suggested calling them the Emanon series, which spells *no name* backwards, a substitute for *Untitled* in jazz circles.

The next year brought both tears and joy. The family experienced more sorrow upon the death of Faith's sister, Barbara. But their spirits were renewed with the birth of Faith's first grandchild — Baby Faith — young Barbara's daughter.

Even before Baby Faith was born, Barbara and Michele talked to her through the walls of Barbara's womb. They wanted to instill the family's rich history of language early on. So it came as no surprise that, at six months, Baby Faith pointed toward one of her grandmother's brand-new <u>abstract</u> paintings and said her first word: "Dah!" From that utterance came the title of a series of six abstract paintings. The Dah series expresses Faith's sorrow in losing her mother and her sister, as well as her joy in gaining a grandchild.

Faith Ringgold. **Dah #3.**
1983. Acrylic on canvas.
72 x 54 inches.

368

QuickREFERENCE

🏠 Home Connection

Ringgold's family worked to help her succeed as an artist. Suggest that students have a conversation with their parents about their mutual goals and how they can work together to achieve them.

Science Link

Ringgold's family talked through Barbara's womb to establish contact with her unborn baby. Invite interested students to research how unborn babies react to various stimuli. Are they really able to hear and respond to human communication?

Visual Literacy

Invite students to share their responses to *Dah #3*. What in general do they like or dislike about abstract art?

More than twenty years had passed since Ringgold had set out to become a professional artist. On her own and with Birdie, she had developed an audience for her art across the country. Finally, in 1986, she began working with a New York art dealer who showcases the works of women and ethnic minority artists. At last she had a market for selling her art. Now Ringgold could focus strictly on *doing* art.

Just as Ringgold was experiencing newly found freedom in her career, *Groovin' High* shows jubilant movement. Dancers shift in polyrhythms, an African way of having a variety of rhythms around you at the same time. Even the figures are different sizes, moving in different directions and in different spaces. In the African tradition of the Kuba people of Zaire, Ringgold sewed her favorite motif — four triangles in a square — and quilted them together to form the border. If you look closely, you can see that she also strengthened the painted canvas by stitching rows of large squares across it. Now Ringgold would call herself "a painter who works in the quilt medium."

Faith Ringgold. **Groovin' High.** *1986. Acrylic on canvas; tie-dyed, printed, and pieced fabric. 56 x 92 inches. Collection of Barbara and Ronald Davis Balser.*

369

Social Studies Link

Encourage students to use a map of Africa to find Zaire at the heart of the continent. Explain that it is three times the size of Texas and that the Kuba people are just one of many ethnic groups in the country.

M I N I L E S S O N

Noting Details

Teach/Model

Help students see that this selection is full of details, some of which are more important than others. First, have them note several from page 369, such as:

- Dates: In 1986, Ringgold began working with an art dealer.

- Examples: *Groovin' High* shows how Ringgold's art has evolved.

- Images: triangles in a square

- Quotations: "a painter who works in the quilt medium"

Model this process with a Think Aloud.

Think Aloud

Robyn Montana Turner gives a lot of different details. Some of them seem more important than others, like the one about the art dealer. It seems important because it's a kind of breakthrough for Ringgold. Now her work is being shown in public.

Practice/Apply

Invite students to note details on another page of the selection and record them. Have them circle the ones they consider most important.

Full lesson/Reteaching, pp. 385A–385B; Theme 3

Minilessons, p. 391; Themes 1, 3

Interact *with* Literature

Reading Strategies

 **Summarize**

This is a good point to ask students to pause and summarize the events of Ringgold's life *before* she began to work in the quilt medium. Ask them to summarize what led her to this turning point in her career. They might express their summaries in various ways:

- one or two sentences written independently or in pairs
- a paragraph written collectively by a small group
- a shared summary spoken orally by volunteers from the whole class
- a storyboard of three to five frames, which summarizes the most important events in pictures

Working on her quilted paintings, Ringgold realized that she had more to say than images alone could convey. She felt a need to write down stories. After all, she had grown up listening to Willi tell family stories in the oral tradition of their heritage.

One day, Ringgold thought of a way to publish her stories through her art. She would write her stories onto her quilts. Then everyone who saw her artwork would also read her "story quilts."

The stories on Ringgold's quilts are dilemma tales. They present problems without solutions. In this way, Ringgold follows an African tradition in which the storyteller does not make judgments. Instead, she leaves the audience with questions that might have many answers.

Church Picnic tells and shows the story of an African American gathering in Atlanta, Georgia, in 1909. The event takes place during the time of Willi's childhood, a time when southern African Americans were hopeful about the future. The banner on the ground lets us know that this is a church picnic in the urban south. The picnickers sit on patterned blankets and turn their eyes to the focal point of the composition — the minister and a young woman dressed in pink.

The storyteller is the woman seated beside her son, who touches her shoulder, in the upper right of the quilt. Later, at home, the storyteller describes the picnic to her daughter, Aleathia, whom she assumes is in another room.

Ringgold wrote the words exactly as she imagined that they were said — in a southern dialect. For example, the mother says, "The Reverend and Miss Molly was sure 'nuff in love at the picnic. The way he took

370

Self-Assessment

Invite students to reflect on their reading of the story so far, with questions such as: How well am I following the story of this artist? Have my predictions/questions been appropriate and helpful?

QuickREFERENCE

★★★ Multicultural Link

Story Quilts Writing on quilts dates to the 1800s, when *album quilts* were popular. Album quilts carried well-known quotations, Bible verses, lines of poetry, and/or the names of the people who created the quilt.

 Journal

After they've read the selection, invite students to write their own "dilemma tales" (tales that present problems without solutions) based on personal experiences.

her in his arms, and she look up at him so tender. They in love chile."

Midway through the story, the mother realizes her daughter is not at home after all, but nevertheless continues to talk to herself. Later, just before Aleathia returns, we learn that she too is in love with the reverend, and that she stayed away from the picnic to avoid the pain of seeing him with Miss Molly. With no solution in mind, the mother consoles herself by saying, "God don't give us no more than we can bear."

Faith Ringgold. **Church Picnic.** *1988. Acrylic on canvas; pieced fabric borders. 74½ x 75½ inches. Collection of the High Museum, Atlanta, Georgia. Gift of Don and Jill Childress through the 20th Century Art Acquisition Fund. Ringgold wrote the story of the Church Picnic story quilt on cotton canvas, which she sewed onto the top and bottom of the quilt. It hangs in the permanent collection of the High Museum, in Atlanta.*

371

MEETING INDIVIDUAL NEEDS

Students Acquiring English

Storytelling Focus students' attention on the sentence *One day, Ringgold thought of a way to publish her stories through her art.* This refers, of course, to the literal writing of words on quilts, but it also suggests that each quilt "tells a story." Let students choose and study their favorite quilts from the selection and tell oral stories based on the images they contain.

Compare and Contrast

REVIEW & MAINTAIN

Teach/Model

Invite students to turn back to pages 368 and 369 to compare and contrast *Dah #3* and *Groovin' High.* As they make observations, have them note whether they compare (find similarities) or contrast (find differences). For example:

- The colors are oranges, golds, and blues. (compare)

- Both use acrylic on canvas. (compare)

- *Groovin' High* is realistic; *Dah #3* is abstract. (contrast)

Practice/Apply

Have students use two other examples of Ringgold's art to complete a compare-and-contrast chart.

	Title and date	Title and date
subject matter/ inspiration		
colors/tones		
media		
border		
mood		
other details		

SKILL FINDER

Full lesson/Reteaching, Theme 6

Minilessons, Themes 3, 5, 6

Interact *with* Literature

 **Guided Reading**

Comprehension/Critical Thinking

1. Why did Ringgold write stories on her quilts? (She couldn't convey everything she wanted to say with images; she had a need to tell stories.)

2. How did Faith Ringgold draw upon African culture in *Groovin' High*? (She shows dancers shifting in polyrhythms, an African way of having a variety of rhythms around you at once; she uses a motif from Zaire—four triangles in a square.)

3. Who is Cee Cee Prince? (She is a fictional character from the story quilt *Harlem Renaissance Party*. She shares many qualities with Ringgold herself.)

4. Which piece of Ringgold's art do you like most so far? Give your reasons.

Predicting/Purpose Setting

Remind students to revise or add to their predictions or purpose-setting questions as they continue to read the selection.

(Opposite page)
Faith Ringgold. **Harlem Renaissance Party.** *Bitter Nest: Part II. 1988. Acrylic on canvas; printed, tie-dyed, and pieced fabric. 94½ x 82 inches.* The *Harlem Renaissance Party* story quilt is one among five quilts in the Bitter Nest series. Seated around the table are: Celia (left); Florence Mills (singer and comedienne); Aaron Douglass (painter); Meta Warrick Fuller (sculptor); W. E. B. Du Bois (organizer and writer); Cee Cee's husband; Richard Wright (writer); Countee Cullen (poet, novelist, playwright); Zora Neale Hurston (novelist, folklorist, anthropologist); Alain Locke (philosopher and writer); Langston Hughes (poet and writer); and Cee Cee.

372

To dress the characters in the *Church Picnic* story quilt, Ringgold recalled the clothes people wore to church when she was young — Sunday-best dresses, hair-ribbon bows, white socks, patent-leather shoes, starched shirts, suits, and ties. After church, families had picnics in the parks of Harlem. They brought picnic baskets, linen napkins, fine tablecloths, china plates, glasses, and sterling silverware.

Like *Church Picnic*, several of Ringgold's story quilts celebrate mealtime in the African American community. To create them, she drew from her imagination, her knowledge of historical events, and memories.

A favorite memory was of Willi's Sunday evening desserts — sweet-potato pie, pound cake, or peach cobbler. Sometimes the family would have company for this special treat. Of course, Willi's table was formally set. On Sunday evening, the children got to listen to the radio.

The elegant table setting and the dressed-up guests of *Harlem Renaissance Party* are reminders of the Sunday evening desserts and Sunday afternoon picnics from Ringgold's childhood. But this story quilt is about a fictional event and character — a deaf woman named Cee Cee Prince, who stands in a colorful African dress that she has quilted.

Even though Cee Cee comes from Ringgold's imagination, she is a lot like Ringgold in real life. They both adore quilting colorful wall hangings, coverlets, and bags. Like Ringgold, Cee Cee likes to dance and perform. Cee Cee is married to a dentist, however, who sits at the head of the table. Their daughter, Celia, seated left of Cee Cee, shrinks from embarrassment because her mother loves to dance to her own music and wear a mask in front of the distinguished dinner guests.

Informal Assessment

If students' responses indicate that they are understanding the selection, have them finish reading it independently or cooperatively. If they still need help, have them answer questions on page 378.

Quick REFERENCE

 Home Connection

Invite students to talk with their parents to recall memorable family meals like the one pictured on page 373. If they were to prepare a story quilt of the event, what would it show?

 Challenge

Research Encourage students to research and report on the Harlem Renaissance figures depicted in this quilt. Students might read poems by Countee Cullen or Langston Hughes or summarize *Their Eyes Were Watching God* by Zora Neale Hurston. Others might find pictures that show the artwork of Aaron Douglas or Meta Warrick Fuller.

The guests are famous artists from the era of the Harlem Renaissance. During this time, from 1919 to 1929, African American painters, sculptors, musicians, poets, novelists, and dramatists flocked together in Harlem. Their art left a rich cultural legacy. Indeed, Ringgold's invention of the story quilt reflects that same spirit of being creative and true to yourself.

373

Interact *with* Literature

Reading Strategies

▶ **Evaluate**

Ask students to imagine them-selves at the performance of *Faith Ringgold's Over 100 Pounds Weight Loss Performance Story Quilt*. How do they think this performance might affect them? Would they think it was weird? Powerful? Moving? Exciting? Unpleasant? Do they think the performance—as it is described here—was worthwhile? Why or why not? Make sure they give reasons for their answers.

Faith Ringgold. **Change: Faith Ringgold's Over 100 Pounds Weight Loss Performance Story Quilt.** *1986. Photo etching on canvas. 57 x 70 inches. Detail below.* Ringgold traveled around the country to perform live dramatizations of the story and images on this quilt.

During the late 1980s, Ringgold performed *Change: Faith Ringgold's Over 100 Pounds Weight Loss Perform-ance Story Quilt* on stages across the United States. Audiences first viewed the quilt, which features photographs of Faith's life with the story that explains how she overcame her weight problem. Then they watched her act out the story on stage.

The performance needed only a few props. As she recited the words of the story quilt, Ringgold dragged around a black plastic bag filled with a hundred pounds of water to show the heavy burden she had been carry-ing as body weight. "I can CHANGE. I can do it. I can do it. I can CHANGE. I can CHANGE. Now!" she chanted to the beat of African drums. The story quilt and performance remind the audience that with determination people can change their lives.

374

QuickREFERENCE

Media Literacy

Performance art usually features a live artist presenting personal mate-rial and often includes video, sound, lighting effects, and props. Students might know of some contemporary examples that they can describe to the class.

Health Link

One hundred pounds is a lot of weight to lose! Invite students to research and distinguish between safe weight-loss techniques and dieting methods that might prove dangerous to their health.

Dancing on the George Washington Bridge has a similar message — that of being free and able to reach your highest goals. This story quilt is one in a series of five, which Ringgold designed to show women claiming the bridges of New York and San Francisco. Recalling her childhood fascination with the George Washington Bridge, she considered it to be a "magnificent masculine structure." Onto her story quilt, she now would paint fifteen women flying, dancing, laughing, and singing above that bridge and the skyline. Their colorful patterned dresses unite the canvas with the patterned cloth border.

Faith Ringgold. **Dancing on the George Washington Bridge.** *The Woman on a Bridge Series. 1988. Acrylic on canvas; pieced fabric borders. 68 x 68 inches. Collection of Roy Eaton.*
Ringgold likes the way bridges are formed because they remind her of quilts floating in air. She sees their triangles as being little quilt patches of air separated by the girders.

375

Social Studies Link

The 4760-foot George Washington Bridge is the sixth-longest suspension bridge in the world. Students might investigate one specific type of bridge—suspension, cantilever, steel arch, truss, cable-stayed—and report on how it is built.

Interact
with
Literature

Reading Strategies

▶ Summarize

Discuss with students how they might summarize the information about the French Collection to make sure they understand it. The information continues through page 382. Model the summarizing process, using a Think Aloud.

Think Aloud

The French Collection is a series of twelve story quilts about a fictional character, Willia. She's kind of like Faith Ringgold, but she does things that Faith Ringgold never got to do, like study art for many years in Paris. In the quilts, Ringgold shows how she feels about the great masters of art and about how women like her have always felt excluded from their world. In these quilts, African American women find their places in the world of art. The French Collection is the last of Ringgold's story quilts.

Leonardo da Vinci. **Mona Lisa.** *Paris, Louvre.* SCALA/ ART RESOURCE, NEW YORK (K 80332). Leonardo da Vinci was a well-known artist of the Renaissance period in Europe. He lived about five hundred years ago. His paintings are carefully preserved in museums such as the Louvre. The *Mona Lisa* is so popular that people stand in line to see it.

In 1991, Ringgold traveled to Paris to begin working on a series of story quilts called the French Collection. These twelve story quilts tell the adventures of an African American woman named Willia Marie Simone, who was born in Faith's imagination. She does things Ringgold never did but would like to have done — such as study art for years by herself in Paris. Willia's story makes us aware of the struggle that all women artists have faced in the male-centered art world.

The story starts in 1920, when sixteen-year-old Willia leaves Harlem to become an artist in Paris. Willia's mother has a sister, Aunt Melissa, who wants Willia to develop her artistic talents. So she has suggested the trip and has given Willia five hundred dollars to help with expenses. Years later, Willia will send her two children to live with Aunt Melissa because Willia is determined to become a professional artist in Paris. She eventually becomes a world-famous painter and enjoys being among the inner circles of Parisian artists.

In *Dancing at the Louvre*, Willia helps her friend Marcia take her three daughters to visit the Louvre, a historic museum in Paris. The children dance in front of the familiar painting the *Mona Lisa*, by Leonardo da Vinci.

By posing the children as dancers beneath the *Mona Lisa*, Ringgold revealed her feelings about European art. Traditionally African Americans and women were not included among the inner circles of European artists. So Ringgold depicted the figures in this piece observing European art with interest but also with lightheartedness. Even Ringgold's Mona Lisa, with her half-smile, seems to be amused at the romping and dancing below. She appears to understand Ringgold's intent for these

376

 Multicultural Link

Paris, the capital of France, has long been considered the art capital of the world. During the nineteenth and early twentieth centuries, young artists from the United States and all over the world were attracted to Paris's Montmartre district, where a special atmosphere of freedom allowed new styles to develop.

Social Studies Link

The Louvre Originally built as a palace for the king of France in about 1200, the Louvre is the most famous art museum in the world. It covers more than forty acres, has eight miles of galleries, and contains more than a million works of art.

viewers to appreciate European art, as long as they do not take it too seriously.

As models for this story quilt, Ringgold used photographs of her own family. Marcia and her children look like Ringgold's daughter Barbara and her children, Baby Faith, Teddy, and Martha. Willia Marie resembles Ringgold's mother as a young woman. In fact, Willia's personality was inspired by Ringgold's memories of Willi. Willia Marie's story is written across the top and bottom of the quilt. A patterned border frames the brightly painted canvas.

Faith Ringgold. **Dancing at the Louvre.** *The French Collection, Part I. 1991. Acrylic on canvas; pieced fabric borders. 73½ x 80½ inches.* Ringgold used artistic freedom to reproduce the paintings that hang in the Louvre. She purposely altered the colors and frames — even the sizes of the reproductions. For example, in real life, the *Mona Lisa* is smaller than it appears on the story quilt. Perhaps Ringgold enlarged the piece because of its importance in the story.

377

Art Link

Mona Lisa Probably the most famous portrait ever painted, the *Mona Lisa* shows Lisa del Gioconda, the wife of a Florence merchant. Leonardo da Vinci actually intended to show the woman's face moving into or out of a smile.

Interact with Literature

Guided Reading

Comprehension/Critical Thinking

1. How does Faith Ringgold's *Harlem Renaissance Party* reflect the Harlem Renaissance? (It shows the major African American artists who contributed to the movement. It also reflects the period's creativity and spirit.)

2. What is the theme or message that Faith Ringgold expresses in her *Over 100 Pounds Weight Loss* quilt? (With determination, people can change their lives.)

3. What do bridges, especially the George Washington Bridge, represent for Ringgold? (A bridge is a way to get somewhere. For Ringgold, bridges might represent reaching a goal.)

4. Who is Willia Marie Simone, and what does she tell you about Faith Ringgold? (Ringgold created Simone to do things that Ringgold would have liked to have done. From her, we learn about Ringgold's dreams and disappointments.)

Predicting/Purpose Setting

Ask students to predict how this selection will end.

Vincent van Gogh.
Sunflowers. *1888. Munich, Neue Pinakothek.*
SCALA/ART RESOURCE, NEW YORK.
Dutch painter Vincent van Gogh (1853–1890) never knew that his artwork would someday become famous. Today his paintings are popular throughout the world.

Another quilt in the French Collection tells the story of Willia at a meeting of an imaginary group called the National Sunflower Quilters Society of America. African American women who changed history work on a quilt of sunflowers. Standing in the sunflower field is Dutch artist Vincent van Gogh, who painted many still life images of sunflowers during his lifetime.

When the sun goes down, the women finish piecing their quilt. The story reads that van Gogh "just settled inside himself, and took on the look of the sunflowers in the field as if he were one of them." In this way, Ringgold contrasts the way that some men traditionally have created art — alone with their paints — with the method of the women quilters, who work as a team.

Diagram of #4 The Sunflowers Quilting Bee at Arles. *Reprinted by permission of Melissa McGrath.*

1. Madame Walker, businesswoman
2. Sojourner Truth, social reformer
3. Ida Wells, journalist
4. Fannie Lou Hamer, civil rights activist
5. Harriet Tubman, abolitionist
6. Rosa Parks, civil rights activist
7. Mary McLeod Bethune, educator
8. Ella Baker, civil rights activist
9. Vincent van Gogh

378

Informal Assessment

Oral Reading Ask volunteers to choose a paragraph or two from the selection so far to read aloud. See the Oral Reading Checklist in the *Teacher's Assessment Handbook* for criteria.

QuickREFERENCE

Background: FYI

Vincent van Gogh (1853–1890) is better known than any other painter. In 1987, *Sunflowers* was sold at auction to an anonymous buyer for 39.9 million dollars. During his tragic life, however, the Dutch artist sold only one painting.

Faith Ringgold. **#4 The Sunflowers Quilting Bee at Arles.** *The French Collection, Part I. 1991. Acrylic on canvas; pieced fabric. 74 x 80 inches. Private collection.*

379

Genre
Biography

Teach/Model

Write the word *biography* on the board and ask a volunteer to define it. (the story of someone's life written by someone else) Invite students to brainstorm as many elements of biographies (what they include) as possible, such as

- important dates and events in chronological order

- facts about the person's family

- photographs of important events and people

- stories about the person's experiences

- facts about the person's culture and community

- opinions about the person's personality and contributions

Practice/Apply

Encourage students or pairs of students to prepare and present brief biographical sketches of the African American women listed at the bottom of page 378. Invite students to explain how each woman "changed history."

Interact
with
Literature

2

Faith Ringgold. **Matisse's Chapel.** *The French Collection, Part I. 1991. Acrylic on canvas; pieced fabric borders. 74 x 79½ inches.*
The bright colors, flat shapes, exciting patterns, and simple lines of Matisse's chapel are present in Ringgold's story quilt. Again, she used artistic freedom to reproduce the art of a European male artist. It is interesting to note that Ringgold painted Ralph, the brother she never knew, on Willi's lap.

The Chapel of Vence.
Photograph by Hélène Adant. Rights reserved.
From his wheelchair, Matisse used his scissors as he would have used a chisel, carving with color the large paper shapes as designs for stained glass windows of the chapel.

380

QuickREFERENCE

★★★ Multicultural Link

Henri Matisse (1869–1954) was the leader of *fauvism*, a movement in modern painting marked by vivid colors and a free treatment of form. Matisse's work has a decorative quality similar to the art of the Middle East. The Chapel of Vence, also called the Chapel of the Rosary, is located in Vence, France. It was designed and decorated by the artist between 1948 and 1951.

As Ringgold traveled in France to gather ideas for the French Collection, she visited a chapel designed by Henri Matisse, a well-known French artist. *Matisse's Chapel* became a story quilt based on an imaginary gathering of Faith's own relatives in the chapel. In the story quilt, they are known, of course, as Willia Marie's family.

At the time that Ringgold painted *Matisse's Chapel*, everyone in the image had died. From photographs and memories, she re-created their likenesses. Their talk is of slavery. Their hearts are bitter. But their pride is still alive.

Faith Ringgold's mother, Willi Posey, with her sisters, Bessie and Edith. *c. 1920s.*

Diagram of Matisse's Chapel.
Reprinted by permission of Melissa McGrath.

Faith Ringgold's grandfather Professor Bunyon Posey. *c. 1880s.*

1. Ida Posey, grandmother
2. Susie Shannon, great-great-grandmother
3. Betsy Bingham, great-grandmother
4. Professor Bunyon Posey, grandfather
5. Aunt Janie, grandaunt
6. Uncle Peter, granduncle
7. Barbara Knight, sister
8. Willi Posey (Jones), mother
9. Ralph, brother who died as a baby
10. Andrew Louis Jones, Sr., father
11. Andrew Louis Jones, Jr., brother
12. Uncle Hilliard
13. Uncle Cardoza
14. Aunt Edith
15. Aunt Bessie
16. Mildred, cousin
17. Ida Mae, cousin
18. Baby Doll Hurd, grandmother
19. Rev. Jones, grandfather

Faith Ringgold's uncle Cardoza Posey in his World War I uniform. *1919.*

381

 Home Connection

Invite students and their parents to imagine a get-together between themselves and their ancestors, living and dead. Who exactly would attend? They might use the opportunity to look at and identify old photographs if they are available.

 Students Acquiring English

In the spirit of Matisse's Chapel, invite students to make collages of family photographs to share with their classmates. Encourage them to photocopy old photographs to prevent loss or damage.

Interact
with
Literature

 Guided Reading

Comprehension/Critical Thinking

1. Who are the women of the National Sunflower Quilters Society? (The women were all influential African American leaders who changed history.)

2. Why did Faith Ringgold decide to stop making story quilts? (Publishers asked her to write and illustrate her stories as children's books instead.)

3. Faith Ringgold did not want to sacrifice "one iota" of her blackness, her femaleness, or her humanity to become a successful artist. Give examples from her art that show she has achieved this goal.

Faith Ringgold and Baby Faith. *1989. Photograph © Lucille Tortora.* Ringgold has received six honorary doctorates from several colleges and universities. Other awards include a Caldecott Honor for her children's book *Tar Beach*, a John Simon Guggenheim Memorial Foundation Fellowship, the Coretta Scott King Award for Illustration, and the Arts Award for Painting and Sculpture from the National Endowment for the Arts. Her name was on a *New York Times* list of Ten Major Women Artists, and her artwork is published in books for both children and adults. In this portrait, she embraces her granddaughter Baby Faith.

The French Collection became the last of Ringgold's quilts with a story written on the fabric. Just as Ringgold had hoped, publishers asked her to write and illustrate her stories as children's books. Her artwork can be found in the permanent collections of many museums throughout the world. Many private collectors, including Oprah Winfrey and Bill Cosby, own her work.

Today Ringgold divides her year between teaching as a full professor and doing her art. Until recently, she had a studio in the garment district of Manhattan, where Willi Posey first taught her to sew. Reminiscing, Ringgold says, "The neighborhood has a lot of memories for me because I used to go down there, and she'd take me into factories to buy fabric by the bolt. She would get a kick out of the fact that my studio was down there for a while."

Now Ringgold enjoys a new studio and home in Englewood, New Jersey, which is across the George Washington Bridge from Harlem. Reflecting upon a time long ago when she was even too young to sew with a machine, she says with a smile, "I still love that bridge."

382

Self-Assessment

Ask students if they think the reading strategies they used helped them better understand and enjoy the selection. Ask them to evaluate the entire selection in terms of the information presented, the organization of the text, and their own enjoyment.

Background: ᶠʏɪ

Caldecott The Caldecott Medal is an annual award given to the most distinguished picture book published for children. It was named after Randolph Caldecott (1846–1886), an English illustrator.

Vocabulary

Iota Explain that *iota* is the ninth letter of the Greek alphabet and corresponds to our letter *i*. Since the letter is small, the word *iota* has come to mean "a very tiny amount."

★★★ Multicultural Link

Invite students to discuss or write about how they can affirm their own ethnic background or sex while struggling to achieve a goal. Why is it important not to sacrifice aspects of one's background?

After I decided to be an artist, the first thing that I had to believe was that I, a black woman, could be on the art scene without sacrificing one iota of my blackness, or my femaleness, or my humanity.

— **Faith Ringgold**

ABOUT
Robyn Montana Turner

In fourth grade, Turner read a biography of Jane Addams, a social reformer from Chicago who won the 1931 Nobel Peace Prize. Addams, who had a professional career outside her home, inspired Turner's professional interests in teaching, writing, and art education. The biography of Faith Ringgold is one of Turner's series titled *Portraits of Women Artists for Children*. She says, "The series sprung from my collective experiences as mother, teacher, writer, editor, feminist, and artist. In many ways I've been researching this series all my life. There's a part of us in each of these books. I hope you find yours."

More About the Author

Robyn Montana Turner

A writer and consultant on the subject of multicultural art education for young people, Robyn Montana Turner holds a master of arts degree in Media Education and a doctorate in Curriculum and Instruction from the University of Texas at Austin. She writes of her growing up, "Aside from my teachers, two nurses, and the director of the local blood bank, I didn't know one woman whose professional career extended beyond the home." Her biographies of women artists represent her attempt to rectify a "limited understanding of just exactly what women were capable of doing with their lives and of the professional contributions they could make." The former elementary school teacher lives in Austin, Texas.

383

MEETING INDIVIDUAL NEEDS

Extra Support

Rereading Suggest that students who have difficulty understanding Faith Ringgold's development reread the selection, keeping in mind the three main parts: (1) early ideas about art, (2) a new art form: the story quilt, and (3) The French Collection.

Interact
with
Literature

Responding Activities

 ### Personal Response

Ask students to tell which examples of Faith Ringgold's art they liked most and to give reasons.

Anthology Activities

Students can choose an activity from pages 384–385.

Literature Discussion

- What inspires artists like Faith Ringgold?

- What do you think Ringgold's future artwork will be like?

Selection Connections

Invite students to complete the part of the chart on *Literacy Activity Book* pages 147–148 that refers to *Faith Ringgold*.

Informal Assessment

Responses should indicate a familiarity with Ringgold's artwork and her efforts to express her heritage.

Additional Support:

- Use Guided Reading questions to review and, if necessary, reread.

- Have students summarize the selection.

Crafting Your

Make a Story Quilt

Tell a Story of Your Own

Using construction paper — or cloth if you wish — draw the design for a story quilt that tells a story from your own life or imagination. Like Faith Ringgold, you might combine scraps of your life and experience that didn't actually exist in the same time and place. Write a short description of what your design means and display the design or the quilt for others to see.

Make a Time Line

First, Then, Next

Make a time line of Faith Ringgold's life by attaching several sheets of paper lengthwise. On them, draw a long horizontal line and divide it into five-year segments, beginning in 1930 and continuing up to the present. Use as many details from the selection as possible to show the important events of Ringgold's life. Include any major world events that you know happened during her lifetime, too. (Like your own birthday!) Display your time line in your classroom.

384

 ### Quick**REFERENCE**

Media Literacy

On-line Resources Encourage students to use on-line resources at a local library to find recent magazine and newspaper articles about Ringgold's latest publications or work.

Students
Acquiring English

MEETING INDIVIDUAL NEEDS

Let students acquiring English make visual story quilts. Then pair them with native English speakers who can help them add a written dimension to their quilts in English.

RESPONDING

Own Ideas

Write a Poem

Words to Weave

Skim through the selection and choose what you think are the ten most important words or phrases. Then try to use all ten in a short poem about Faith Ringgold, her art, and what she means to you. Along with a brief introduction to *Faith Ringgold*, combine it with your classmates' poems on a bulletin board in your school.

Write a Comparison

Never Give Up

Like Milo in *The Phantom Tollbooth* (pages 334–355), Faith Ringgold sometimes found that her life as an artist slowed down to a near standstill. What are some of the obstacles that she had to overcome to get her life moving again? Who or what is the Watchdog that helps her get out of her Doldrums? Write a brief comparison of how the two people — one fantastic, one real — move on with their life journeys after being temporarily stuck.

385

Comprehension Check

To check student comprehension, use these questions and/or *Literacy Activity Book* page 160.

1. Why did Ringgold decide to change her art style from traditional painted canvases to story quilts? (She wanted to use materials of her heritage: fabric, beads, and storytelling.)

2. Based on her story quilts and other paintings, what do you think Faith Ringgold values most? (Answers will vary: family, heritage, expression of her own ideas, breaking through traditional rules, storytelling.)

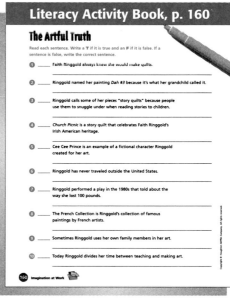

Literacy Activity Book, p. 160

The Artful Truth

Read each sentence. Write a **T** if it is true and an **F** if it is false. If a sentence is false, write the correct sentence.

1. _____ Faith Ringgold always knew she would make quilts.

2. _____ Ringgold named her painting *Dah #3* because it's what her grandchild called it.

3. _____ Ringgold calls some of her pieces "story quilts" because people use them to snuggle under when reading stories to children.

4. _____ *Church Picnic* is a story quilt that celebrates Faith Ringgold's Irish American heritage.

5. _____ Cee Cee Prince is an example of a fictional character Ringgold created for her art.

6. _____ Ringgold has never traveled outside the United States.

7. _____ Ringgold performed a play in the 1980s that told about the way she lost 100 pounds.

8. _____ The French Collection is Ringgold's collection of famous paintings by French artists.

9. _____ Sometimes Ringgold uses her own family members in her art.

10. _____ Today Ringgold divides her time between teaching and making art.

160 Imagination at Work

 Home Connection

Art Exhibits Encourage students to organize a family outing to an art gallery or museum OR watch a videotape that provides an art museum tour. Suggest that they use the concepts and vocabulary from *Faith Ringgold* to discuss the art with their parents and siblings.

 Portfolio Opportunity

- Comprehension Check: Save *Literacy Activity Book* page 160.
- Save students' time lines, story quilts, poems, or comparisons.

Instruct *and* Integrate

Comprehension

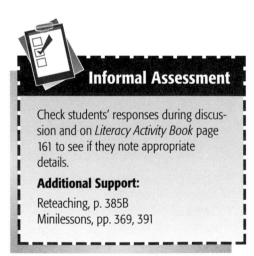

Informal Assessment

Check students' responses during discussion and on *Literacy Activity Book* page 161 to see if they note appropriate details.

Additional Support:

Reteaching, p. 385B
Minilessons, pp. 369, 391

 Noting Details

LAB, p. 161

Teach/Model

Invite students to share real-life situations in which paying attention to details made a big difference. Explain that noting details will also help with reading. Note that details can help them:

- visualize characters and events
- predict outcomes
- make inferences
- understand important ideas

Ask students to note details of Ringgold's French Collection quilts on pages 376–381. What do these suggest about Ringgold's artistic purpose?

Think Aloud

In each of these quilts, I notice that Faith Ringgold has combined her own personal history with the work of famous artists–da Vinci's *Mona Lisa,* van Gogh's *Sunflowers,* and the chapel designed by Matisse. It's as if Ringgold is saying, "Think about the artwork of women and African Americans as you do that of white European men." This is an important idea in her work that the details make me see.

Note that one of Ringgold's goals is to preserve her own and her family's experiences and achievements. As students note details about this idea, have a volunteer list them on Transparency 4–9. For example:

Practice/Apply

- Have students complete *Literacy Activity Book* page 161.

- Have students also choose one detail from *Faith Ringgold* and tell or write how it helps them understand the selection.

Page	Title	Detail
377	*Dancing at the Louvre*	main character is modeled on Ringgold's mother
379	*#4 The Sunflowers Quilting Bee at Arles*	African American women work as a team while van Gogh stands alone

SKILL FINDER   Minilessons, pp. 369, 391; Themes 1, 3

Reteaching | Noting Details

Invite students to note details about the actual historical figures as well as the imaginary characters who appear in Ringgold's artwork. You may want to write questions such as these on the board:

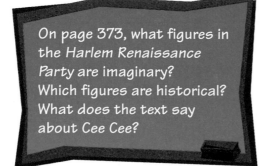

On page 373, what figures in the Harlem Renaissance Party are imaginary? Which figures are historical? What does the text say about Cee Cee?

(Only Cee Cee Prince, her husband, and her daughter are imaginary; the others are actual historical figures who contributed to African American culture in Harlem.)
(She is a lot like Ringgold herself.)

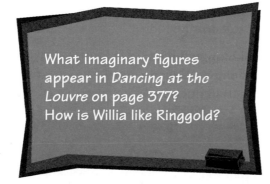

What imaginary figures appear in *Dancing at the Louvre* on page 377? How is Willia like Ringgold?

(Willia Marie Simone, her friend Marcia, and Marcia's daughters)
(She is an African American artist who did the things that Ringgold would have liked to have done.)

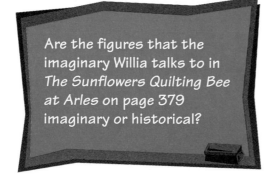

Are the figures that the imaginary Willia talks to in *The Sunflowers Quilting Bee at Arles* on page 379 imaginary or historical?

(historical)

As students note these details, ask students to think about, discuss, and write what the ideas suggest to them. (Answers will vary. Ringgold likes to mix historical and imaginary characters; Ringgold creates imaginary characters like herself so she can "be there" to experience important historical and cultural happenings.)

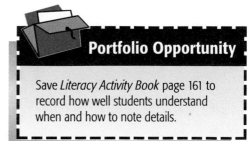

Portfolio Opportunity

Save *Literacy Activity Book* page 161 to record how well students understand when and how to note details.

Instruct *and* Integrate

Writing Skills and Activities

Transparency 4–10

A Biographical Sketch

Remembering Benjamin Franklin

*Early to bed and early to rise makes
a man healthy, wealthy, and wise.*

Do you recognize this saying? It is from *Poor Richard's Almanack*, a publication of weather forecasts, sayings, humorous stories, jokes, and proverbs. The publication, first appearing in 1732, was created by Benjamin Franklin. During his lifetime of 84 years, he was an author, printer, scientist, inventor, philosopher, educator, diplomat and statesman!

Born in Boston on January 17, 1706, Benjamin Franklin was one of seventeen children and went to school only two years. He very quickly stood out in his family, however, as he read books and studied on his own. In 1718, when he was 12, young Franklin was sent to work in the print shop of his half-brother, James.

Throughout his teens, Franklin served as apprentice to James and learned a great deal about the printing business. During this time, he also became an accomplished writer. Franklin wrote under the pen name of Mrs. Silence Dogood and secretly submitted letters to the weekly newspaper James had started. The letters were clever and humorous and became a popular feature. When James finally discovered the real author of the letters, however, he was not pleased. It was the end of Franklin's work with him. The year was 1723.

Literacy Activity Book, p. 162

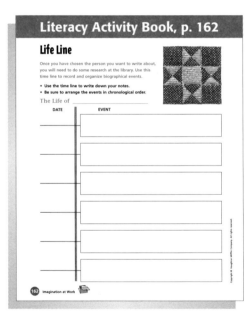

Life Line

Once you have chosen the person you want to write about, you will need to do some research at the library. Use this time line to record and organize biographical events.

• Use the time line to write down your notes.
• Be sure to arrange the events in chronological order.

The Life of _____

Informal Assessment

Check students' writing for focus and continuity. Do they present prominent events in the person's life? Do they use time-sequence words correctly?

Writing a Biographical Sketch

LAB, p. 162

Teach/Model

A biographical sketch is a written profile summarizing important events in a person's life. Encourage students who have read biographies or biographical sketches to describe the kinds of information they learned.

Display Transparency 4–10 and have volunteers read it aloud.

After reviewing this portion of a biographical sketch on American statesman and scientist Benjamin Franklin, provide students with some guidelines for writing their own biographical sketches.

• Choose a person who interests you, someone you would want to know. Look up facts about your subject: the person's birthday and birthplace; when and where he or she lived; his or her schooling.

• Find out what experiences helped shape your subject. What forces or situations shaped this person, made him or her unique?

• Begin your sketch with an anecdote about the person. You might choose an incident from the person's life or include a famous quotation from your biographical subject.

• Present at least two events from the person's life that you think best reveal your subject's character or achievements.

Practice/Apply

Assign the activity Write a Biographical Sketch. Remind students to include important dates and time-clue words when writing their biographical sketches.

Writing Activities

Students can use the **Student Writing Center** for all their writing activities.

Write a Biographical Sketch

Invite students to write biographical sketches. Suggest that they select one of the famous people referred to in the selection as having influenced Faith Ringgold, another famous person who interests them, or someone they know personally, such as a family member. Have them use *Literacy Activity Book* page 162 to help them plan their biographical sketches. *(See the Writer's Craft Minilesson on page 365.)*

Write an Art Review

Have students look through the selection and choose a work of art that they particularly like. Ask students to write a review of the art. Their review should include:

- the title of the artwork
- the artist's name
- facts about what the work represents
- the materials used
- notes about the artist's style and the use of color
- writer's opinion of the work

Create an Award

Invite students to design and write their own special award for Faith Ringgold. Suggest that students review the selection before deciding on the form of the award and the words they will put on it. Students can display their awards on the bulletin board.

Portfolio Opportunity

- Save *Literacy Activity Book* page 162 to record students' understanding of writing a biographical sketch.
- Save responses to activities on this page for writing samples.

Instruct *and* Integrate

Word Skills and Strategies

Literacy Activity Book, p. 163

Quilting Bee

Below is one completed quilt and one that hasn't been put together yet. Cut out the pieces of the incomplete quilt and assemble it. Make sure that each definition in your new quilt is in the same place as the word it defines in the already-finished quilt.

INTERACTIVE LEARNING

Structural Analysis

Word Roots *graph* and *ven*

LAB, p. 163

Teach/Model   Remind students that many English words are based on ancient Greek and Latin words. Explain that the meaning of a root affects the meaning of the word it is in. Readers who know these roots can figure out the meanings of many words. Write the roots *graph* and *ven* on the board. Explain that *graph* comes from a Greek word meaning "to write, draw, or record," and that *ven* comes from a Latin word meaning "to come." Then write these sentences on the board. Ask volunteers to come to the board to underline words containing *graph* or *ven*.

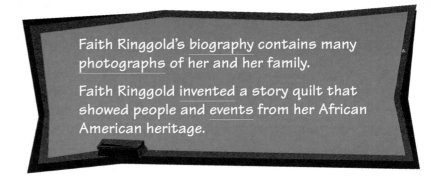

Faith Ringgold's bio<u>graph</u>y contains many photo<u>graph</u>s of her and her family.

Faith Ringgold in<u>ven</u>ted a story quilt that showed people and e<u>ven</u>ts from her African American heritage.

Discuss how the meaning of the root in each underlined word is related to the meaning of the word. (A biography is the written story of a person's life; photographs are recorded pictures; to invent is to come up with something new; and events are things that come to pass.)

Practice/Apply   ***Cooperative Learning***   Have students work in small groups to find the word roots in these words and discuss the ways in which the meaning of the root is related to the meaning of the word as a whole. Encourage students to use dictionaries.

adventure	autobiography	geography	choreograph
convene	convenience	graphite	intervene
invention	mimeograph	paragraph	prevent
revenue	seismograph	souvenir	telegraph

Informal Assessment

Use Practice/Apply to check students' understanding of the word roots *graph* and *ven*.

Additional Support:

Reteaching, p. 385F

Reteaching | **Word Roots *graph* and *ven***

Explain that the word root *graph* comes from an ancient Greek word meaning "to write, draw, or record," and that *ven* is a root that comes from a Latin word meaning "to come." Write these words on the board. Briefly discuss the meaning of each word, and ask students to explain how the meaning of the root is related to the meaning of the word.

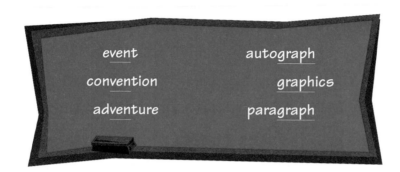

event   auto<u>graph</u>

con<u>ven</u>tion   <u>graph</u>ics

ad<u>ven</u>ture   para<u>graph</u>

M I N I L E S S O N

Dictionary
Word Forms

Teach/Model

Write this sentence on the board:

Faith Ringgold decided to use cloth frames as a way of enhancing her art.

Underline *enhancing* and tell students that if they wanted to find the meaning of this word in the dictionary, they would have to look up *enhance*, the base word of *enhancing*. Point out that the final *e* of *enhance* is dropped when an *-ing* ending is added. Tell students that they need to watch out for changes in spelling when they are trying to figure out the base word for an unfamiliar word. Tell them also that looking up a base word will tell them how to spell other forms of the word.

Display Transparency 4–11 and point out the base words and inflected forms of *create, discovery,* and *medium.* Ask students what spelling changes they notice between base words and the words with endings.

Practice/Apply

Write these words on the board: *picnicker, appreciates, savviest,* and *harmonized.* Ask students to look up each word to find the base word and any other forms listed in each entry.

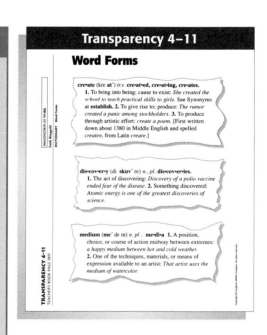

Transparency 4–11

Word Forms

cre·ate (krē āt´) *tr.v.* **cre·at·ed, cre·at·ing, cre·ates.**
1. To bring into being; cause to exist: *She created the school to teach practical skills to girls.* See Synonyms at **establish. 2.** To give rise to; produce: *The rumor created a panic among stockholders.* **3.** To produce through artistic effort: *create a poem.* [First written down about 1380 in Middle English and spelled *createn*, from Latin *creare.*]

dis·cov·er·y (dĭ skŭv´ rē) *n., pl.* **dis·cov·er·ies.**
1. The act of discovering: *Discovery of a polio vaccine ended fear of the disease.* **2.** Something discovered: *Atomic energy is one of the greatest discoveries of science.*

medium (mē´ dē m) *n. pl .* **me·di·a 1.** A position, choice, or course of action midway between extremes: *a happy medium between hot and cold weather.* **2.** One of the techniques, materials, or means of expression available to an artist: *That artist uses the medium of watercolor.*

Portfolio Opportunity

Save *Literacy Activity Book* page 163 to record students' understanding of the word roots *graph* and *ven.*

Instruct *and* Integrate

Building Vocabulary

Vocabulary Activities

Art Words

Have students work in pairs to find art-related words in the selection. Possible words include *paint, canvas, sculptures, gallery, exhibits, abstract, images, motif, pattern, design, still life, medium,* and *studio.* Students may add other art-related words they know to the list. Then ask students to select a word from the list to illustrate with drawings or photos clipped from magazines. Ask students to write a caption using one or more art-related words for the illustrations they create. (Example: "Abstract sculptures were on exhibit at the gallery.") Students' illustrations may be displayed on a bulletin board.

Imagination at Work

Have students find the list of creative careers on page 373 of the selection: "painters, sculptors, musicians, poets, novelists, and dramatists." The group can brainstorm additions to the list, such as choreographer, composer, fashion designer, filmmaker, chef, photographer, and storyteller. You may wish to divide the list and give students time to discuss in small groups how people in each of these professions use their imaginations.

Number Prefixes

Write the selection words *divide, dilemma,* and *polyrhythms* on the board. Then ask students if they recall what these terms had to do with Faith Ringgold's work. (Ringgold divides her time between teaching and creating art; Ringgold was interested in African dilemma tales and in the polyrhythms of African music.) Circle the prefix *di-,* explaining that it means "two": *divide* means to separate into two parts, and a *dilemma* presents a problem involving two choices. Circle the prefix *poly-* and explain that it means "many": African dancers often move to more than one beat at a time.

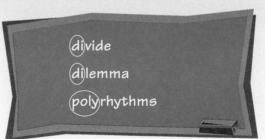

Literacy Activity Book, p. 165

Meaning Match

Find the word in the paint box on the right that belongs in the same category as a word in the paint box on the left. Color the matching circles.

Use this page to review Selection Vocabulary.

Spelling

M I N I L E S S O N

TESTED SKILL

Plurals of Words Ending with *o*

LAB, pp. 166–167

Spelling Words

*heroes   solos
*studios   pianos
*radios   echoes
*potatoes   stereos
mottoes   volcanoes

Challenge Words

mementos
tuxedos
ghettos
avocados
vetoes

*Starred words or forms of the words appear in *Faith Ringgold.*

Write the following pairs of word on the board:

studio	solo	hero
studios	solos	heroes

- Point out that *studio* ends with a vowel plus *o*. *Solo* and *hero* end with a consonant plus *o*. Note that the plurals of these words are formed by adding *-s* to *studio* and *solo,* and *-es* to *hero*. Explain that when a noun ends with a vowel plus *o*, the plural is formed by adding *-s*. Then tell students that when a noun ends with a consonant plus *o*, they must remember whether to add *s* or *-es*.

- Write the Spelling Words on the board. Say the words and have students repeat them.

Literacy Activity Book, p. 166

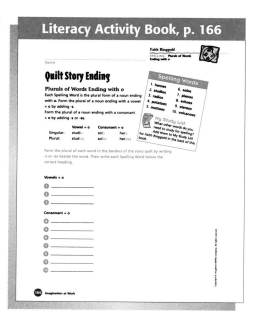

Literacy Activity Book, p. 167

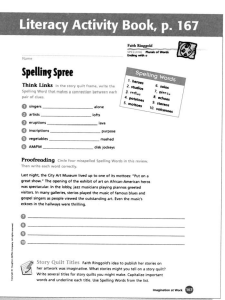

Spelling Assessment

Pretest

Say each underlined word, read the sentence, and then repeat the word. Have students write only the underlined words.

1. She painted pictures of national heroes.
2. Our class went to see artists' studios.
3. People listened more to radios before TV.
4. My favorite dinner is steak with potatoes.
5. We learn state mottoes in Social Studies.
6. Aimee had two solos in the recital.
7. Uncle Max makes a living tuning pianos.
8. The teacher's voice echoes in the gym.
9. Portable stereos are not allowed in school.
10. Only active volcanoes are dangerous.

Test

Spelling Words Use the Pretest sentences.

Challenge Words

11. Penguins look as if they're wearing tuxedos!
12. Carlos saves mementos in a shoebox.
13. If the president vetoes a law, it doesn't pass.
14. Many large cities have ghettos.
15. These avocados aren't ripe yet.

SKILL FINDER

Daily Language Practice, p. 385J

Reading-Writing Workshop, p. 399E

MEETING INDIVIDUAL NEEDS

Challenge

Challenge Words Practice Have students use the Challenge Words to write sentences from an art critic's review of a gallery opening.

Instruct *and* Integrate

Grammar

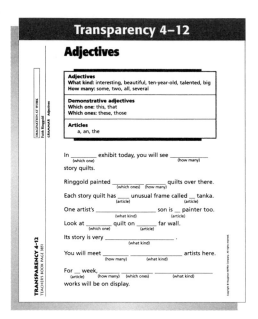

Transparency 4–12

Adjectives

Adjectives
What kind: interesting, beautiful, ten-year-old, talented, big
How many: some, two, all, several

Demonstrative adjectives
Which one: this, that
Which ones: these, those

Articles
a, an, the

In _____ exhibit today, you will see _____
(which one)   (how many)
story quilts.

Ringgold painted _____ _____ quilts over there.
(which ones) (how many)

Each story quilt has ____ unusual frame called __ tanka.
(article)   (article)

One artist's _____ son is __ painter too.
(what kind)   (article)

Look at _____ quilt on _____ far wall.
(which one)   (article)

Its story is very _____ .
(what kind)

You will meet _____ _____ artists here.
(how many)   (what kind)

For __ week, _____ _____ _____
(article) (how many) (which ones)   (what kind)
works will be on display.

Literacy Activity Book, p. 169

Fancy Stitches

Literacy Activity Book, p. 168

Complete a Quilt

Adjectives	what kind / how many	The **big** painting is **colorful**. / There are **many** colors in **one** painting.
Demonstrative adjectives	which one / which ones	I like **that** painting over there. / He prefers **these** quilts right there.
Articles		The quilt tells a story with **an** illustration.

Adjectives Match each numbered type of adjective in the sentences with an adjective of the same type from the box. Write the adjectives in the quilt squares.

I am making (1. article) (2. what kind) quilt.
I will paint (3. how many) (4. what kind) decorations.
The design of (5. which one) quilt will be (6. what kind).
Perhaps someday people will know me as (7. which one)
(8. what kind) artist.

several	unusual
a/an	delightful
famous	this
colorful	that

160 Imagination at Work

Informal Assessment

Responses to the activities should indicate a general understanding of adjectives.

Additional Support:
Reteaching, p. 385J

INTERACTIVE LEARNING

Adjectives
LAB, pp. 168–169

> • An **adjective** modifies, or describes, a noun or a pronoun. It can tell what kind, which one, or how many.
>
> • The **articles** *a, an,* and *the* are special adjectives. *A* and *an* refer to any item in a group; *the* refers to a specific item or items.
>
> • **Demonstrative adjectives** tell which one. *This* and *these* point out items nearby; *that* and *those* point out items farther away. *This* and *that* refer to one item; *these* and *those* refer to more than one.

Teach/Model   Write the following sentence on the chalkboard:

> Artists painted women in dresses.

Then have volunteers take turns rewriting the sentence at the chalkboard, adding and underlining one or more words in answer to each of these questions:

• What kinds of dresses were they? (Samples: *colorful, flowered, cotton*)

• How many women did artists paint? (Samples: *twelve, several, many*)

• Which artists painted women? (Samples: *Those, These*)

Introduce and discuss the terms *adjective* and *demonstrative adjective.* You may want to point out that demonstratives are adjectives only before nouns, as in *those artists.* Then elicit from students that many adjectives are used after linking verbs. Invite volunteers to describe the dresses in sentences, using linking verbs. (Sample: *The dresses were colorful.*) Next, write this sentence:

> Faith had <u>the</u> desire to be <u>an</u> artist even as <u>a</u> child.

Introduce and discuss *articles,* eliciting that *an* is used before a vowel sound and *a* before a consonant sound. Solicit other examples.

SKILL FINDER

Reading-Writing Workshop, p. 399E

Writing Skills, p. 396D; Grammar, p. 396J

INTERACTIVE LEARNING *(continued)*

Display Transparency 4–12. Review the adjectives, and have students use them to complete the sentences. Elicit that two- or three-word adjectives may be hyphenated before nouns. (Samples: *well-known, ten-foot*) You may want to have students add their own sentences, using adjectives.

Practice/Apply   ***Cooperative Learning:* Abstract Art** Discuss with students what abstract art is. Then have students work in pairs to design and draw a piece of abstract art. Suggest that they plan the work by writing questions that begin *What kind, How many,* and *Which one/ones* and then answering with sentences that contain adjectives, demonstrative adjectives, and articles.

Writing Application: Word Pictures Play a piece of classical, jazz, or other type of music, instrumental only. Ask students to think of how the music makes them feel and what images come to mind as they listen. Suggest that they write a paragraph describing the music and what it makes them think of. Encourage them to use specific, vivid adjectives, demonstrative adjectives, and articles.

Students' Writing Have students check their writing in process to be sure they have used articles and demonstrative adjectives correctly and to see where they can add adjectives.

Reteaching

Adjectives

Prepare a set of 16 or 20 cards of various colors, and write a different article, demonstrative adjective, or adjective on each one. Then post a large sheet of butcher paper and write *Adjective Quilt* at the top. Have each student choose a card, name the kind of adjective (Sample: *friendly*—adjective that tells what kind), paste the card on the butcher paper, and write the word in a sentence on the chalkboard. Review and reteach adjectives, articles, and demonstrative adjectives as students respond.

Daily Language Practice

Focus Skills

Grammar: Articles and Demonstrative Adjectives

Spelling: Plurals of Words Ending with *o*

Each day write one sentence on the chalkboard. Have each student write the sentence correctly on a sheet of paper. Tell students to check for the correct use of articles and demonstrative adjectives and for misspelled words. Have students correct their own paper as a volunteer corrects the sentence on the chalkboard.

1. Art from a studioes of several artists inspired her.
Art from **the studios** of several artists inspired her.

2. The echoz of her heroes are strong in this story quilts.
The **echoes** of her heroes are strong in **these** story quilts.

3. In those quilt you can almost hear pianose playing for the dancers.
In **that** quilt you can almost hear **pianos** playing for the dancers.

4. It would be easy to find soloes for an violin.
It would be easy to find **solos** for **a** violin.

5. People in the first half of these century listened to raidos daily.
People in the first half of **this** century listened to **radios** daily.

3

Instruct
and
Integrate

Communication Activities

Listening and Speaking

Dialect

Read aloud the sentences from pages 370–371 in which the author records some of the words from the story quilt *Church Picnic*. Find examples of dialect in this passage, such as *sure 'nuff* and *chile*. Invite students to tell what these words would be in standard English, the English that is used and written most often in the United States. (*sure enough* and *child*) To further explore dialect, have students:

Read other portions of the story that appears in the border of *Church Picnic* and find other examples of southern dialect.

Read and listen to passages from books that contain examples of other dialects—Appalachian, Scottish, cowboy Western, or New England Yankee English.

Listen to a tape recording that uses dialect, especially in humor.

Listening to Jazz and Blues

Just as Faith Ringgold was learning to draw on her African heritage as a visual artist, other innovative artists were expressing similar ideas through music. Make available recordings by Duke Ellington, Charlie Parker, Bessie Smith, Louis Armstrong, Billie Holiday, Robert Johnson, Leadbelly, Howlin' Wolf, John Coltrane, or Dizzy Gillespie.

Tips for Listening to Music

- Find a quiet place with few distractions.
- Close your eyes. Concentrate only on the sound.
- Let yourself picture images the music suggests.
- Try to imagine what instruments are being played.
- Try to picture the people making the music.

Viewing

Ringgold's Books

Share with the class a copy of Faith Ringgold's Caldecott-honor picture book *Tar Beach* or her more recent *Aunt Harriet's Underground Railroad in the Sky*. Invite students to comment on the illustrations, using what they have learned about Ringgold's artistic style, media, and inspirations.

Looking at Quilts

Have students look again at the reproductions of the story quilts that appear on pages 371–380. Use the following prompts to explore their reactions to the quilts.

- Which story quilt has the greatest visual impact on you? What makes it so striking?

- Which story quilt do you find most interesting or unusual? What interests you most about it?

- Does viewing one of the quilts leave you with strong feelings or emotions? Explain.

3

Instruct *and* Integrate

Cross-Curricular Activities

Book List

Art

Stitching Stars: The Story Quilts of Harriet Powers
by Mary E. Lyons

Careers

Painting: Behind the Scenes
by Andrew Pekarik

Talking with Artists
by Pat Cummings

Materials

- 8–10" squares of cloth
- scissors
- fabric paints
- embroidery thread
- pins
- sewing needle

Art

Quilt Making

Some students may wish to make a quilted wall hanging that tells a collective story. Stitchery and/or fabric paints can be used to make picture blocks for piecing together and quilting.

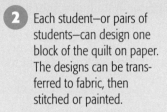

1 Students can choose or write a collective story. They should work cooperatively to choose the parts of the story to illustrate on the quilt.

2 Each student—or pairs of students—can design one block of the quilt on paper. The designs can be transferred to fabric, then stitched or painted.

3 Perhaps parent or community volunteers can help several interested students arrange the blocks and sew them together. The completed hanging may be presented to the school for exhibition.

Social Studies

The Harlem Renaissance

Have students research, plan, and present a multimedia program to celebrate the works of such Harlem Renaissance writers as W.E.B. Du Bois, Zora Neale Hurston, Langston Hughes, and James Weldon Johnson. If they are obtainable, include recordings of the renowned singers Roland Hayes and Paul Robeson as well as the works of composers Duke Ellington, Louis Armstrong, and W. C. Handy in the program.

Math

Symmetry

Display a variety of traditional quilt block patterns like the ones shown here. Remind students that a line of symmetry divides a figure into two equal parts that are exact mirror images. Have students find the lines of symmetry in each of the displayed patterns. Distribute graph paper and colored markers or pencils and challenge students to create new patterns with differing lines of symmetry.

Careers

Artists Everywhere!

Let students explore art careers of all kinds: professional musicians, graphic designers, interior decorators, chefs, florists, model makers, architects, potters, choreographers, actors—the list is nearly infinite. If possible, invite representatives from the community to speak to your class. Students might also do short reports about various careers in the field of art, answering questions such as these:

- Exactly what does this artist do?

- What skills and/or education does this art require?

- Does this kind of artist work alone or with others?

- Who are some famous artists of this kind?

Study Skill

Index

Teach/Model

The purpose of an index is to help readers locate information on a topic. For example, if they are looking for information about Bessie Smith in an American history book, they might find:

Smith, Adam, 158–159
Smith, Alfred E., 512, 535, 536, 589
Smith, Bessie, 521–522, *p*522
Smith, Jedediah, 205
Smith, Joseph, 222
Smith, Margaret Chase, *p*667
Smith, Sidney, 190

They might also look under "jazz" or "Harlem Renaissance" to find information about this musician. An index may use abbreviations such as *p* for picture or *m* for map.

Practice/Apply

Have students study and use indexes whenever they do research. You might ask volunteers to bring in examples of indexes to share with the class. What do all indexes have in common? How do they vary?

 Full lesson, p. H2; Theme 6

Activating Prior Knowledge

Ask students to think about the word *gallery.* What does it mean? What images does it suggest? Has anyone ever visited a gallery? When? Where? What kinds of things might they expect to find in a gallery? What does a gallery look like? Finally, after students have explored through discussion the literal definition of the word, ask them to think about what a *gallery of ideas* might mean. What might one look like?

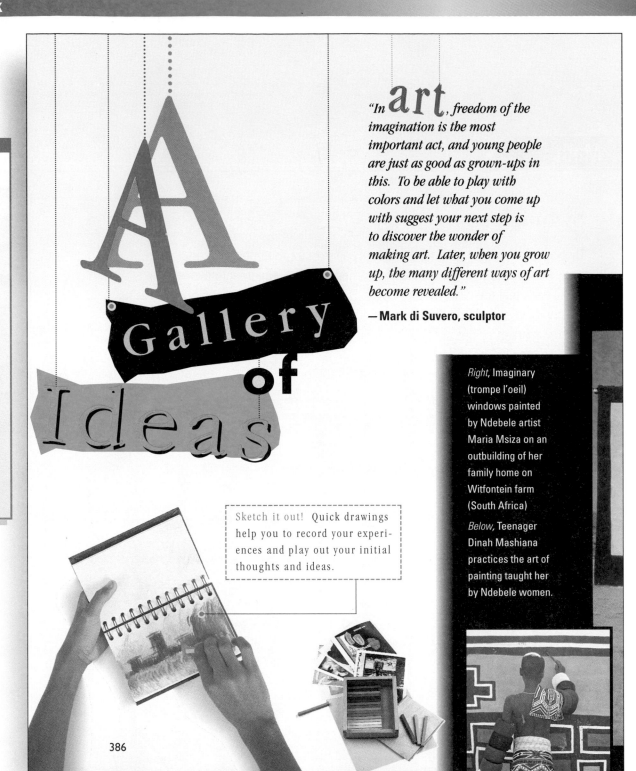

"In **art**, *freedom of the imagination is the most important act, and young people are just as good as grown-ups in this. To be able to play with colors and let what you come up with suggest your next step is to discover the wonder of making art. Later, when you grow up, the many different ways of art become revealed."*

— **Mark di Suvero, sculptor**

Right, Imaginary (trompe l'oeil) windows painted by Ndebele artist Maria Msiza on an outbuilding of her family home on Witfontein farm (South Africa)

Below, Teenager Dinah Mashiana practices the art of painting taught her by Ndebele women.

Sketch it out! Quick drawings help you to record your experiences and play out your initial thoughts and ideas.

386

Through discussion, help students see that this gallery uses

- Photographs of famous pieces of art with captions to explain them

- Images of young people creating art, along with boxed suggestions

- Italicized quotations by famous artists

Help students understand that they should read or study the three formats a bit differently, at different paces, and for different purposes.

Keep them coming! Accidental results can bring meaningful surprises.

Above, Swiss artist Etienne Delessert's watercolor palette shows his remarkable doodling. Delessert, award-winning children's book illustrator, writer, publisher, and filmmaker, is seriously interested in computer-generated imagery.

"My first memory is of the brightness of light, light all around."
—Georgia O'Keeffe, painter

Interact with Literature

Research Reports

Suggest that pairs of students choose one of the artists represented on these pages as the subject for a short report that they present to the rest of the class. Encourage them to include

- a short biography of the artist
- another sample of his or her work
- their opinion of his or her art

Journal

From the "works" in this gallery, ask students to choose their favorite and use it as a jumping-off point for a journal entry. Ask them to express their own ideas about the piece specifically and about the process of making art in general. What kinds of visual art do they enjoy most? Why?

Right, **Claes Oldenburg.** *Floor Cone (Giant Ice-Cream Cone),* 1962. Synthetic polymer paint on canvas filled with foam rubber and cardboard boxes. The Museum of Modern Art, New York. "When you can't speak the verbal language you have to depend on your vision and on representing things —the language of seeing."

Above, **Meret Oppenheim.** *Object (Breakfast in Fur),* 1936. Overall height 2⅞". The Museum of Modern Art, New York

"I wasn't content
with imagining things.
I wanted to build them myself."

— **Red Grooms, sculptor**

Start a collection! Enhance your creative ideas by gathering colors, shapes, textures as they catch your eye.

Interact with Literature

Background: FYI

- For generations, Ndebele women of southern Africa have produced art of remarkable richness and variety.

- Joan (*hoh AHN*) Miró (*mee ROH*) (1893–1983) used his imagination to help invent a new style of art called *surrealism* in the 1920s.

- Alexander Calder (1898–1976) invented many huge public mobiles.

Get inspired! Listen to music to expand your imagination. Draw or paint to music and ideas will come.

Left, **Alexander Calder.** *Little Clown, the Trumpeter,* 1926–31.
"Calder's art is eternally young. He plays, he amuses himself, and in so doing invests his art with life and force . . ."
—James Johnson Sweeney, art critic

Left, Calder roars with the lion from his famous miniature circus.

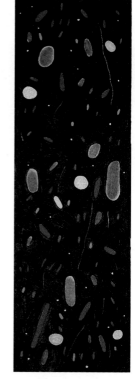

Above, **Joan Miró.** *The Song of the Vowels.* 1966. Oil on canvas, 144" x 45¼". The Museum of Modern Art, New York.
Miró uses abstract elements — line, shape, and color — to represent musical ideas and to suggest a musical range from full notes to tiny accents. The title refers to a French poem, "Vowels," by Rimbaud, which matches colors to vowels (A to black, E to white, I to red, O to blue, and U to green).

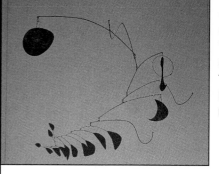

Left, **Alexander Calder.** *Red Gongs.* Mobile, 1951. Overall length approximately 12'. The Metropolitan Museum of Art, New York

389

Instruct and Integrate

Math

Dimensions Make sure that students understand the difference between two-dimensional and three-dimensional art. Have them point out the pieces of art on these pages that are examples of each.

Art

Art Play Encourage students to follow at least one of the pieces of advice given in the boxes on these pages and see where their imaginations take them.

Writing

Writing As Art How many ways can students compare the process of making visual art with the process of writing? For example, help them see that prewriting can sometimes be like doodling; displaying finished products in a gallery is like publishing. Perhaps they can write paragraphs comparing the two means of expression.

Poetry Invite interested students to use one of the pieces of art represented on these pages—combined with their own imaginations—as subjects of original poems. Suggest that their poems try to capture what the piece of art looks like and what it means to them.

SELECTION:
The Moon and I

by Betsy Byars

Other Books by the Author

Wanted . . . Mud Blossom

Bingo Brown and the Language of Love

Summer of the Swans

The Cartoonist

The Dark Stairs: A Herculeah Jones Mystery

- **ALA Notable**
- **SLJ Best Book**
- **Bulletin Blue Ribbon**
- **Texas Bluebonnet Award**

Selection Summary

In this autobiographical excerpt, Betsy Byars blends and explores thoughts about her writing life, her childhood, and observations of a big black snake. As the writer learns about the unexpected turns and twists that her writing process takes, she also learns about patience—all while observing a snake named Moon who becomes a symbol of what she sometimes can't easily find.

Lesson Planning Guide

	Skill/Strategy Instruction	Meeting Individual Needs	Lesson Resources
1 **Introduce** *the* **Literature** *Pacing: 1 day*	**Preparing to Read and Write** Prior Knowledge/Building Background, 389C **Selection Vocabulary,** 389D • resort • patiently • revision • desperate • manuscript • unexpectedly **Spelling Pretest,** 396I • example • discontinue • expect • experience • distance • dissolve • disease • misspell • misunderstand • mischief	**Support in Advance,** 389C **Other Choices for Building Background,** 389C **Students Acquiring English,** 389C **Spelling Challenge Words,** 396I • dissatisfied • exaggerate • misinterpret • disadvantage • mispronounce	*Literacy Activity Book:* Vocabulary, p. 170 **Transparencies:** Building Background, 4–13; Vocabulary, 4–14 **Great Start** CD-ROM software, "Imagination at Work" CD
2 **Interact** *with* **Literature** *Pacing: 1–3 days*	**Reading Strategies** Monitor, 392, 394 Evaluate, 392, 394 **Minilessons** Noting Details, 391 ✓ Author's Viewpoint, 393 Writer's Craft: How to Start, 395	**Choices for Reading,** 392 **Guided Reading,** 392, 394 **Students Acquiring English,** 393, 394, 396 **Challenge,** 395	**Reading-Writing Workshop:** A Personal Essay, 398–399F *Literacy Activity Book:* Selection Connections, pp. 147–148; Comprehension Check, p. 171 **Audio Tape** for Imagination at Work: *The Moon and I* **Student Writing Center,** writing and publishing software
3 **Instruct** *and* **Integrate** *Pacing: 1–3 days*	✓**Comprehension:** Author's Viewpoint, 396B ✓**Writing:** Elaborating with Adjectives, 396D ✓**Word Skills and Strategies:** Word Roots, 396F; Homographs, 396G **Building Vocabulary:** Vocabulary Activities, 396H ✓**Spelling:** Prefixes: *dis-, mis-, ex-,* 396I ✓**Grammar:** Comparing with Adjectives, 396J **Communication Activities:** Listening and Speaking, 396L; Viewing, 396M **Cross-Curricular Activities:** Science, Careers, 396N–396O	**Reteaching:** Author's Viewpoint, 396C **Activity Choices:** Write a Review, How to Start a New Chapter, Write About the Great Outdoors, 396E **Reteaching:** Word Roots: *scrib/script, port,* 396G **Activity Choices:** Words from Writing and Publishing, Word History: *month,* Vocabulary Notebook, 396H **Challenge Words Practice:** 396I **Reteaching:** Comparing with Adjectives, Daily Language Practice, 396K **Activity Choices:** Listening and Speaking, 396L; Viewing, 396M **Activity Choices:** Science, Careers, 396N–396O	**Reading-Writing Workshop:** A Personal Essay, 398–399F **Transparencies:** Comprehension, 4–15, Writing, 4–16; Word Skills, 4–17; Grammar, 4–18 *Literacy Activity Book:* Comprehension, p. 172; Writing, p. 173; Word Skills, p. 174; Building Vocabulary, p. 175; Spelling, pp. 176–177; Grammar, pp. 178–179 **Audio Tape** for Imagination at Work: *The Moon and I* **Channel R.E.A.D.** videodisc: "Heroes of the Marsh" **Student Writing Center,** writing and publishing software

✓ *Indicates* **Tested Skills**. *See page 332F for assessment options.*

1

Introduce *the* Literature

Preparing to Read and Write

Support in Advance

Use this activity for students who need extra support before participating in the whole-class activity.

Symbol-Eyes Draw a hand wearing a wedding ring on the chalkboard and ask students to discuss what ideas the ring represents. (love, marriage, lifelong commitment) Note that the ring is an example of a symbol.

Students Acquiring English

Let students share examples of symbols from their primary languages.

Management Tip

Have other students read independently or write in their journals.

INTERACTIVE LEARNING

Prior Knowledge/Building Background

Key Concepts
Symbolism

Display Transparency 4–13 and ask students to describe what they see literally. (an American flag, thirteen stripes, fifty stars) Note details on the left. Then ask volunteers to tell what *ideas* the image means or suggests to them. (the United States, freedom, patriotism, the government, war) Note these ideas on the right. Help students understand that the flag symbolizes these abstract ideas and that it means different things to different people.

The Writing Process

Initiate a discussion about students' personal writing experiences and the problems they encounter:

- How do they think of ideas?

- What do they do if they can't think of any?

- What decisions do they have to make as they write?

- Do they enjoy writing? Why or why not?

Transparency 4–13

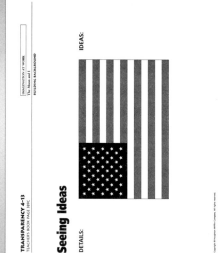

Great Start For students needing extra support with key concepts and vocabulary, use the "Imagination at Work" CD.

Other Choices for Building Background

Snakestorm
Cooperative Learning

Have pairs or small groups of students brainstorm their associations with snakes—real and imaginary. Then have each pair or group contribute one or two ideas or images to a class cluster about snakes.

Partner Interview
Cooperative Learning

First, have pairs work together to develop a questionnaire about writing experiences. Suggest they include questions such as:

- What do you enjoy most about writing?

- What do you enjoy least about writing?

- How do you begin a writing assignment?

Partners can then use the questionnaire to interview each other. You may wish to have students conduct their interviews on audio cassette and then share them with the class.

Selection Vocabulary

Key Words

revision

manuscript

unexpectedly

resort

desperate

patiently

Transparency 4–14	
revision	• process of making changes
manuscript	• original copy of a book or other piece of writing
unexpectedly	• surprisingly; not anticipated
resort	• to do as a last alternative
desperate	• having an extreme desire or need
patiently	• tolerantly; being able to wait

Display the top half of Transparency 4–14. Read each word and its definition. As you do, challenge students to make up a sentence using the word. Then display the whole transparency. Invite volunteers to read each sentence and write the correct Key Word in the blank. Encourage students to explain how they used the context clues.

Vocabulary Practice Have students work independently or in pairs to complete the activity on page 170 of the *Literacy Activity Book*.

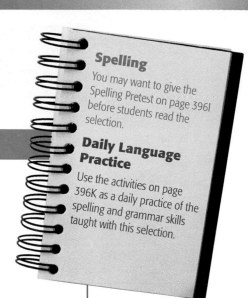

Spelling

You may want to give the Spelling Pretest on page 396I before students read the selection.

Daily Language Practice

Use the activities on page 396K as a daily practice of the spelling and grammar skills taught with this selection.

Transparency 4–14

Write, Rewrite

revision	process of making changes
manuscript	original copy of a book or other piece of writing
unexpectedly	surprisingly, not anticipated
resort	to do as a last alternative
desperate	having an extreme desire or need
patiently	being able to wait

1. The important writing assignment was given _____ to a new writer.

2. Having never written a major news story, the writer was _____ for a strong opening paragraph.

3. After trying several beginnings, she finally had to _____ to an opening question.

4. The story took a long time to complete, but the editor waited _____ for the finished copy.

5. The editor didn't like the ending, so the writer had to make a _____ .

6. The young writer delivered her completed _____ to the editor fifteen minutes before her deadline!

Science Link

Teacher FactFile
Snakes

- Snakes' eating schedules are irregular. After a large meal, they may wait weeks, even a year, before eating again. Despite having teeth, snakes swallow live prey whole—without chewing.

- A snake's home is called a den. Besides sleeping there, snakes use their dens as protection from enemies and weather. They may take over another animal's old burrow, a hollow log, or the space under a rock.

- People may spot snakes on the ground, in trees, or in water. Snakes are cold-blooded; in cold areas, they hibernate in the winter.

Literacy Activity Book, p. 170

Out of Print

Complete the television reporter's notes about a popular novelist with the correct words.

Interact
with
Literature

More About the Author

Betsy Byars

Betsy Byars is a warm, humorous person whose works are loved by young readers and admired by adults. In 1971, Byars won the Newbery Medal for *The Summer of The Swans*, a sensitive account of a girl and her mentally handicapped brother. Although she has dealt with serious issues in many subsequent books, Byars always manages to show the funny side of life as well. Byars has illustrated two of her stories and has had several books adapted for television. The mother of four grown children, Byars currently pilots her own plane and enjoys traveling with her husband, a retired engineer.

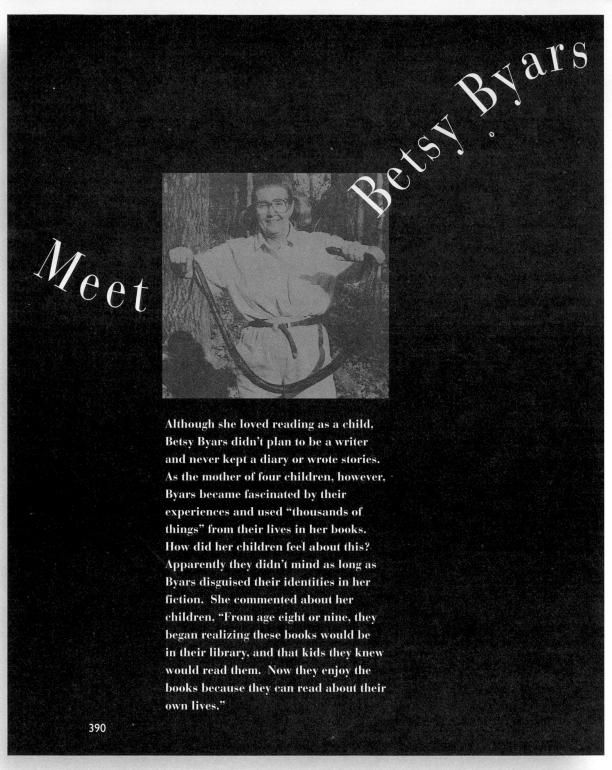

Meet Betsy Byars

Although she loved reading as a child, Betsy Byars didn't plan to be a writer and never kept a diary or wrote stories. As the mother of four children, however, Byars became fascinated by their experiences and used "thousands of things" from their lives in her books. How did her children feel about this? Apparently they didn't mind as long as Byars disguised their identities in her fiction. She commented about her children. "From age eight or nine, they began realizing these books would be in their library, and that kids they knew would read them. Now they enjoy the books because they can read about their own lives."

390

QuickREFERENCE

Background: FYI

Betsy Byars says about writing: "In all of my school years—from grade one through high school, not one single teacher ever said to me, 'Perhaps you should consider becoming a writer.' Anyways, I didn't want to be a writer. Writing seemed boring. You sat in a room all day by yourself and typed."

The Moon and I

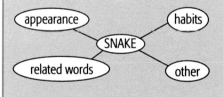

By Betsy Byars

At the log house where she does her writing, Betsy Byars discovered a big black snake and named it Moon. Inspired by her new friend, she wrote a humorous autobiography in which she blends descriptions of her writing life, advice about writing, memories of her childhood, and observations of the snake. This chapter follows eleven others such as "Moonstruck," "Moon in My Hands," and "That Lucky Old Moon."

391

MINILESSON

Noting Details

Teach/Model

REVIEW & MAINTAIN

Noting details is always important, but especially so when a central image (like the snake in this selection) accumulates symbolic meaning. Help students understand that the more details they note about the snake, the more they'll be able to understand how Betsy Byars uses the image to represent an abstract idea.

Practice/Apply

Suggest, even before they begin to read, that students begin a simple list or cluster diagram to note details about the snake they are about to meet.

appearance   habits

SNAKE

related words   other

SKILL FINDER

Full lesson/Reteaching, pp. 385A–385B; Theme 3

Minilessons, p. 369; Themes 1, 3

Interact with Literature

Reading Strategies

▶ **Monitor**
  Evaluate

Student Application Discuss with students what reading strategies they think will be helpful in this selection. If necessary, explain that this short selection is highly symbolic, so they'll need to constantly monitor their reading and evaluate what they've read.

Predicting/Purpose Setting

Have students list questions they may have about the selection. Then have them read to find answers to their questions.

Choices for Reading

| Independent Reading | Cooperative Reading |
| Guided Reading | Teacher Read Aloud |

Guided Reading

Have students read the entire selection with a partner to find answers to their questions. Use the questions on page 394 to check comprehension.

There is no easy way to find a blacksnake that doesn't want to be found. Blacksnakes are secretive, timid, and cautious. I accept that.

Blacksnakes hide when they are digesting food. Their prey is sometimes large and is always swallowed whole. I accept that.

Digestion — which even dissolves the victim's bones — may take a week or more. I accept that, too. Bones are definitely hard to digest.

But come on now, it couldn't take more than a few days to digest a measly lizard or frog.

So where was Moon? I had not seen the snake for over a month, and I had been actively looking for it — putting on boots and wading the length of the creek, trooping through the woods, checking every place I had ever seen it or any place that blacksnakes were known to like.

Summer is a lazy time for snakes — they mostly just hang out — but where?

I really missed Moon!

As the Moon-less days passed, I kept telling myself that Moon was probably somewhere digesting, and I kept reminding myself that all the books said that snakes don't wander, that they pretty much stay in one place until it's time to hibernate, that just because you don't see a snake doesn't mean that it doesn't see you.

And most of all, I kept telling myself that with blacksnakes, like everything in nature, a person must sometimes resort to waiting patiently.

The trouble is that waiting patiently is one of the things I am terrible at. I will do anything to keep from waiting patiently. When I first began to write, it was the thing I really, really hated.

392

Quick**REFERENCE**

Background: **F**YI

Galley proof sheets are the first printed proofs for a book before they have been divided into pages.

Extra Support

Oral Reading Encourage volunteers to read parts of page 393 aloud to hear the strength of the writer's voice, the casual language, and the exclamations. For criteria, see the Oral Reading Checklist in the *Teacher's Assessment Handbook*.

Like:

Like:

I would get one idea for a book, and I would write the book, and I would send it off. There would be rewrites and revisions and galley proof sheets to go over, but finally everything would be done, and then the only thing for me to do was to wait for the next idea.

Sometimes this waiting would go on for months. I would sit around, marking time, waiting like a tick for a dog to come by.

I would get more and more desperate because I always felt that now — now! — I had finally learned something about writing. Now — now! — I was ready to put all this self-taught, hard-earned knowledge into practice. Now I was equipped to write the best book in the entire world.

The only thing that was stopping me was that I didn't have an idea.

Finally, usually just when I had given up all hope, the idea would come, and I would be off — not, of course, writing the best book in the world but the best book I was capable of writing.

As I became more experienced, I learned that I don't need the perfect idea, with all the details in place, I just need an idea with possibilities, something that will allow my imagination to go to work. I now have more ideas than I can ever use. Indeed, I sometimes work on two manuscripts at once.

393

Students Acquiring English

Idioms Ask students what the author means by the idiom *marking time.* (waiting for time to pass) Encourage them to share other idioms they may have heard. You may also wish to discuss the simile, *waiting like a tick for a dog to come by.*

MINILESSON

Author's Viewpoint

Teach/Model

Through discussion, help students understand that an author's relationship to his or her subject—called *author's viewpoint*—is determined by at least three factors:

AUTHOR'S VIEWPOINT		
Point of View	Distance	Attitude

Model thinking about author's viewpoint with a Think Aloud.

Think Aloud

Betsy Byars is writing about two things: Moon and how she writes. She writes using the first person, *I.* She seems really close to both subjects; in fact, sometimes we're inside her head, overhearing her thoughts and feelings. I guess her attitude toward both subjects is kind of playful and affectionate. She likes the snake a lot. She misses him. Despite her problems, she seems to like writing a lot, too.

Practice/Apply

Emphasize that author's viewpoint is not something that can be easily defined. Rather, it is something to think and write about and discuss. It will help to contrast the author's viewpoint in this selection with that in *Faith Ringgold* (pp. 364–383), in which the author's viewpoint is dramatically different.

SKILL FINDER

Full lesson/Reteaching, pp. 396B–396C, Theme 6

Minilessons, p. 417, Themes 5, 6

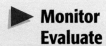

Interact *with* Literature

Reading Strategies

▶ **Monitor**
Evaluate

After reading the first two pages, ask students to pause to monitor their understanding. What relationship exists between the snake named Moon and Byars's other topic—the writing process? Have them evaluate the comparison between the snake and the author's writing ideas.

Guided Reading

Comprehension/Critical Thinking

1. How are the two problems the author talks about alike? How are they different? (Alike: They both involve waiting. Different: a snake vs. an idea)

2. Do you think the author's waiting for an idea for the "best book in the entire world" is appropriate? Why or why not? (Answers will vary but should mention that this is not practical.)

3. What does the last line suggest about Moon? (If Byars waits long enough, Moon will come just as her ideas do.)

Informal Assessment

If students' responses indicate difficulty, read aloud the first two pages and have them reread the rest independently.

Also, I have over the years developed ways to avoid even the smallest of waits.

When I finish one chapter in a manuscript and can't think of a way to start the next one.

I don't just sit around and wait for an idea to come to me. I go after it. I'm sort of like a reporter after a news item.

The first thing I do is go to the library. Then I walk along the shelves, pulling down book after book. I read the first sentence in every chapter.

Nothing.

I keep going. More books. More first lines.

Nothing.

Finally I will come to a chapter that starts with a sentence like **"The phone rang."**

I will snap the book shut. That's it! The phone is going to ring and it's going to be so-and-so, and so-and-so is going to tell what's-his-name that . . .

Before long I'm back in front of my word processor typing away.

When I come to a serious stopping place in a book and can't go on.

This is usually when I, the author, have no idea what's going to happen. I can't even imagine what could happen. I'm stumped.

Once again, I don't just sit there and wait for a solution to come to me.

I sit down with my manuscript. I separate myself (mentally) from being the author of the book. I become the reader of the book.

I start reading.

What I'm looking for is this: What does the reader think is going to happen? What have I led the reader to expect will happen?

For example, I may have spent two hundred words describing a tree just because I felt like describing a tree. But what I was saying to the reader was watch out for this tree! This tree is important! I wouldn't have you read two hundred words about a tree if that tree wasn't going to fall on somebody or somebody wasn't going to fall out of it.

394

QuickREFERENCE

Background: FYI

In *The Moon and I*, Byars eventually finds Moon lying on her driveway. She enjoys watching the snake for about fifteen minutes, before he slithers into a hole beside an old tree stump.

Students Acquiring English

Fork in the Road Ask students to identify clues the author gave to help readers understand the idiom *fork in the road*. Then have students give the meaning for this idiom in their own words. (Sample: a place where I can see two completely different choices)

✸When I come to a fork in the road.

This doesn't happen often, but I occasionally do come to a place where I can see two completely different ways the story can go. And the result will be two completely different books.

This happened in *Cracker Jackson* when Alma and her baby, Nicole, were in the hospital. Alma was going to be all right, but Nicole was in a coma, and I couldn't decide whether Nicole would live or die.

The book would be more powerful if Nicole died — and most writers want a powerful book — but I didn't want Nicole to die.

So I stopped. And I waited.

The answer came <u>unexpectedly</u>. I was giving a talk at a conference, and I was sitting with another author, waiting for the meeting to begin.

Some kids came up to talk to us while we were waiting, and I could hardly concentrate on my conversation because I was listening to hers. She was saying, "I couldn't help it! I just couldn't help it!"

After the kids were gone, I turned to the other author and said, "What was that all about?"

She said, "In one of my books I had a baby that the reader came to care about, and the baby died. Kids ask me why I 'made' the baby die. I tell them I couldn't help it, but they won't accept that."

I thought to myself, Maybe *you* couldn't help it, but I think I can, and when I got home, I went back to my word processor and in the very next chapter Nicole opened her eyes.

The answers always come if I wait, but it still isn't easy for me.

395

MINILESSON

Writer's Craft
How to Start

Teach/Model

Have students recall how Betsy Byars overcomes the obstacle of not being able to start the next chapter. (She reads the first sentences of other books.) Encourage students to discuss ways in which they "get started" or overcome "getting stuck" when they write, which might include

- asking a question and answering it.

- talking to someone else about it.

- starting in the middle; writing the beginning later.

Practice/Apply

Let students combine their ideas into a class poster titled, "What to Do When a Writer Gets Stuck." Encourage them to list and perhaps illustrate five to ten tips and display the poster for all to see.

 Writing Activity: How to Start a New Chapter: Opening Lines, p. 396E

Visual Literacy

Engage students in a discussion of graphic design. Why do the three large phrases appear on the page this way? Why did the designers choose these three phrases? Is the design effective? Why or why not?

 Challenge

Diagrams Invite students to work in pairs to create diagrams showing the four writing obstacles and how Byars overcomes them.

Interact
with
Literature

Responding Activities

Personal Response

- Ask students to write about what they learned about snakes . . . and about writing.

- Allow students to respond in another way of their own choosing.

Anthology Activities

Encourage students to choose activities from Anthology page 396.

Selection Connections

Invite students to complete the part of the chart on *Literacy Activity Book* pages 147–148 that refers to *The Moon and I.*

RESPONDING

Around the Writer's Block

Explore a Simile

Moon Is Like Writing

Although Byars never comes right out with it, she suggests that the blacksnake is like a writing idea. Explore this comparison by brainstorming words and phrases about snakes and then seeing how many might also be true for writing ideas. Or — Brainstorm words about writing ideas and see how many are also true for snakes. Do you think it's a good comparison? Why or why not?

Make an Advice Poster

When I Get Stuck

Byars suggests several techniques that she uses when she gets stuck as a writer. Can you think of even more? Make a poster that includes both her suggestions and yours. Give your poster a title, such as *What To Do When You Can't Write*. Make most of your suggestions serious, but throw in a couple of funny ones, too.

Draw Comparisons

"Waiting patiently"

Byars suggests that "waiting patiently" is the hardest thing for writers (and snake watchers). Think of other examples of people or characters in this theme who "wait patiently." What are they waiting for? Do they get it? How? Is "waiting patiently" difficult for all of them? Do you think it's part of any process in which the imagination is at work? Why or why not?

396

Informal Assessment

Responses should indicate a general understanding of how Byars overcomes obstacles in her writing process and how writers use images symbolically.

Additional Support:

- Reread confusing sections aloud.
- Have students write about what the title means to them.

Quick**REFERENCE**

MEETING INDIVIDUAL NEEDS
Students Acquiring English

Students who have difficulty writing in English may respond to written activities orally, by drawing, by role-playing, or by writing shorter sentences or paragraphs in English.

Home Connection

Invite students to conduct a home survey about waiting. Suggest that they ask family members:

- What do you hate to wait for?
- What do you do to make waiting easier?

More Choices for Responding

Literature Discussion Circle

- What was the author's purpose in writing this selection?

- How do you think Byars will react if Moon never returns?

- How did the conversation Byars overheard affect her writing choice for *Cracker Johnson*?

Create a Story Starter
Cooperative Learning

Have students work in pairs or small groups to think of a topic and beginning for a short story. Then have them trade with another pair or small group and continue the story. Perhaps they could take the story right up until the turning point and then trade with yet another group to finish stories. Ask volunteers to read completed stories aloud.

Comprehension Check

To check selection comprehension, use the following questions or *Literacy Activity Book* page 171.

1. **What did you learn about writing professionally?** (Samples: Professional writers do a lot of revision; professional writers get stuck, too.)

2. **Why does Betsy Byars write about a snake?** (Sample: She's using the snake to say something about writing ideas—they slither away and hide; you must be patient enough to wait for them to appear.)

Diorama Habitat

Have students create dioramas of the habitat of a snake such as Moon. Provide them with an opportunity to use mixed media materials, including clay, for a model. Encourage them to include words or printed paper to capture the two-part meaning of the snake.

1 Have students research the habitats of blacksnakes.

2 Encourage them to use torn newspapers and magazines to create habitats and to suggest that for Betsy Byars, Moon is more than just a snake.

3 What will they use to represent Moon? Remind them to use their imaginations.

Portfolio Opportunity

- For a record of comprehension, save *Literacy Activity Book* page 171.

- For writing samples, save Personal Responses or group stories.

Instruct *and* **Integrate**

Comprehension

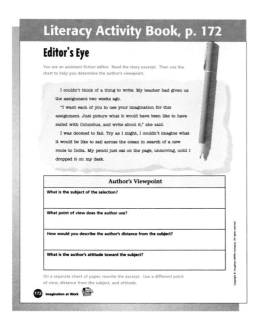

Literacy Activity Book, p. 172

Editor's Eye

You are an assistant fiction editor. Read the story excerpt. Then use the chart to help you determine the author's viewpoint.

> I couldn't think of a thing to write. My teacher had given us the assignment two weeks ago.
> "I want each of you to use your imagination for this assignment. Just picture what it would have been like to have sailed with Columbus, and write about it," she said.
> I was doomed to fail. Try as I might, I couldn't imagine what it would be like to sail across the ocean in search of a new route to India. My pencil just sat on the page, unmoving, until I dropped it on my desk.

Author's Viewpoint

What is the subject of the selection?

What point of view does the author use?

How would you describe the author's distance from the subject?

What is the author's attitude toward the subject?

On a separate sheet of paper, rewrite the excerpt. Use a different point of view, distance from the subject, and attitude.

172 Imagination at Work

Author's Viewpoint

LAB, p. 172

Write *author's viewpoint* on the board and ask students to try to explain what it means. Through discussion, help students understand that viewpoint is *where the author stands in relation to his or her subject.* It is a combination of point of view, distance, and attitude toward the subject.

Point of View	Usually, first person or third person
Distance	Is the author close to the subject or does she "stand" at a distance?
Attitude	How does the author feel about her subject?

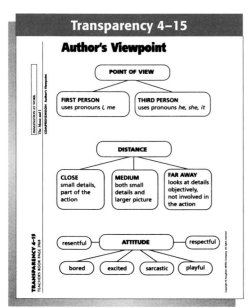

Transparency 4–15

Author's Viewpoint

POINT OF VIEW

FIRST PERSON uses pronouns *I, me*

THIRD PERSON uses pronouns *he, she, it*

DISTANCE

CLOSE small details, part of the action

MEDIUM both small details and larger picture

FAR AWAY looks at details objectively, not involved in the action

resentful — **ATTITUDE** — respectful

bored   excited   sarcastic   playful

Teach/Model

Display Transparency 4–15 and let students discuss the three components of author's viewpoint.

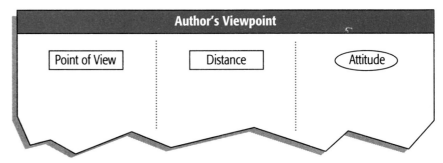

Author's Viewpoint

| Point of View | Distance | Attitude |

- Have a volunteer read the seventh paragraph on page 392. Ask students to name the point of view from which the selection is told. (first person)

- Ask another volunteer to read the first two paragraphs on page 393. Ask students how close they think Betsy Byars is to her subject. (very close) Ask them to locate sentences in which readers are right inside the author's head.

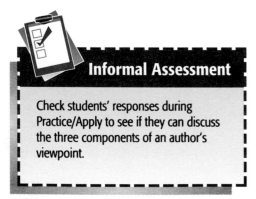

Informal Assessment

Check students' responses during Practice/Apply to see if they can discuss the three components of an author's viewpoint.

SKILL FINDER

Full lesson/Reteaching, Theme 6

Minilessons, pp. 393, 417; Themes 5, 6

INTERACTIVE LEARNING *(continued)*

> Students can use the **Channel R.E.A.D.** videodisc "Heroes of the Marsh" for additional support with Author's Viewpoint.

- Finally, ask students to brainstorm words or phrases that describe how they think Betsy Byars feels about her two subjects—snakes and writing. (sometimes worried, playful, patient, impatient, curious, thoughtful, surprised) Ask if they can come up with one or two words or phrases that describe her attitude in the entire piece.

Practice/Apply
- Have students complete *Literacy Activity Book* page 175.

- Students can also evaluate the author's viewpoint for other selections within this theme.

Reteaching

Author's Viewpoint

Read the following passage aloud to students and ask them to analyze it with respect to the three components of author's viewpoint.

Read Aloud

The poem I was trying to write about my garden wasn't going well. I couldn't find the right words, and the rhythm seemed all wrong. I decided to go for a walk, a climb really, since the hills behind my house were steep. I hiked for about half an hour and looked down at my back yard. There was my garden, rows laid out, sprouts peeking from the earth. From up here, the rectangle of wet, brown dirt looked like a blank page. Words like *hope, promise, compost,* and *fertile* sprouted in my imagination. I realized that I'd been too close to my garden to write about it. I ran down the hill, eager to get back to my word processor.

Sample answers:

Point of View	first person
Distance	author moves from close to far away from the subject (the garden)
Attitude	begins frustrated, ends hopeful and eager

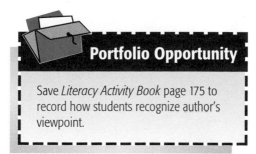

Portfolio Opportunity

Save *Literacy Activity Book* page 175 to record how students recognize author's viewpoint.

Instruct and Integrate

Writing Skills and Activities

Elaborating with Adjectives

① It was a summer day, and the sun shone on the creek in the woods.

② Moon slithered out of the water and across the mud.

③ The blacksnake opened its mouth and grabbed a frog.

④ Byars waded in the creek in her boots, looking for Moon in the water.

⑤ Perhaps Moon slid into a hole near a stump when it heard Byars coming.

TRANSPARENCY 4–16
TEACHER'S BOOK PAGE 396D

INTERACTIVE LEARNING

✓ TESTED SKILL Elaborating with Adjectives

LAB, p. 173

Teach/Model

To elaborate means to describe thoroughly. Remind students that an adjective describes a noun or a pronoun and that it can come before or after the noun it describes. Write these three sentences on the board:

> The blacksnake hid after it ate a meal.
> The timid blacksnake hid after it ate a large meal.
> The blacksnake, timid and cautious, hid after it ate a large meal.

Stress that adjectives are an important part of descriptive writing. Ask students to read each sentence to identify and note the use of adjectives. In the second and third sentences, the adjectives add details that make the sentences clearer and more vivid.

Display Transparency 4–16. Have students suggest adjectives to add to some of the nouns to make the sentences more descriptive and interesting.

Practice/Apply

Assign the activity Write a Review. Remind students to make sure that they use adjectives when writing their reviews to help them describe details from the movie or TV show.

Literacy Activity Book, p. 173

Tell All About It

Help this author complete a chapter in her book by adding adjectives to the sentences.

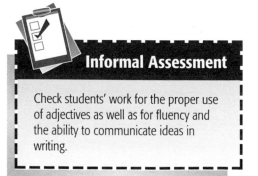

The Adventure Begins

The first day of our camping trip was _____ and _____. After kayaking all day on the _____ river, we were all _____. We ate dinner quickly, and then we lay by the _____ fire and listened to the river. It sounded so _____, I fell asleep immediately.

The next morning I awoke at sunrise. I had never seen a sky so _____. Walking down to the _____ pool in the rocks, I discovered along the shore a bunch of wildflowers. They were _____ with _____ petals. They smelled _____ and reminded me of something I couldn't quite name. The water was _____ and _____. It felt so _____ to take a dip! As I floated on my back I could see on the horizon the _____ mountain we would climb that day.

"Won't the view be _____ from up there," I said to myself. Just then I heard the _____ cry of a bird. Above me a red-tailed hawk soared. I knew then it was going to be a _____ day!

Imagination at Work 173

Informal Assessment

Check students' work for the proper use of adjectives as well as for fluency and the ability to communicate ideas in writing.

SKILL FINDER

Reading-Writing Workshop, pp. 398–399F

Grammar, pp. 396J, 385I

Writing Activities

Write a Review

Ask students to write a review about a movie or television show they have seen that concerns a relationship between a person and an animal. The animal could be wild, like a bear or a wolf, or domesticated, like a cat or a horse. Remind them to use adjectives to describe the animals and their relationships to people.

How to Start a New Chapter: Opening Lines

Invite students to select one of their favorite books or a book that they would like to read. Ask students to read the first line in every chapter of the book they have chosen. Then have them write the first paragraph for the chapter of a new book based on one of these opening lines. After they finish their paragraphs, students can share them with the class. *(See Writer's Craft Minilesson on page 395.)*

Write About the Great Outdoors

Invite students to write a descriptive paragraph about a walk in the park. Ask them to use adjectives to describe what they see and feel. Encourage students to elaborate: Who is walking with them? What types of plants or trees do they see? What kinds of animals? Is there a stream, a lake, or a fountain? What season is it? What time of day?

3

Instruct and Integrate

Word Skills and Strategies

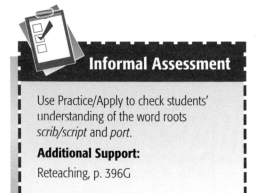

Literacy Activity Book, p. 174

Writer's Block

Writers often brainstorm ideas before they begin to write. One idea sometimes leads to another. What word does each group of words below make you think of? Choose a word from the snake and write it in the blank.

1. ticket agent, pilot, baggage handler _____
2. actor, stage, curtain _____
3. Egypt, documents, parchment _____
4. suitcase, ticket, currency _____
5. meteorologist, sportscaster, cameraperson _____
6. doodle, sketch, scrawl _____
7. print, carve, engrave _____
8. greeting, body, salutation _____

174 Imagination at Work

Structural Analysis
Word Roots *scrib/script* and *port*
LAB, p. 174

Teach/Model

Write the following word lists on the board:

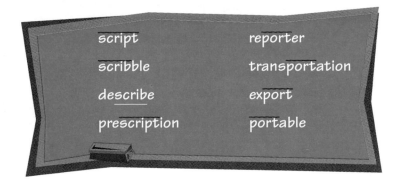

script	reporter
scribble	transportation
describe	export
prescription	portable

Underline *script* or *scrib* in each word in the first list. Explain that *script* and *scrib* come from a Latin word meaning "to write." Underline *port* in each word in the second list, explaining that this root comes from a Latin word meaning "to carry."

Then write the sentence below on the chalkboard and ask students to look for words in the sentence that could be added to each list. (*important, manuscript*)

> Betsy Byars learned important things about writing a manuscript.

Have a volunteer go to the chalkboard to add these words to the appropriate list. Remind students that the meaning of a root affects the meaning of the word it is in and that knowing the roots can help readers figure out the meaning of unfamiliar words.

Practice/Apply

Cooperative Learning Have students work in small groups to discuss how the meaning of the root is related to the meaning of each word in the lists above. Suggest that they use a dictionary to check their ideas.

Informal Assessment

Use Practice/Apply to check students' understanding of the word roots *scrib/script* and *port*.

Additional Support:

Reteaching, p. 396G

Reteaching | # Word Roots *scrib/script* and *port*

Cooperative Learning Tell students that the word root *scrib* or *script* comes from a Latin word that means "to write." Then explain that the root word *port* comes from a Latin word that means "to carry." Tell students that many English words can be formed using these roots. List the words below on the chalkboard. Have students make two columns headed *scrib/script* and *port* on a piece of paper. Ask them to work in small groups to find the roots in these words and list them in the correct columns.

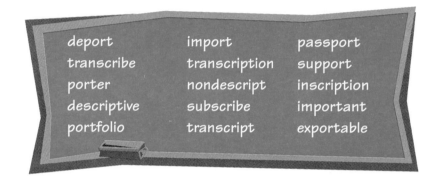

deport	import	passport
transcribe	transcription	support
porter	nondescript	inscription
descriptive	subscribe	important
portfolio	transcript	exportable

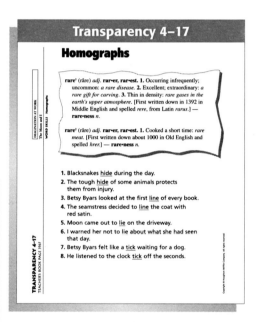

Transparency 4–17

Homographs

rare¹ (râre) *adj.* **rar·er, rar·est. 1.** Occurring infrequently; uncommon: *a rare disease.* **2.** Excellent; extraordinary: *a rare gift for carving.* **3.** Thin in density: *rare gases in the earth's upper atmosphere.* [First written down in 1392 in Middle English and spelled *rere*, from Latin *rarus.*] — **rare·ness** *n.*

rare² (râre) *adj.* **rar·er, rar·est. 1.** Cooked a short time: *rare meat.* [First written down about 1000 in Old English and spelled *hrer.*] — **rare·ness** *n.*

1. Blacksnakes <u>hide</u> during the day.
2. The tough <u>hide</u> of some animals protects them from injury.
3. Betsy Byars looked at the first <u>line</u> of every book.
4. The seamstress decided to <u>line</u> the coat with red satin.
5. Moon came out to <u>lie</u> on the driveway.
6. I warned her not to lie about what she had seen that day.
7. Betsy Byars felt like a <u>tick</u> waiting for a dog.
8. He listened to the clock <u>tick</u> off the seconds.

M I N I L E S S O N

Dictionary
Homographs

Teach/Model

Tell students that homographs are words that are spelled the same way and may be pronounced the same way, but come from different roots. Because their origins are different, homographs are listed separately in a dictionary. Display Transparency 4–17. Use the entries for *rare* to point out

- the superscript numerals ¹ and ²

- the etymology at the end of each entry

Then have students tell which homograph, *rare¹* or *rare²*, is being used in this sentence:

> Betsy Byars enjoyed watching Moon because she knew such moments would become *rare*. *(rare¹* includes the meaning "uncommon.")

Practice/Apply

For each sentence on Transparency 4–17, have students look up the underlined homograph in the dictionary and tell which meaning is being used.

Portfolio Opportunity

Save *Literacy Activity Book* page 174 to record students' understanding of the word roots *scrib/script* and *port.*

Instruct
and
Integrate

Building Vocabulary

Vocabulary Activities

Words from Writing and Publishing

Have students work in pairs to look through *The Moon and I* for all the terms they can find that are related to the fields of writing and publishing. Have students list the words from the selection and then brainstorm others. Ask each pair to share items from their list to build a master list of words from writing and publishing on the chalkboard.

Word History: *month*

Share this word history.

Tell students that in England long ago, the word for the moon sounded like MOH-nah. Because the moon takes about 30 days to go through a complete cycle, that period was called by a related word, which sounded like MOH-nath. Ask students what modern English word has grown from the Old English word. (*month*)

Examples of Writing and Publishing Terms

- rewrites
- revisions
- galley proof sheets
- manuscript
- chapter
- word processor
- typing
- author
- reader
- describing

Vocabulary Notebook

Ask students whether they think professional writers, such as Betsy Byars, keep a "vocabulary notebook." Remind students that Betsy Byars described glancing at sentences in books to get writing ideas. Encourage them to discuss some ways that they could use their Vocabulary Notebooks as sources of ideas for stories and other works. Ask students to go through their notebooks and jot down several ideas for stories, essays, or poems.

Literacy Activity Book, p. 175

Swirling Words

Read the clues. Then fill in the words on the snake's scales.

1. changes in your writing to make it better
2. surprising way some books end
3. to do something when nothing else works
4. opening sentence or paragraph
5. frustrated or without hope
6. what you do to get new ideas
7. finished work you send to your publisher
8. how you wait in a calm way

resort
revisions
manuscript
unexpectedly
desperate
lead
brainstorm
patiently

Imagination at Work 175

Use this page to review Selection Vocabulary.

Spelling

M I N I L E S S O N

Spelling Words

*example   *dissolve
*discontinue *disease
*expect   misspell
*experience   misunderstand
*distance   mischief

Challenge Words

dissatisfied
exaggerate
misinterpret
disadvantage
mispronounce

*Starred words or forms of the words appear in *The Moon and I.*

TESTED SKILL Prefixes *dis-, mis-, ex-*
LAB, pp. 176–177

- Write *discontinue, expect,* and *misunderstand* on the board. Underline the prefixes *dis-, ex-,* and *mis-*. Tell students that a prefix is a word part that is added to the beginning of a base word or a word root and adds meaning to a word.

- Remind students that a base word is a word that can stand alone. Ask which words on the board contain base words. *(discontinue; misunderstand)* Explain that a word root is a word part that has meaning but cannot stand alone. Ask which word has a word root. *(expect)* Note that *dis-* can mean "not;" *mis-* can mean "incorrectly." *Ex-* plus *spect,* "to look out at," has come to mean "to look forward to."

- Write the Spelling Words on the board. Note that each Spelling Word has the prefix *dis-, ex-,* or *mis-*. Say the words and have students repeat them.

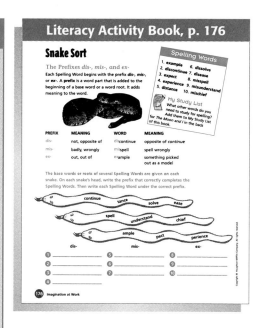

Literacy Activity Book, p. 176

Snake Sort

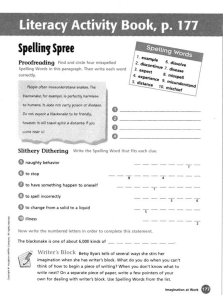

Literacy Activity Book, p. 177

Spelling Spree

Spelling Assessment

Pretest

Say each underlined word, read the sentence, and then repeat the word. Have students write only the underlined words.

1. Give an example of her work.
2. The bookstore will discontinue the series.
3. I didn't expect the story to end that way.
4. The author wrote about her experience
5. The mountain rises in the distance.
6. Sprinkle salt on the sidewalk to dissolve ice.
7. One character in the story suffers from a rare disease.
8. Do famous writers ever misspell words?
9. Don't misunderstand the point of the story.

10. The boy in the book makes mischief.

Test

Spelling Words Use the Pretest sentences.

Challenge Words

11. Sara felt dissatisfied with the story's ending.
12. I like to exaggerate the truth when I write.
13. Sometimes readers misinterpret the author.
14. Being famous can be a disadvantage too.
15. People always mispronounce my last name.

SKILL FINDER

Daily Language Practice, p. 396K

Reading-Writing Workshop, p. 398–399F

 **Challenge**

Challenge Words Practice Have students use the Challenge Words to suggest story ideas to writers suffering from writer's block.

3

Instruct *and* Integrate

Grammar

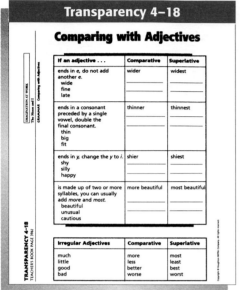

Transparency 4–18

Comparing with Adjectives

If an adjective . . .	Comparative	Superlative
ends in e, do not add another e. wide fine late	wider	widest
ends in a consonant preceded by a single vowel, double the final consonant. thin big fit	thinner	thinnest
ends in y, change the y to i. shy silly happy	shier	shiest
is made up of two or more syllables, you can usually add *more* and *most.* beautiful unusual cautious	more beautiful	most beautiful

Irregular Adjectives	Comparative	Superlative
much	more	most
little	less	least
good	better	best
bad	worse	worst

Literacy Activity Book, p. 179

Picture Forms

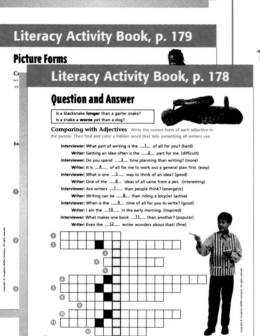

Literacy Activity Book, p. 178

Question and Answer

Is a blacksnake **longer** than a garter snake?
Is a snake a **worse** pet than a dog?

Comparing with Adjectives Write the correct form of each adjective in the puzzle. Then find and color a hidden word that tells something all writers use.

Interviewer: What part of writing is the ___1___ of all for you? (hard)
  Writer: Getting an idea often is the ___2___ part for me. (difficult)
Interviewer: Do you spend ___3___ time planning than writing? (more)
  Writer: It is ___4___ of all for me to work out a general plan first. (easy)
Interviewer: What is one ___5___ way to think of an idea? (good)
  Writer: One of the ___6___ ideas of all came from a pet. (interesting)
Interviewer: Are writers ___7___ than people think? (energetic)
  Writer: Writing can be ___8___ than riding a bicycle! (active)
Interviewer: When is the ___9___ time of all for you to write? (good)
  Writer: I am the ___10___ in the early morning. (inspired)
Interviewer: What makes one book ___11___ than another? (popular)
  Writer: Even the ___12___ writer wonders about that! (fine)

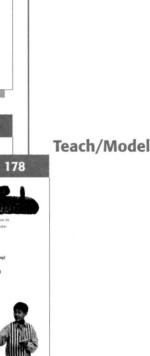

178 Imagination at Work

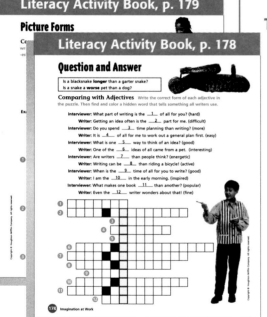

Informal Assessment

Responses to the activities should indicate a general understanding of comparative and superlative adjectives.

Additional Support:

Reteaching, p. 396K

Comparing with Adjectives

LAB, pp. 178–179

TESTED SKILL

- Use the **comparative form** (*-er*) of an adjective to compare two people, places, things, or ideas. Use the **superlative** form (*-est*) of an adjective to compare three or more. Sometimes the spelling of an adjective changes when *-er* or *-est* is added.
- Use *more* to form the comparative and *most* to form the superlative of most adjectives of two or more syllables.
- Some adjectives have completely different forms in the comparative and superlative.

Teach/Model

Write the adjectives *tall, taller,* and *tallest* on the chalkboard. Have four students of different heights come to the front of the room and arrange themselves in order of height. Ask volunteers to write sentences on the board comparing the students' heights. (Sample: *Juan is taller than Andrea.*) Then elicit from students that *-er* is added to an adjective to compare two things and that *-est* is added to compare three or more. Introduce the terms *comparative* and *superlative forms.*

Write this sentence on the chalkboard:

Blacksnakes are secretive.

Ask students for the comparative and superlative forms of *secretive.* (Add *more* and *most.*) Elicit that the comparative and superlative of most adjectives of two or more syllables can be formed by adding the words *more* and *most.* Have students offer other, similar adjective examples.

SKILL FINDER

Reading-Writing Workshop, p. 399E

Writing Skill, pp. 396D–396E

INTERACTIVE LEARNING (continued)

Teach/Model Display Transparency 4–18. Review the spelling changes for regular adjectives, and discuss the forms of the irregular adjectives. Call on volunteers to fill in the blanks and to offer additional examples of adjectives. Have volunteers use the adjective forms in oral sentences.

Practice/Apply ***Literacy Activity Book*** Refer students to the Handbook at the back of the *Literacy Activity Book* for a chart of adjective forms.

Cooperative Learning: **Adjective Shuffle** Prepare 20 cards. On each one write an adjective. (Samples: *happy, remarkable, bad*) Group students in teams of three. Have each team take a card. Have one member use the adjective, one the comparative, and one the superlative form aloud in a sentence. Then have students write the forms on the card.

 Writing Application: Comparison and Contrast Suggest that students write a paragraph that compares waiting for three events to happen, such as a birthday, a vacation, and a visit from someone special to them. Have them use comparative and superlative forms of adjectives. Ask volunteers to read aloud their paragraphs.

Students' Writing Have students check their writing in process for the correct use and spelling of adjective forms.

Daily Language Practice

Focus Skills

Grammar: Comparing with Adjectives
Spelling: The Prefixes *dis-, mis-,* and *ex-*

Each day write one sentence on the chalkboard. Have each student write the sentence correctly on a sheet of paper. Tell students to check for correct comparative and superlative forms of adjectives and for misspelled words. Have students correct their own paper as a volunteer corrects the sentence on the chalkboard.

1. The author presents a more broader idea than the experiance of looking for a snake.
   The author presents a **broader** idea than the **experience** of looking for a snake.

2. She could exspect a gooder look at the snake after a rain than before.
   She could **expect** a **better** look at the snake after a rain than before.

3. A snake's way of digesting is unusualer than that of some other animals because it will disolve the bones of its food.
   A snake's way of digesting is **more unusual** than that of some other animals because it will **dissolve** the bones of its food.

4. The worstest thing of all is to missunderstand the example that Moon gives.
   The **worst** thing of all is to **misunderstand** the example that Moon gives.

5. Blacksnakes seem the most timidest of all when they stay at a distanse from people.
   Blacksnakes seem the **timidest** of all when they stay at a **distance** from people.

Reteaching | ## Comparing with Adjectives

On the chalkboard, draw a cartoonish snake form, large enough to fit eight adjectives vertically, representing all the ways in which comparatives are formed. Use the adjectives to reteach the formation of comparative and superlative forms. To the right of the snake write the headings *Comparative Forms* and *Superlative Forms*. Have students write the correct forms under the headings and make up sentences using the forms. Continue the activity by having students replace the adjectives with others.

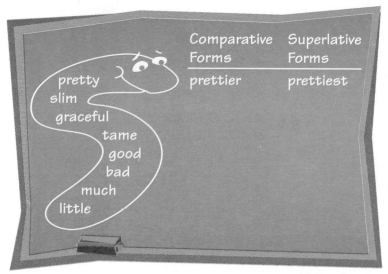

Communication Activities

Questions for Writers

How did you get started being a writer?

What kinds of things do you write?

Did you enjoy writing when you were young?

What is a typical day like for you?

What do you do when you get stuck?

Listening and Speaking

Visit from an Author

Invite a local author to your class to talk with students about what it is like to be a professional writer. Encourage students to prepare questions beforehand. Encourage volunteers to tape-record or videotape the visit—with the writer's permission—for other classes to hear and/or see.

How-to Writing Books

Invite students to give short presentations of books about writing, a variety of which are available in local bookstores and/or libraries. What kinds of advice do they offer? How do they seem to be like *The Moon and I?* How are they different? In their oral presentations, have them include

- the name of the author and title of the book

- a brief summary

- a dramatic reading of a passage they found interesting or helpful

- where they found the book and how others can get it

Viewing

Symbols and Signs

We live in a visual world, one in which single visual images often convey large abstract ideas. Invite students to explore the world of signs and symbols that surrounds them.

Materials
- paper
- markers
- yarn

2 Have students find signs and symbols in their environment.

1 Show students examples of signs and symbols, such as a peace symbol, Uncle Sam, and a school crossing.

3 Students can combine the images on a bulletin board or reproduce them and hang them from the ceiling of the classroom.

Snakes Alive!

Let students observe a live snake—or the next best thing, a book or video about snakes. Ask students to write in their journals about what they observe, noting as many specific details as possible.

Noting Details

- What color is it? How big is it?

- What do its eyes look like? Its mouth? Its skin? Its tail?

- What kind of snake is it? Where does it live?

Portfolio Opportunity

Save students' posters and any recordings they might have made in a portfolio for class projects.

Instruct
and
Integrate

Cross-Curricular Activities

Book List

Science

The Moon
by Isaac Asimov

All About the Moon
by David Adler

The Moon
by George Michael

Snakes
by Seymour Simon

Amazing Snakes
by Alexandra Parsons

Poisonous Snakes
by Seymour Simon

Careers

Young Person's Guide to Becoming a Writer
by Janet E. Grant

What's Your Story? A Young Person's Guide to Writing Fiction
by Marion Dane Bauer

Market Guide for Young Writers
by Kathy Henderson

Choices for Science

Snake Take

Invite interested students to prepare a report or poster about snakes: their habitats, habits, food, lifespans, appearances, and unique characteristics. Encourage them to use a variety of resources and to include photographs if possible. Also encourage them to find out if any black-snakes live in your area.

Why Moon?

Why do students think Betsy Byars names her snake Moon? Perhaps it's because the moon goes through phases, too, just as artists do, waiting for inspiration. Have students prepare a series of illustrations that show the various phases of the moon. When is it hidden? When is it in full view? What causes these phases to appear? Have students check the calendar, of course, to see what phase of the moon you are experiencing right now.

New Moon	Waxing Cresent	First Quarter	Waxing Gibbous	Full Moon	Waning Gibbous	Last Quarter	Waning Cresent

Choices for Careers

Books: Idea to Sale

Cooperative Learning

With the help of the library, have students list and research various kinds of jobs in the book publishing business and compile a class chart or bulletin board showing how they work together to sell books.

Materials
- markers
- construction paper

2 Assign pairs or groups of students to each job. With library resources—or the help of a local publisher— they can find out details about each and how each one fits into the big picture.

1 Have pairs of students find out and list the various jobs: WRITER, EDITOR, PROOFREADER, DESIGNER, ELECTRONIC PUBLISHER, PRINTER, BINDER.

3 The class can make a flow chart of WHERE BOOKS COME FROM by combining a short written report and an illustration of each stage.

Be a Publisher!

Have groups of students work together on such small publishing projects as the following:

- a flier announcing an upcoming school event

- an informational brochure dealing with a topic such as bike safety

- a newsletter for parents

Summer's Bounty

Building Background

Write the word *bounty* on the board and ask volunteers to tell what it means. (a huge amount, an abundance) Then ask students to picture a bounty of summer fruits and vegetables. As they name examples, list them on the board. Finally, ask a volunteer to read May Swenson's poem aloud as others follow along.

About the Poet

American poet May Swenson (1919–1989) published ten volumes of poetry and won numerous awards. She has been called "a master sculptor in the medium of language." She herself saw her poems as "iconographs," that is, pictures painted in words. "Summer's Bounty" is a good example.

Poetry Response

Let students respond freely to the poem OR offer prompts such as these:

- What makes this a poem?
- How does the poem's appearance on the page add to its meaning?
- How should you read the stanzas? Left to right or up and down? Why?
- What do you think May Swenson means by this poem?
- Are there any lines you don't understand? Which ones?

berries of Straw nuts of Brazil
berries of Goose nuts of Monkey
berries of Huckle nuts of Pecan
berries of Dew nuts of Grape

berries of Boisen beans of Lima
berries of Black beans of French
berries of Rasp beans of Coffee
berries of Blue beans of Black

berries of Mul beans of Jumping
berries of Cran beans of Jelly
berries of Elder beans of Green
berries of Haw beans of Soy

apples of Crab melons of Water
apples of May melons of Musk
apples of Pine cherries of Pie
apples of Love cherries of Choke

nuts of Pea glories of Morning
nuts of Wal rooms of Mush
nuts of Hazel days of Dog
nuts of Chest puppies of Hush

MAY SWENSON

Summer's Bounty

Genre

Concrete Poetry

Teach/Model

Remind students that concrete poems express part of their meaning through the appearance of the words on the page. They appeal to the eye as well as the ear and the imagination. Encourage students to let their imaginations loose as they think about and discuss the shape of "Summer's Bounty." Ask them how the poem is a picture painted in words. They may come up with ideas such as these:

- The lines suggest the stacks of fruit and vegetables in a market.

- The groups of four lines suggest the four seasons of the year.

- The rows and columns look like a calendar.

- The poem is layered like a fancy cake, fruit salad, or parfait.

Practice/Apply

Have students engage their own imaginations by writing concrete poems of their own. Be sure to display them so others can appreciate their appearances. Students Acquiring English may want to write poems in their primary language.

Reading-Writing Workshop

A Personal Essay

About the Workshop

This workshop includes specific suggestions and ideas to help you guide students through the process of writing a personal essay. Minilessons deal with focus, using examples to elaborate, and openings and closings. These elements form the basis for the assessment criteria at the end of the workshop.

Keep these considerations in mind:

- A personal essay is subjective; it expresses the writer's own viewpoint.
- A personal essay is informal and conversational in tone and personalized in voice and style.
- Although a personal essay may include opinions, it is not written to persuade.
- **Students Acquiring English** Brainstorm words that signal opinion.

Connecting to *The Moon and I*

Review with students that Betsy Byars expresses some of her thoughts about writing in *The Moon and I.* Tell students that they are going to write a personal essay in which they can express their thoughts on a subject.

Introducing the Student Model

Have students discuss whether an imagination can change one's world and how. Then have them read Sabrina Dwight's essay and discuss the questions on page 399.

BE A WRITER

Imagination Changes My World

A Personal Essay by Sabrina Dwight

Can imagination add fun to your life? Sabrina thinks so. In this essay she shares her thoughts on using imagination to brighten a boring or a lonely day.

Sabrina Dwight
Gertrude Scott Smith School
Aurora, Illinois

"I like being creative," said Sabrina when she wrote this essay in the sixth grade. Sabrina also likes writing stories, reading, running, and playing the flute. In the future she would like to become a lawyer.

SKILL FINDER

PREWRITING/DRAFTING

Workshop Minilessons	Theme Resources
• Keeping to the Focus, p. 399A • Using Examples, p. 399B • Openings and Closings, p. 399C	• Author's Viewpoint, pp. 393, 396B–396C, 417 *Writing* • How to Start, p. 395 • Elaborating with Adjectives, p. 396D

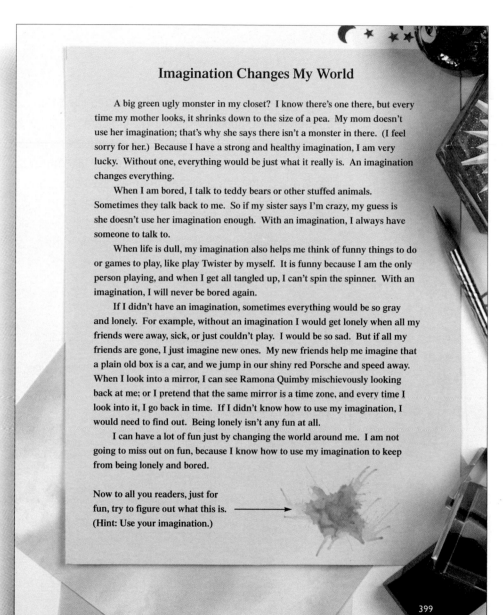

Imagination Changes My World

A big green ugly monster in my closet? I know there's one there, but every time my mother looks, it shrinks down to the size of a pea. My mom doesn't use her imagination; that's why she says there isn't a monster in there. (I feel sorry for her.) Because I have a strong and healthy imagination, I am very lucky. Without one, everything would be just what it really is. An imagination changes everything.

When I am bored, I talk to teddy bears or other stuffed animals. Sometimes they talk back to me. So if my sister says I'm crazy, my guess is she doesn't use her imagination enough. With an imagination, I always have someone to talk to.

When life is dull, my imagination also helps me think of funny things to do or games to play, like play Twister by myself. It is funny because I am the only person playing, and when I get all tangled up, I can't spin the spinner. With an imagination, I will never be bored again.

If I didn't have an imagination, sometimes everything would be so gray and lonely. For example, without an imagination I would get lonely when all my friends were away, sick, or just couldn't play. I would be so sad. But if all my friends are gone, I just imagine new ones. My new friends help me imagine that a plain old box is a car, and we jump in our shiny red Porsche and speed away. When I look into a mirror, I can see Ramona Quimby mischievously looking back at me; or I pretend that the same mirror is a time zone, and every time I look into it, I go back in time. If I didn't know how to use my imagination, I would need to find out. Being lonely isn't any fun at all.

I can have a lot of fun just by changing the world around me. I am not going to miss out on fun, because I know how to use my imagination to keep from being lonely and bored.

Now to all you readers, just for fun, try to figure out what this is. ⟶
(Hint: Use your imagination.)

399

SKILL FINDER

PROOFREADING

Theme Resources	**Theme Resources**
Grammar	*Spelling*
• Principal Parts of Regular and Irregular Verbs, pp. 357I–357J	• Plurals of Words Ending with *f*, p. 357H
• Adjectives, pp. 385I–385J	• Plurals of Words Ending with *o*, p. 385H
• Comparing with Adjectives, pp. 396J–396K	• Prefixes *dis-*, *mis-*, and *ex-*, p. 396I
• Avoiding Double Negatives, pp. 419I–419J	• Prefixes *per-*, *pre-*, and *pro-*, p. 419H

Discussing the Model

Reading and Responding

• What is the main point of Sabrina's essay? (Imagination changes her world.)

• In what two major ways does Sabrina's imagination change her world? (keeps her from being bored and lonely)

• Do you agree that Sabrina is lucky to have a strong imagination? Explain.

• What do you like best about this essay?

Reading As a Writer

• Why does Sabrina's opening pull you right in? (clever; arouses curiosity)

• Sabrina tells about talking to stuffed animals and playing Twister by herself. How do these examples make her essay better? (clarify her thoughts)

• Why is Sabrina's ending suitable? (fits the topic; fun)

Characteristics of Personal Essays

Elicit these characteristics:

• *Purpose:* to share thoughts

• A main focus idea

• Thoughts about the focus idea, supported with examples

• An interesting opening that introduces the topic; a closing that finishes the essay

Reading-Writing Workshop (continued)
A Personal Essay

Keeping to the Focus

Resource: Anthology, pp. 392–393, 399

- With the class, make an idea map of *The Moon and I.* First, have students find the main point, or *focus idea,* of the essay. (Betsy Byars hates waiting.) **Which sentences state this idea?** (p. 392, last paragraph)

hates waiting

tries to make ideas happen when she:

can't start

can't continue

can't decide

- Help students see that all her thoughts and points *support and expand on* the focus idea.

- Ask whether these points would keep to the essay's focus:

  what she likes about writing (no)
  how to write a good first line (no)
  what to do when she can't think of a title (yes)

- Have students map the focus idea and supporting thoughts in Sabrina's essay on page 399. Have students note which sentence states the focus idea. (*Focus idea:* Imagination changes her world—last sentence in first paragraph; *Supporting thoughts/points:* keeps her from being bored, lonely.)

Warm-up ## Panel Discussion

Invite students to suggest topics they would like to discuss, such as peer pressure or the quality of TV shows. Organize students into small groups to hold panel discussions. Suggest a few questions to help each group get started, and request that a student recorder take notes. Circulate among the groups. After ten or fifteen minutes, ask each group to share some of their thoughts. Help students understand that no idea is right or wrong because each one is an opinion. Discuss which ideas could be the focus for an essay and which thoughts would support those focus ideas.

Prewriting

LAB, pp. 180-181

Choose an Essay Topic Students brainstorm, discuss, and choose essay topics.

- **List Topics** Have students list three to five topics that they would like to express their thoughts about.

- **Think and Discuss** Have students discuss their topics with partners and then answer these questions about each idea: Do I have interesting points to make? Can I think of good examples to explain my thoughts? Do I really want to write about this?

Help with Topics

Titles

Share these titles of essays by famous writers. Encourage the class to brainstorm others.

"Hair" by Marcia Aldridge
"Reflections on Horror Movies" by Robert Brustein
"Bagel" by Leo Rosten
"Self-Reliance" by Ralph Waldo Emerson
"On Being an American" by H. L. Mencken
"My Face" by Robert Benchley

Idea Starters

Invite students to freewrite in response to these (or other) prompts.

I get a little nervous when . . .
I just can't understand why . . .
If I could be anyone, I would be . . .
The most difficult thing to do is . . .
I like being a girl/boy because . . .

Prewriting *(continued)*

Plan the Essay

Students explore their focus ideas, plan, and discuss their essays.

- **Explore Ideas** Have students brainstorm, freewrite, or use graphic organizers to explore their focus ideas and identify two or three supporting thoughts or points.

- **List Examples** Have students list two examples for each point.

- **Make Idea Maps** Have students organize their thoughts.

Help with Planning

An Idea Web

Students can use a web to explore their focus ideas. One branch might become the focus idea.

- leads to day-dreaming
- live in a fantasy world
- ideas don't work out

IMAGINING CAN BE RISKY

Talk Show

Cooperative Learning

Suggest that interviewing a partner about one's own topic might help students explore their thoughts.

Students Acquiring English This strategy is good for these students.

Literacy Activity Book, p. 180

What Do You Think?

Essay Topics Does one of these topics suggest an essay idea to you?

Clouds	Reading
Broccoli	What Makes Me Happy
The Right/Wrong Pet	A Holiday I Hate
Studying	Being Fair
Growing Up Isn't Easy	Looking on the Bright Side
Choosing the Right Shoes	

My Personal Essay Topics
Write five ideas that you might like to write about in a personal essay.

Ask yourself these questions about each idea you listed.

- Can I think of good examples to explain my thoughts?
- Do I really want to write about this?
- Do I have interesting points to make?

Now circle the topic that you will write about.

180 Imagination at Work

Literacy Activity Book, p. 181

Put on Your Thinking Cap

Use this diagram to plan your essay. Write your focus idea in the center. Around it list your thoughts about your focus idea. In the outside circle, add examples to support each thought.

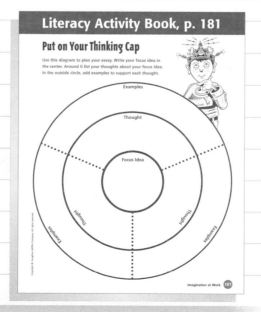

Examples

Thought

Focus Idea

Imagination at Work 181

Using Examples

Resource: Anthology pp. 394–395, 399

- Have students turn to page 394. Read aloud the paragraph beginning *I don't just sit around and wait. . . .* Ask students to review the remaining text down to the next star and explain its purpose. (It's an example that supports the first starred statement.)

- Ask students what examples Byars provides to support her second starred point. (sample questions she asks herself; an example situation of having many words that describe a tree, which means the tree must be important)

- Ask students what kind of example Byars used to support her third point. (a personal experience)

- Help students conclude that examples are necessary to clarify and strengthen their thoughts and points about their focus ideas.

- Discuss with students the examples Sabrina used on page 399. As in *The Moon and I,* these examples also focus on her own actions and experiences. Discuss how other essay topics, such as an essay about a career choice, might include different kinds of examples, such as facts, lists, and the experiences of others.

Reading-Writing Workshop (continued)
A Personal Essay

Openings and Closings

Resource: Anthology pp. 391–395, 399

- Discuss why Byars's opening is effective even though at first it seems unrelated to her focus idea. (Her impatience in waiting for Moon leads to her impatience in general and when writing.) Which sentences make this transition? (p. 392, last two paragraphs) Point out that the opening concludes with her focus idea.

- Explain that describing an experience is one interesting way to open an essay. Review how Sabrina opened her essay. (with an intriguing question) Discuss other interesting ways to open an essay. (quotation, dialogue, a definition, anecdote, a startling statement) How might Sabrina or Betsy Byars have used them?

- Discuss why Sabrina's final two paragraphs make a good closing. (sum up her focus idea; leave reader thinking)

Self-Assessment

Have students evaluate their essays, using the Revising Checklist.

Drafting

Students use their notes and other planning aids to help them draft.

Help with Drafting

Drafting Strategies

Focus on Paragraphs Encourage students to keep in mind "New thought, new paragraph." Examples should go in the same paragraph as the thought they support.

Focus on Fluency Remind students that neatness does not count in a draft but ideas do. Encourage them to cross out sentences that aren't working, replace examples, and let their thoughts flow.

Tone

Encourage students to think about the tone of their essay. Will it be funny? annoyed? serious? enthusiastic? curious? something else?

Their Own Voice

Suggest that students think of themselves talking to their audience as they write.

Revising

LAB p. 182

Students revise their essays and discuss them in writing conferences.

Revising Checklist

- ☐ Does the opening present the focus idea?
- ☐ Do all my points and thoughts keep to the focus idea?
- ☐ Did I use good examples to explain each point or thought?
- ☐ Does the closing sum up the focus idea and make the essay seem finished?

Revising *(continued)*

Writing Conference

Cooperative Learning Students read their essays aloud to you or to one or more classmates. They can use the Questions for a Writing Conference to guide their discussions.

Questions for a Writing Conference

* What do you like about this essay?

* Is the opening interesting? Does it clearly state the focus idea?

* Does each point or thought keep to the focus of the essay?

* Do the examples clearly explain each point? Should different examples be used? Are more examples needed?

* What parts are unclear?

* Could the closing be improved?

* What other revisions might be helpful?

Help with Revising

Revising Strategies

Highlighting Using different highlighters, students can mark the sentences related to each thought in a given color. Are thoughts mixed together?

Reading Aloud Encourage students to read aloud their essays to themselves and to listen carefully. (Help them audiotape the readings, if possible.) Do the essays clearly express their thoughts?

Openings

Suggest that students write several openings, using different devices (such as a question, an anecdote, or a definition), and try them out on classmates.

TECH TIPS Suggest that students use the Copy function to duplicate text that they would like to revise. They can then compare the different versions.

Additional Questions for Writing Conferences

These questions may be useful during teacher-student conferences.

* Why do you think or feel this way? Can you give more explanation?

* Does this example really support this point? What other example could you use?

* What does this part [or sentence] have to do with your focus idea [or the thoughts in this paragraph]?

* What do you mean when you say . . . ?

* How can you close the essay so that it doesn't just stop?

If your class is using the **Student Writing Center,** to write, illustrate, and publish their work to share with others.

Literacy Activity Book, p. 182

Does It Work?

Reread and revise your essay, using the Revising Checklist. Then use the Questions for a Writing Conference to help you discuss your essay with a classmate.

Revising Checklist

❑ Does the opening present the focus idea?

❑ Do all my points and thoughts keep to the focus idea?

❑ Did I use good examples to explain each point or thought?

❑ Does the closing sum up the focus idea and make the essay seem finished?

Questions for a Writing Conference

* What do you like about this essay?
* Is the opening interesting? Does it clearly state the focus idea?
* Does each point or thought keep to the focus of the essay?
* Do the examples clearly explain each point? Should different examples be used? Are more examples needed?
* What parts are unclear?
* Could the closing be improved?
* What other revisions might be helpful?

Write notes to help you remember comments and suggestions made during your writing conference.

My Notes

182 Imagination at Work

Reading-Writing Workshop (continued)
A Personal Essay

Students using the **Student Writing Center** can use the spell-check feature when editing their documents.

Proofreading

Students proofread their essays, using the Proofreading Checklist and the proofreading marks in the Handbook of the *Literacy Activity Book.*

Grammar/ Spelling Connections

- **Checking Verbs, Adjectives, and Negatives** Remind students to check that they have used the correct forms of verbs and the correct forms of adjectives when comparing. Also remind them to avoid double negatives. *pp. 357I–357J, 385I–385J, 396J–396K, 419I–419J*

- **Spelling** Remind students to double-check the spelling of plurals ending with *f* or *o* as well as words having the prefixes *dis-, mis-, ex-, per-, pre-,* or *pro-. pp. 357H, 385H, 396I, 419H*

Publishing and Sharing

Students title their essays, decide how they will share them, and make neat final copies. Remind them to check that they have included all changes.

Ideas for Publishing and Sharing

IMAGINATION CHANGES EVERYTHING

A big green ugly monster in my closet? I know there's one there, but every time my mother looks, it shrinks down to the size of a pea. My mom doesn't use her imagination; that's why she says there isn't a monster in there. (I feel sorry for her.) Because I have a strong and healthy imagination, I am very lucky. Without one, everything would

Words of Wisdom

Show pictures of illuminated manuscripts. Suggest that students create ornamental letters and borders for their final papers. Students could state their focus idea as a maxim and use it for their title.

Thought for the Day

Each morning invite one student to read aloud his or her essay. Make an audio or video recording.

Class Book

Students might enjoy collecting their essays in a class book with a beautiful cover to preserve them.

More Ideas for Publishing and Sharing

Collage

Students can create a complementary visual representation of their thoughts in the form of a collage.

Group Discussion

If several students wrote about the same topic, invite them to lead a class discussion about it.

Self-Assessment

- What do you like best about your essay?
- Do you think your essay really communicates your ideas? If not, why not?
- Which examples work best? Why?
- Are you happy with your opening and closing? Why or why not?
- Which revisions improved your essay the most?
- What was most difficult: organizing your thoughts? writing an interesting opening and closing? finding the right words to say what you mean? thinking of examples?
- What did you learn about writing?

Reflecting/Self-Assessment

Use the Self-Assessment questions, or questions of your own, to help your students reflect on and evaluate their experience in writing an essay. They can discuss or write their responses.

Evaluating Writing

Use the criteria below to evaluate students' essays.

Criteria for Evaluating Personal Essays

- The opening engages the reader and presents the focus idea.
- The essay explores several thoughts or points related to the focus idea.
- Examples are used to strengthen and explain each thought or point.
- The closing makes the essay feel finished.

Portfolio Opportunity

- Save students' final copies to show their understanding of writing personal essays.
- Save students' planning aids and drafts to show their use of the writing process.
- Save the recording from Thought for the Day to show students' oral fluency and expression.

Sample Scoring Rubric

1	2	3	4
The paper is not a personal essay, or it meets the criteria only minimally. The focus idea is unclear and poorly developed, with little or no elaboration. The discussion is unfocused and undeveloped.	The essay includes a focus idea, but the presentation of ideas is sketchy or somewhat disorganized. The opening and/or closing are weak or inappropriate. More elaboration is needed.	The essay has a clear focus. The writer's thoughts are organized and supported, although more elaboration would be helpful. The essay includes an appropriate opening and closing. The essay might rate a 4 except for significant spelling, usage, or mechanics errors.	The essay meets all the evaluation criteria. It is well organized, thoughtful, and supported by strong examples. The opening and closing are interesting and effective. The essay has a minimum of spelling, mechanics, and usage errors.

Activating Prior Knowledge

Invite volunteers to name and describe (or demonstrate, if willing) as many kinds of dance as they can. (tap, ballet, modern, rock, country western, ballroom) Then ask:

- What live performances, TV shows, or films have you seen in which dance is an important part?

- What do you think it takes to be a professional dancer? (Samples: talent, training, dedication, confidence)

Savion Glover:

Savion Glover hunches way forward in his chair, talking about basketball. Dressed in sneakers, no-fit jeans, too-big T-shirt, and backward baseball cap, he seems primed for a quick game. But Glover isn't on the court. He's sitting in his dressing room at the Virginia Theatre on Broadway, where he costars in *Jelly's Last Jam.*

400

Making the Rules

by Robert Sandla

If Glover looks like the guy next door, don't be fooled: At age nineteen, he is a Broadway veteran who has literally grown up onstage, with the kind of rock-solid, so-fast-you're-not-sure-you're-hearing-it-right tap technique that has even blasé dancers racing to catch up. He's a brilliant, even avant-garde tapper, kicking up sparks, rattling out torrents of sound dense with rhythm, sailing through more pointe work than Pavlova. What makes Glover a star is that he makes tap look so easy.

Savion Glover as young Jelly Roll Morton, the famous composer, taps up sparks in *Jelly's Last Jam.*

Jelly's Last Jam tells the life story of Jelly Roll Morton, the African American pianist and composer who wrote a slew of popular tunes in the 1920s and eventually claimed to have "invented" jazz all by himself. Glover plays Morton as a smug young man growing up in New Orleans, where he is raised in a high-class Creole household but rediscovers his ethnic heritage in the music and culture of Africa. He shares the role with Gregory Hines, who plays Morton as a tortured adult and won a Tony Award for his performance.

Glover made his Broadway debut in *The Tap Dance Kid* when he was twelve; by the time he was fifteen, the *New York Times* had proclaimed him a "tap dance master." In 1989 he starred in the long-running revue *Black and Blue,* where he

401

Interact with Literature

Encourage students to respond to this article on their own, or offer prompts such as these:

• What does the title mean?

• What are the differences between "taking class" and improvisation? If you were a dancer, which one would you rather do? Why?

• How is dance like other kinds of art? How is it different?

• How is Savion Glover like Jelly Roll Morton? How is Jelly Roll Morton like Faith Ringgold? (See pp. 364–383.)

• What are three questions you'd ask Savion Glover if you could?

Interact with Literature

Background: FYI

The author describes Glover as *sailing through more pointe work than Pavlova. Pointe work* refers to ballet; *sur les pointes* means (in French) "on the toes." Anna Pavlova (1881–1931) was a famous Russian ballerina, known for her graceful style and delicate form. You might suggest that the author chose the name *Pavlova* for alliteration as well as for her famous ability.

Vocabulary

blasé: indifferent or bored; a word borrowed from the French

avant-garde: the latest or newest trend in a field; also a French word

Creole: native to Louisiana but of French ancestry

spontaneous: not planned or forced

endures: lasts

elite: the best of a group

improvisational: composed on the spur of the moment

camaraderie: friendship

aesthetic: of or pertaining to beauty and art

articulated: spoken clearly and effectively

tangible: real, quantifiable

bucolic: relating to country life; rural, rustic

hoofer: a slang term for dancer

more than held his own with such tap greats as Bunny Briggs, Lon Chaney, and Jimmy Slyde. The previous year he had appeared in the film *Tap* with Hines, who has said of him: "I call Savion 'The Man' because he is certainly the one who is going to take tap into the future. *He* is where tap dance is going."

If he is the future, Glover carries on one tap tradition that endures among the elite: He doesn't take class. A loose, highly improvisational form handed down from dancer to dancer in easygoing camaraderie, tap evolves as it gets passed along. In fact, Glover carries on the aesthetic philosophy articulated — shouted, actually — by a character in *Jelly's Last Jam* when young Jelly proudly asserts that he can play *Il Trovatore*: "That ain't no music. The notes is written out telling you what's going to come next. That's like waking up in the morning knowing you going to be alive at the end of the day."

A young Savion plays around on a photo shoot for a national magazine.

"Every night Gregory and I have an improvisation that we do together," Glover says about a showstopping competition number with Hines. "Gregory, Ted Levy, and I made the dance together, and we came up with so many steps, so many ideas, that we had to cut a lot. So I'm glad we're not nailed down to the same steps every performance. A lot of the time, I don't even like to work with a band. I like everything to be spontaneous. If it's going to happen, let it happen."

Has he *ever* been nervous?

"No." He pauses. "Actually, I was nervous twice: When I did my first performance in *The Tap Dance Kid;* and once when Gregory called me on stage at the Apollo Theater to dance with him. We decided what to do as we went along."

Though Glover doesn't take class, he teaches where he was taught, at Broadway

402

Dance Center. "It was supposed to be a nice, slow class, but I don't have patience," he says. "I like things to be done yesterday. I'm giving my students stuff that I do when I perform instead of the basic stuff."

Glover now plans to attend New York University, but he was once torn between tap and sports: "I had wanted to go to college in Syracuse so bad, just to play basketball. I gave it some thought and if I was to stop dancing for a basketball season — well, I chose not to. Staying in New York City, I can perform and go to college."

Though he's starring in a Broadway show, Glover lives with his family in New Jersey. The one tangible measure of his success is that he has moved from Newark, a city with a tough reputation, to the comparatively bucolic Montclair. "People say, 'You're out of Newark,' but I am there every day, playing basketball with the same friends in the same playground. I was born and raised there. People think once you get a certain amount of money you're going to move up on a hill and not be bothered. I think if I was to do that I'd go crazy. My house in Montclair is so quiet, sometimes I'll say, 'Where's the buses? Where's the trucks making noise?' I really wanted to get my mom out of Newark so she can chill out. Newark can be hard."

Glover's five-year plan makes him sound like the hoofer next door: "Hopefully, my girlfriend will be coming out of college. I really want to get married, start a family, and I want to keep performing. I'll be acting, singing, making movies — directing. I'll be happy, just living."

Left, Savion and Jimmy Slyde improvise on stage in a December 1992 performance of *Ted Levy and Friends* at the New School in New York City.

Below, In the same performance, Savion holds his own with the legends of tap.

403

✎ Writing

Students might enjoy researching a favorite dance form or dancer and writing an article for a magazine entitled Dancing Arts. Have interested students publish a copy of the magazine to share with classmates.

Social Studies

Students might research one of the proper nouns (such as Jelly Roll Morton, Gregory Hines, Tony Awards) mentioned in the article and choose their own way to present the information gathered, orally and/or visually.

Music/Dance

- Invite students to work alone or with others to choose a piece of music and *choreograph* a dance and perform it for others.

- Some people might take exception to Jelly Roll Morton's comment about the opera *Il Trovatore*. Suggest that interested students listen to the opera and decide for themselves whether or not it is music. (The opera was composed in the latter 1800s by Giuseppi Verdi. He died in 1901.)

SELECTION:
The Wright Brothers

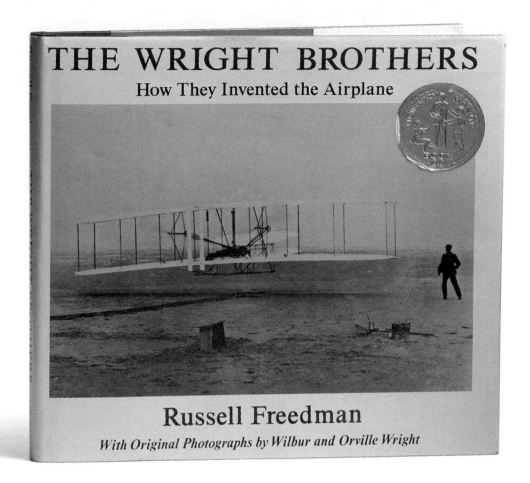

THE WRIGHT BROTHERS
How They Invented the Airplane

Russell Freedman

With Original Photographs by Wilbur and Orville Wright

by Russell Freedman

Other Books by the Author

Kids at Work: Lewis Hine and the Crusade Against Child Labor

Eleanor Roosevelt: A Life of Discovery

Lincoln: A Photobiography

Franklin Delano Roosevelt

Cowboys of the Wild West

An Indian Winter

- Newbery Honor
- Boston Globe–Horn Book Honor
- SLJ Best Book
- ALA Notable
- Bulletin Blue Ribbon
- Booklist Editors' Choice
- Booklist Top of the List

Selection Summary

Before making the first machine-powered aircraft to fly, the Wright brothers worked on designing and building gliders. In 1901, Wilbur and Orville realized that the calculations they had been using to construct a new glider were unreliable. Deciding to rely on their own direct observations, they built a wind tunnel and used it to test models of different types of wings. With the data they collected they designed their biggest glider yet and assembled it at Kitty Hawk. The new glider performed beautifully for the most part, but occasionally spun out of control. Orville reasoned that pressure built up on the tail, throwing the whole glider off balance. The brothers solved the problem by installing a movable tail rudder.

Lesson Planning Guide

	Skill/Strategy Instruction	Meeting Individual Needs	Lesson Resources
1 **Introduce** *the* **Literature** *Pacing: 1 day*	**Preparing to Read and Write** Prior Knowledge/Building Background, 403C **Selection Vocabulary,** 403D • calculations • data • accuracy • absorbed • systematic • tedious • stabilize **Spelling Pretest,** 419H • prepare • process • perform • problem • perfect • propose • persist • preview • profession • prehistoric	**Support in Advance,** 403C **Other Choices for Building Background,** 403C **Students Acquiring English,** 403C **Spelling Challenge Words,** 419H • propel • precaution • perception • prosecute • persecute	***Literacy Activity Book:*** Vocabulary, p. 183 **Transparency:** Vocabulary, 4–19 **Great Start** CD-ROM software, "Imagination at Work" CD
2 **Interact** *with* **Literature** *Pacing: 1–3 days*	**Reading Strategies** Summarize, 406, 410 Evaluate, 406, 410, 414 **Minilessons** Study Skill: K-W-L, 405 Making Judgments, 407 Writer's Craft: Using Primary Sources, 409 ✔ Text Organization, 411 Problem Solving/Decision Making, 413 Genre: Narrative Nonfiction, 415 Author's Viewpoint, 417	**Choices for Reading,** 406 **Guided Reading,** 406, 408, 412, 416 **Students Acquiring English,** 412, 415, 418 **Extra Support,** 406, 414, 416 **Challenge,** 407	**Reading-Writing Workshop:** A Personal Essay, 398–399F ***Literacy Activity Book:*** Selection Connections, pp. 147–148; Comprehension Check, p. 184 **Study Skills:** KWL, 405, H3 **Audio Tape** for Imagination at Work: *The Wright Brothers* **Student Writing Center,** writing and publishing software
3 **Instruct** *and* **Integrate** *Pacing: 1–3 days*	✔ **Comprehension:** Text Organization, 419A **Writing:** Answering an Essay Question, 419C ✔ **Word Skills & Strategies:** Absorbed Prefixes, 419E; Think About Words, 419F **Building Vocabulary:** Vocabulary Activities, 419G ✔ **Spelling:** Prefixes *per-, pre-,* and *pro-,* 419H ✔ **Grammar:** Avoiding Double Negatives, 419I **Communication Activities:** Listening and Speaking, 419K; Viewing, 419L **Cross-Curricular Activities:** Science, Social Studies, 419M–419N	**Reteaching:** Text Organization, 419B **Activity Choices:** Write On!, Shared Writing: Write a Song, Figure It Out, 419D **Reteaching:** Absorbed Prefixes, 419F **Activity Choices:** Aviation Terms, Word Root *vert/vers*, Word History: *atmosphere*, 419G **Challenge Words Practice:** 419H **Reteaching:** Avoiding Double Negatives, Daily Language Practice, 419J **Activity Choices:** Listening and Speaking, 419K; Viewing, 419L **Activity Choices:** Science, Social Studies, 419M–419N	**Reading-Writing Workshop:** A Personal Essay, 398–399F **Transparencies:** Comprehension, 4–20; Writing, 4–21; Grammar, 4–22 ***Literacy Activity Book:*** Comprehension, p. 185; Writing, p. 186; Word Skills, p. 187; Building Vocabulary, p. 188; Spelling, pp. 189–190; Grammar, pp. 191–192 **Study Skills:** Almanac, 419N, H4 **Audio Tape** for Imagination at Work: *The Wright Brothers* **Student Writing Center,** writing and publishing software

✔ *Indicates Tested Skills. See page 332F for assessment options.*

Introduce *the* Literature

Preparing to Read and Write

Support in Advance

Use this activity for students who need extra support before participating in the whole-class activity.

Photo Flight Preview the photographs in this selection of the Wright brothers' test flights. Encourage students to talk about what the photographs mean to them. Ask students about their own experiences with flight: flying in a plane, flying a kite, making a model airplane or glider, releasing helium balloons, or watching birds in flight. Ask them how and when they think airplanes were invented.

Management Tip
Have other students engage in self-selected silent reading during this activity.

Students Acquiring English
Help students to define terms used in the context of aviation, such as *glider, lift, drag, warped, elevator, wind tunnel, spokes,* and *blades*. Pantomime when possible.

Great Start
For students needing extra support with key concepts and vocabulary, use the "Imagination at Work" CD.

INTERACTIVE LEARNING

Prior Knowledge/Building Background

Key Concept
Aviation
Inventors and
Pioneers

Find out how much your students already know about the history of aviation. Do they know about the Wright brothers, Wilbur and Orville? How do they suppose the Wright brothers came up with their ideas? What is the relationship between imagination and invention? Where do they think the longing to fly comes from?

Ask a volunteer to define the word *pioneer*. Copy the following Venn diagram on the board and have students compare *pioneers* and *inventors*. Note that, often, people describe inventors as types of pioneers.

PIONEERS — INVENTORS
Journey to new lands | DISCOVERERS ADVENTURERS INNOVATORS | Journey to new discoveries

Other Choices for Building Background

Comparing Planes and Gliders

Extra Support Have students design paper airplanes out of a single sheet of paper, and then have a competition for "sustained flight." Have students discuss why they think certain airplanes flew farther than others. Then have students survey photographs of the Wright brothers' glider. Ask them to draw a picture of the glider next to one of a modern plane. Have them write captions to compare and contrast gliders and planes.

✎ Quick Write

Refer to the photographs on pages 414–417. Explain that there is no engine; the glider is riding aloft on wind power alone. Ask students to imagine what that must be like. Then let them write for five minutes in response.

Selection Vocabulary

Key Words

calculations

data

systematic

tedious

accuracy

stabilize

absorbed

Display Transparency 4–19.

- Pronounce the words with students and encourage those who are familiar with any of the words to define them or use them in context in a sentence.

- Model using context clues to determine which word belongs in Step 2 of Creating an Invention. Then ask volunteers to tell where the other Key Words belong.

- Encourage students to identify the context clues that helped them decide.

Vocabulary Practice Have students work independently or in pairs to complete the activity on page 183 of the *Literacy Activity Book*.

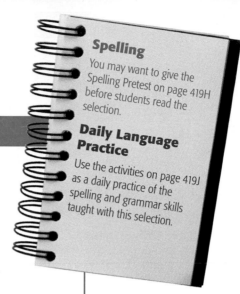

Spelling

You may want to give the Spelling Pretest on page 419H before students read the selection.

Daily Language Practice

Use the activities on page 419J as a daily practice of the spelling and grammar skills taught with this selection.

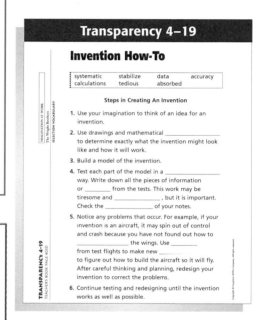

Transparency 4–19

Invention How-To

| systematic | stabilize | data | accuracy |
| calculations | tedious | absorbed | |

Steps in Creating An Invention

1. Use your imagination to think of an idea for an invention.
2. Use drawings and mathematical _____ to determine exactly what the invention might look like and how it will work.
3. Build a model of the invention.
4. Test each part of the model in a _____ way. Write down all the pieces of information or _____ from the tests. This work may be tiresome and _____, but it is important. Check the _____ of your notes.
5. Notice any problems that occur. For example, if your invention is an aircraft, it may spin out of control and crash because you have not found out how to _____ the wings. Use _____ from test flights to make new _____ to figure out how to build the aircraft so it will fly. After careful thinking and planning, redesign your invention to correct the problems.
6. Continue testing and redesigning until the invention works as well as possible.

Social Studies

Teacher FactFile
History Link

Balloons were the first aircraft to carry human beings aloft successfully. The brothers Joseph and Jacques Montgolfier (mahnt GAHL fee ur) invented hot-air balloons in France in 1783; Jacques Charles (sharl) invented the hydrogen balloon.

In 1853, the British inventor Sir George Cayley created the first glider to carry a human being into the air. The Wright brothers built and tested many gliders before inventing powered aircraft.

The Wright brothers made the first successful flight of an aircraft with a motor in 1903.

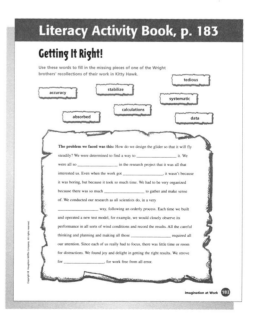

Literacy Activity Book, p. 183

Getting It Right!

Use these words to fill in the missing pieces of one of the Wright brothers' recollections of their work in Kitty Hawk.

tedious · accuracy · stabilize · systematic · absorbed · calculations · data

The problem we faced was this: How do we design the glider so that it will fly steadily? We were determined to find a way to _____ it. We were all so _____ in the research project that it was all that interested us. Even when the work got _____, it wasn't because it was boring, but because it took so much time. We had to be very organized because there was so much _____ to gather and make sense of. We conducted our research as all scientists do, in a very _____ way, following an orderly process. Each time we built and operated a new test model, for example, we would closely observe its performance in all sorts of wind conditions and record the results. All the careful thinking and planning and making all those _____ required all our attention. Since each of us really had to focus, there was little time or room for distractions. We found joy and delight in getting the right results. We strove for _____, for work free from all error.

Imagination at Work 183

Interact *with* Literature

More About the Author

Born in San Francisco in 1929, Russell Freedman wrote for newspapers, television, and advertising agencies before becoming a highly respected author of over thirty-five nonfiction books for young people. For many years, most of Freedman's books dealt with aspects of animal behavior, from *Animal Fathers* to *Hanging On: How Animals Carry Their Young*. In 1980, Freedman wrote a book on the immigrant experience, using historic photographs. Since then, Freedman has written a number of books on American history, including the first nonfiction book to win the Newbery Medal in over thirty years, *Lincoln: A Photobiography*. *The Wright Brothers* was a Newbery Honor book.

THE WRIGHT BROTHERS
How They Invented the Airplane
Russell Freedman
With Original Photographs by Wilbur and Orville Wright

THE WRIGHT BROTHERS

MEET RUSSELL FREEDMAN

While reading the *New York Times* one day, Russell Freedman learned that Orville and Wilbur Wright had taken photographs of their first flights. Intrigued, Freedman tracked down the original negatives in the Library of Congress. The images so fascinated Freedman that he decided to write about the famous aviators. "While I was working on my book, I visited their hometown, Dayton, Ohio, where I had a chance to examine the reconstructed 1905 Wright Flyer at Carillon Park and work the controls myself.... It helped me understand (and explain to my readers) exactly how the pilot navigated that early airplane."

Quick REFERENCE

Visual Literacy

Ask students why they think the Wright brothers took photographs of test flights. Help students understand that the brothers used these pictures as part of the data that helped them see how well their gliders worked.

Background: FYI

A plane stays aloft because its weight is spread over a large surface area. As an object falls, it pushes against air particles, which in turn resist this push. This creates a counterforce of equivalent resistance along the surface area, pushing the plane up.

HOW THEY INVENTED THE AIRPLANE

In 1899, Orville and Wilbur Wright, hard-working brothers from Dayton, Ohio, began to study bird flight, aviation, and early gliding experiments. First they made tests on kites and tethered gliders. Then in 1901, they made manned test glides at their camp at windy Kitty Hawk on North Carolina's Outer Banks and in Ohio. But when their glider continued to spin out of control, they closed their Kitty Hawk camp early and returned sadly to Dayton. At this point Wilbur doubted that a successful manned flight would take place in his lifetime.

405

MINILESSON

Study Skill
K–W–L

Teach/Model

Make sure your students know the K-W-L strategy to help them better understand, organize, and retain new information.

Explain what K–W–L stands for:

*What Do I **K**now?*

*What Do I **W**ant to Find Out?*

*What Did I **L**earn?*

Practice/Apply

Create the following chart on the chalkboard for students to copy and use while reading the selection. Encourage them to focus on what they want to know about the history of aviation or the Wright brothers. They fill in the K and W sections of the chart before they begin reading, and then complete the L column when they have finished the selection.

K	W	L
What Do I **K**now?	What Do I **W**ant to Find Out?	What Did I **L**earn?

SKILL FINDER   Full lesson, p. H3

Interact with Literature

Student Application

Have students discuss the strategies they plan on using to read this piece of historical nonfiction. Ask for volunteers to explain why they have chosen a certain reading strategy, and how they think it will help them.

Predicting/Purpose Setting

Have students predict what sorts of problems the Wright brothers will encounter as they try to perfect the controlled flight of their glider, and how they will overcome them.

Choices for Reading

Independent Reading	Cooperative Reading
Guided Reading	Teacher Read Aloud

Guided Reading

Have students read to the end of page 408. Use the questions on page 408 to check students' comprehension.

BACK TO THE DRAWING BOARD

Wilbur and Dan Tate launch the 1902 glider with Orville at the controls.

The experiments that Wilbur and Orville had carried out with their latest glider in 1901 were far from encouraging. Reflecting on their problems, Wilbur observed: "We saw that the calculations upon which all flying machines had been based were unreliable, and that all were simply groping in the dark. Having set out with absolute faith in the existing scientific data, we were driven to doubt one thing after another, till finally, after two years of experiment, we cast it all aside, and decided to rely entirely on our own investigations."

In the gaslit workroom behind their bicycle shop, Wilbur and Orville began to compile their own data. They wanted to test different types of wing surfaces and obtain accurate air-pressure tables. To do this, they built a wind tunnel — a wooden box 6 feet long with a glass viewing window on top and a fan at one end. It wasn't the world's first wind tunnel, but it would be the first to yield valuable results for the construction of a practical airplane.

 Quick**REFERENCE**

Visual Literacy

Because a glider has no engine, it must be lifted and accelerated to give it enough speed to stay in the air. In the photograph, the men at the sides of the glider had to run with it to launch it.

Extra Support

Vocabulary *Solder* is a mixture of metals that, when melted and allowed to reharden, is used to join two other pieces of metal. *Galvanized* iron is iron coated with zinc.

The materials needed to make model wings, or *airfoils,* and the tools to shape them were right at hand. Using tin shears, hammers, files, and a soldering iron, the brothers fashioned as many as two hundred miniature wings out of tin, galvanized iron, steel, solder, and wax. They made wings that were thick or thin, curved or flat, wings with rounded tips and pointed tips, slender wings and stubby wings. They attached these experimental airfoils to balances made of bicycle spokes and old hacksaw blades. Then they tested the wings in their wind tunnel to see how they behaved in a moving airstream.

For several weeks they were absorbed in painstaking and systematic lab work — testing, measuring, and calculating as they tried to unlock the secrets of an aircraft wing. The work was tedious. It was repetitious. Yet they would look back on that winter as a time of great excitement, when each new day promised discoveries waiting to be made. "Wilbur and I could hardly wait for morning to come," Orville declared, "to get at something that interested us. *That's* happiness."

The Wrights knew that they were exploring uncharted territory with their wind-tunnel tests. Each new bit of data jotted down in their notebooks added to their understanding of how an airfoil works. Gradually they replaced the calculations of others with facts and figures of their own. Their doubts vanished, and their faith in themselves grew. When their lab tests were finally completed, they felt confident that they could calculate in advance the performance of an aircraft's wings with far greater accuracy than had ever before been possible.

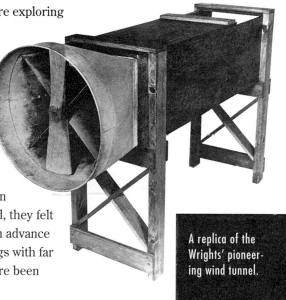

A replica of the Wrights' pioneering wind tunnel.

407

Challenge

Encourage interested students to research and build a model wind tunnel like the one the Wright brothers used to test wing designs. Students can use their journals to document the process.

M I N I L E S S O N

Making Judgments

REVIEW & MAINTAIN

Teach/Model

To make a judgment is to form an opinion. Readers can observe a character's behavior and actions to evaluate a character's personality. Have students reread the first two paragraphs on page 407. Then ask them what judgments they can make about the Wright brothers, based on the facts they have read. (The Wright brothers were patient, careful, methodical workers, very committed to their work.)

Practice/Apply

Have students make a judgment about the Wright brothers based on the following sets of facts.

Facts:
- The brothers stopped using other people's data and tested everything for themselves.
- They believed that they could calculate in advance the performance of an aircraft's wings.
- Even when the glider crashed, they were not discouraged.

Judgment:
(They were determined, self-sufficient, and self-confident.)

SKILL FINDER

Full lesson/Reteaching, Theme 5

Minilessons, p. 337; Theme 5

Interact *with* Literature

Guided Reading

Comprehension/Critical Thinking

1. For what purpose did the Wright brothers use the wind tunnel?
(to test different wing models in a moving airstream)

2. Why did they become more self-confident as they made their tests?
(Sample answers: because they were relying on their own observations; because they knew the tests were thorough)

3. Why was the testing tedious and exciting at the same time? (The work was time consuming and repetitive, but the brothers were making new discoveries and becoming more sure of how an airfoil works.)

Predicting/Purpose Setting

Encourage students to discuss what they think of the Wright brothers' work. Ask students if they need to revise their predictions. Have them continue reading to the end of page 413.

Informal Assessment

If students' responses to the Guided Reading questions indicate that they comprehend the selection, let them continue reading independently.

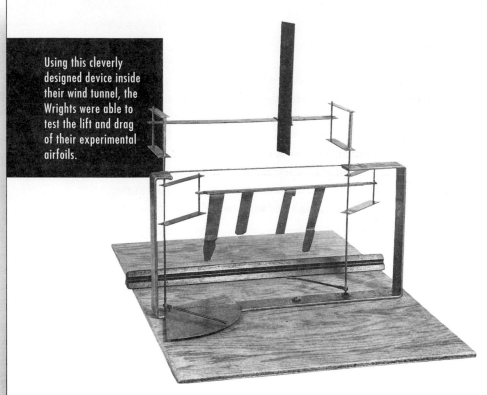

Using this cleverly designed device inside their wind tunnel, the Wrights were able to test the lift and drag of their experimental airfoils.

Armed with this new knowledge, they designed their biggest glider yet. Its wings, longer and narrower than before, measured 32 feet from tip to tip and 5 feet from front to rear. For the first time, the new glider had a tail — two 6-foot-high vertical fins, designed to help stabilize the machine during turns. The hip cradle developed the year before to control wing warping was retained. The craft weighed just under 120 pounds.

With growing anticipation, Wilbur and Orville prepared for their 1902 trip to the Outer Banks. "They really ought to get away for a while," Katharine wrote to her father. "Will is thin and nervous and so is Orv. They will be all right when they get down in the sand where the salt breezes blow. . . . They think that life at Kitty Hawk cures all ills, you know.

408

QuickREFERENCE

Vocabulary

Words have different meanings in aviation. *Lift* is the aerodynamic force (the action of air) that opposes gravity, thus keeping a plane aloft. *Drag* is the aerodynamic force that opposes, or works against, a plane's forward movement, slowing it down.

Science Link

Warping is the twisting of a plane's wings to compensate for gusts of wind which would otherwise tip the plane sideways. In warping, the movable part of one wing twists up, while the same part of the other wing twists down.

The Wright brothers figured out this control mechanism after watching turkey vultures twist their wingtips when wind hit them. All modern aircraft employ warping.

"The flying machine is in process of making now. Will spins the sewing machine around by the hour while Orv squats around marking the places to sew [the cotton wing covering]. There is no place in the house to live but I'll be lonesome enough by this time next week and wish I could have some of their racket around."

The brothers reached the Outer Banks at the end of August with their trunks, baggage, and crates carrying the glider parts. At Kill Devil Hills, they found that their wooden shed from the year before had been battered by winter storms. They set to work making repairs and remodeling the building, so they could use it instead of a tent as their new living quarters.

"We fitted up our living arrangements much more comfortably than last year," Wilbur reported. "Our kitchen is immensely improved, and then we have made beds on the second floor and now sleep aloft. It is an improvement over cots. We also have a bicycle which runs much better

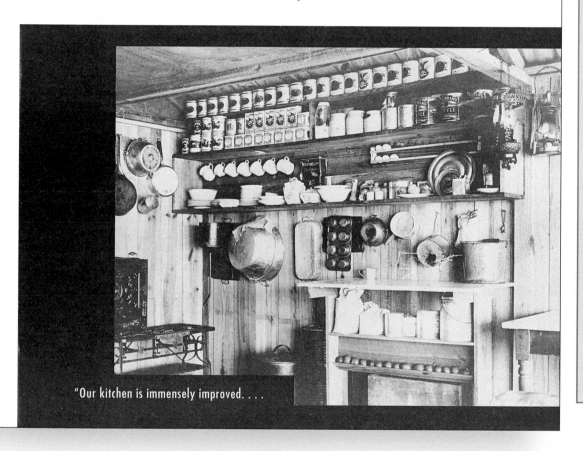

"Our kitchen is immensely improved. . . ."

SKILL FINDER · Writing Activity: Write On!, p. 419D

M I N I L E S S O N

Writer's Craft

Using Primary Sources

Teach/Model

A primary source is any form of information that comes directly from people involved in a historical event. Primary sources include photographs, letters, diary or journal entries, contemporary publications, and oral histories or recollections.

Ask students what primary sources Freedman uses in this selection. (excerpts from the Wright brothers' correspondence and journals, and photographs they took of their Kitty Hawk quarters and of their test flights)

Practice/Apply

Have students work with a partner to list other primary sources used in the selection (see the blue text). Have students compare their lists. (quotations from conversations between Wilbur and his father, p. 412; personal recollections, p. 414; quoted descriptions of the Wright brothers' lives and experiments)

Background: FYI

Kitty Hawk The Wright brothers chose this coastal test site in North Carolina because its steady winds and the gentle terrain of sand dunes made launching and flying the craft easy. People who fly hang gliders today look for similar sites.

Interact *with* **Literature**

"...and we have made beds on the second floor and now sleep aloft."

over the sand than we hoped, so that it takes only about an hour to make the round trip to Kitty Hawk instead of three hours as before. There are other improvements . . . so we are having a splendid time."

By the middle of September they had assembled their new glider and were ready to try it out. This year they took turns in the pilot's position, giving Orville a chance to fly for the first time. To begin with, they were very cautious. They would launch the machine from the slope on Big Hill and glide only a short distance as they practiced working the controls. Steering to the right or left was accomplished by warping the wings, with the glider always turning toward the lower wing. Up-and-down movements were controlled by the forward elevator.

In a few days they made dozens of short but successful test glides. At this point, things looked more promising than ever. The only mishap occurred one afternoon when Orville was at the controls. That evening he recorded the incident in his diary:

"I was sailing along smoothly without any trouble . . . when I noticed that one wing was getting a little too high and that the machine was slowly sliding off in the opposite direction. . . . The next thing I knew was that the wing was very high in the air, a great deal higher than before, and I thought I must have worked the twisting apparatus the wrong way. Thinking of nothing else . . . I threw the wingtips to their greatest angle. By this time I found suddenly that I was making a descent backwards

410

QuickREFERENCE

Vocabulary

To warp the plane, cables control the *ailerons,* flexible flaps on the wing. *Elevators* are the horizontal stabilizers on the tail; they move together, up or down, to control the plane's *pitch,* the direction of the plane's nose and tail up or down.

Flying the 1902 glider as a kite.

411

Text Organization

Teach/Model

Have students discuss how the author has organized the text. Make sure they point out examples. For example, the author has used time as an organizer to convey the sense that the Wright brothers were making progress. On page 410 there are phrases like *By the middle of September* and *In a few days.*

Ask volunteers to explain the difference between the text in black (the author narrating) and the text in blue (material from primary sources).

Practice/Apply

Have students set up a chart similar to the one shown here to list the main events of the selection in time order and to note the words and phrases that tell when each event happened.

Time Clue	Event

SKILL FINDER

Full lesson/Reteaching, pp. 419A–419B

Minilessons, p. 373, Themes 3, 6

Interact *with* Literature

 **Guided Reading**

Comprehension/Critical Thinking

1. What would you have told Orville if you had witnessed his accident? (Responses will vary.)

2. Look at the picture and caption on page 411. Why do you think the brothers flew the glider as a kite? (Samples: to test the plane's stability and control; to better observe how forces of air act on the glider)

3. When the brothers installed a movable tail, what problem were they solving, and how? (They were preventing the aircraft from spinning out of control. The movable tail wing served as a rudder to guide the glider.)

Predicting/Purpose Setting

For students who continue using Guided Reading, instruct them to read to the end of the selection. Use the questions on page 416 to check their comprehension.

---

toward the low wing, from a height of 25 or 30 feet. . . . The result was a heap of flying machine, cloth and sticks in a heap, with me in the center without a bruise or scratch. The experiments thereupon suddenly came to a close till repairs can be made. In spite of this sad catastrophe we are tonight in a hilarious mood as a result of the encouraging performance of the machine."

A few days' labor made the glider as good as new. It wasn't seriously damaged again during hundreds of test glides, and it repeatedly withstood rough landings at full speed. Wilbur and Orville became more and more confident. "Our new machine is a very great improvement over anything we had built before and over anything anyone has built," Wilbur told his father. "Everything is so much more satisfactory that we now believe that the flying problem is really nearing its solution."

And yet the solution was not yet quite at hand. As they continued their test flights, a baffling new problem arose. On most flights, the glider performed almost perfectly. But every so often — in about one flight out of fifty — it would spin out of control as the pilot tried to level off after a turn.

"We were at a loss to know what the cause might be," wrote Wilbur. "The new machine . . . had a vertical tail while the earlier ones were tailless; and the wingtips were on a line with the center while the old machines had the tips drawn down like a gull's wings. The trouble might be due to either of these differences."

First they altered the wingtips and went back to Big Hill for more test flights. Again, the glider spun out of control during a turn. Then they focused their attention to the machine's 6-foot-high double-vaned tail, which was fixed rigidly in place. They had installed this tail to help stabilize the glider during turns, but now, it seemed, something was wrong.

Lying in bed one sleepless night, Orville figured out what the problem was. The fixed tail worked perfectly well most of the time. During some turns, however — when the airspeed was low and the pilot failed to level off soon enough — pressure was built up on the tail, throwing the glider off balance and into a spin. That's just what happened to Orville the day of his accident. The cure was to make the tail movable — like a ship's rudder or a bird's tail.

412

Vocabulary

In a *banked turn* the pilot tilts the plane to one side, leaning into the direction of the turn. This method helps control the plane by offsetting the centrifugal force, just as a bicycle rider leans into the direction of the turn when rounding a curve.

 Students Acquiring English

If possible, point out a *rudder* on a toy boat or in the photograph of a sailboat. Explain that the rudder helps to direct the course of a boat. You cannot steer without one.

The next morning at breakfast, Orville told Wilbur about his idea. After thinking it over for a few minutes, Wilbur agreed. Then he offered an idea of his own. Why not connect the new movable tail to the wing-warping wires? This would allow the pilot to twist the wings and turn the tail at the same time, simply by shifting his hips. With the wings and tail coordinated, the glider would always make a smooth banked turn.

They removed the original tail and installed a movable single-vaned tail 5 feet high. From then on, there were no more problems. The movable tail rudder finally gave the Wright brothers complete control of their glider. "With this improvement our serious troubles ended," wrote Wilbur, "and thereafter we devoted ourselves to the work of gaining skill by continued practice."

As the brothers worked on their glider, their camp was filling up with visitors again. Their older brother Lorin arrived at the end of September to see what Wilbur and Orville were up to. Then Octave Chanute showed up again, along with two other gliding enthusiasts. Now six bunks were jammed into the narrow sleeping quarters up in the rafters. At night, the sounds of Wilbur's harmonica, Orville's mandolin, and a chorus of male voices drifted across the lonely dunes.

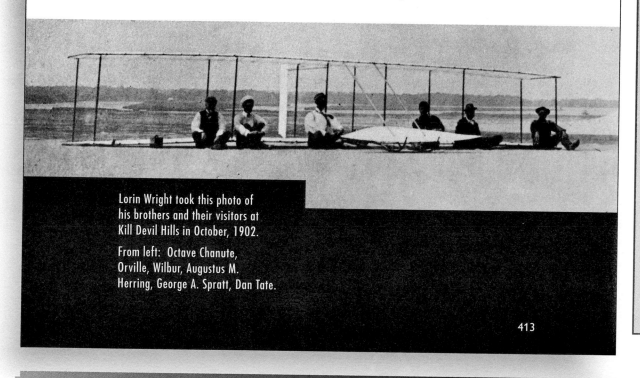

Lorin Wright took this photo of his brothers and their visitors at Kill Devil Hills in October, 1902.

From left: Octave Chanute, Orville, Wilbur, Augustus M. Herring, George A. Spratt, Dan Tate.

413

MINILESSON

Problem Solving and Decision Making

REVIEW & MAINTAIN

Teach/Model

Ask students to discuss the process inventors must use when they come upon a problem, or when things don't happen as expected. (They go back to the drawing board, review and revise plans, test out various components until it works right.)

Have students cite examples of how Orville and Wilbur decided to solve problems they encountered during the test flights of the glider. Although the brothers were systematic in their approach, they also relied on intuition and their imagination. Ask volunteers to explain how the brothers' imagination helped their invention.

Practice/Apply

Ask students to list the steps the brothers took to solve one problem. Have them conclude with the solution the brothers reached.

SKILL FINDER

Full lesson/Reteaching, Theme 2

Minilesson, Theme 2

Background: FYI

Octave Chanute was born in France but raised in the United States. His pioneering work with gliders greatly influenced Orville and Wilbur. Data from Chanute's glider flights was instrumental in their initial designs for aircraft.

Interact *with* Literature

"When the wind rose to 20 miles an hour, gliding was a real sport. . . ."

With their movable tail rudder, the Wrights felt confident that their glider could master the winds. They practiced flying at every opportunity, staying on at their camp until late in October, long after all their visitors had left. "Glides were made whenever weather conditions were favorable," Wilbur recalled. "Many days were lost on account of rain. Still more were lost on account of light winds. Whenever the breeze fell below six miles an hour, very hard running was required to get the machine started, and the task of carrying it back up the hill was real labor . . . but when the wind rose to 20 miles an hour, gliding was a real sport, for starting was easy and the labor of carrying the machine back uphill was performed by the wind."

One day they had a wind of about 30 miles an hour and were able to glide in it without any trouble. "That was the highest wind a gliding machine was ever in, so that we now hold all the records!" Orville wrote home. "The largest machine ever handled . . . the longest distance glide (American), the longest time in the air, the smallest angle of descent, and the highest wind!!! Well, I'll leave the rest of the 'blow' till we get home."

414

QuickREFERENCE

That season the Wrights had designed, built, and flown the world's first fully controllable aircraft. The three-dimensional system of aircraft control worked out by the brothers is the basic system used even today in all winged vehicles that depend on the atmosphere for support.

Except for an engine, their 1902 glider flew just as a Boeing 747 airliner or a jet fighter flies. A modern plane "warps" its wings in order to turn or level off by moving the ailerons on the rear edges of the wings. It makes smooth banking turns with the aid of a movable vertical rudder. And it noses up or down by means of an elevator (usually located at the rear of the plane).

Wilbur and Orville made hundreds of perfectly controlled glides in 1902. They proved that their laboratory tests were accurate. The next step was to build a powered airplane. "Before leaving camp," Orville wrote, "we were already at work on the general design of a new machine which we proposed to propel with a motor."

415

Students Acquiring English

Have students obtain a picture or diagram of a modern plane, such as the Boeing 747, and point out the location of the ailerons, the rudder, and the elevator.

MINILESSON

Genre
Narrative Nonfiction

Teach/Model

Ask volunteers to define *nonfiction* and *narrative*. (Nonfiction refers to writing that gives information about people that really lived and about things that really happen. A *narrative* is any story told or written.) Have students identify and discuss aspects of this selection that make it an example of narrative nonfiction.

- It is about the experience of real people as they lived and worked.

- It recounts and enlivens actual events in the early days of aviation.

- It is based on historical facts.

- The author doesn't make up any detail to tell this story: Instead, he uses primary sources such as photographs and journal entries.

Practice/Apply

Have students work with partners to review the selection and find passages about the personal experiences of the Wright brothers that they believe bring to life the history of aviation.

Interact *with* Literature

416

🔖 Guided Reading

Comprehension/Critical Thinking

1. Which of the Wright brothers' major achievements in 1902 impressed you most? (Samples: built a wind tunnel for testing airfoils; built and tested new glider; installed wing warping mechanism and rudder to improve stability; set new records for gliding; flew first fully controllable aircraft)

2. The Wright brothers gathered data to figure out several things. Name a few. (how airfoils behaved in an airstream; how different parts of a glider affected its control; how gliders behaved in flight)

3. Why do you think the brothers tested gliders before trying to build a powered plane? (Sample: Gliders were simpler, and the problems they presented would also occur in powered planes.)

4. What problems might the brothers have encountered when they began testing a plane with a motor? (Samples: how the extra weight of the motor affected the plane; how to make the motor reliable in flight)

Self-Assessment

Ask students to evaluate how effective their chosen reading strategies were. Encourage them to discuss and compare what worked best for them.

Quick**REFERENCE**

Visual Literacy

Help students see how these pictures were shot in sequence and show a single flight of the glider coming down a slope. Ask why the glider is shown at different angles. (First, it is coming toward the photographer; then it is moving away.)

🔖 Extra Support

Rereading Encourage students who would most benefit to read aloud with a partner. Have them reread the passages they found confusing and take turns summarizing information in text and in photographs.

Wilbur making a right turn in the 1902 glider.

417

Author's Viewpoint

REVIEW & MAINTAIN

Teach/Model

Ask students to describe the viewpoint of author Russell Freedman. Suggest that his tone is *objective*, not influenced by emotion or personal prejudice. Although the work of the Wright brothers greatly inspired and intrigued Freedman, his viewpoint is impartial. He has written a nonfiction narrative that reconstructs an exciting time in the lives of two inventors and pioneers in aviation. Freedman informs the readers; his writing lets people form their own opinions. Have students discuss what makes this author's viewpoint objective:

- He sticks to the facts.

- He doesn't make any judgments.

- He relies on primary sources.

Practice/Apply

Have students work in pairs to discuss selections in the rest of the theme. Ask them to describe the authors' viewpoints.

SKILL FINDER

Full lesson/Reteaching, p. 396B; Theme 6

Minilessons, p. 393, Themes 5, 6

Science Link

Ask students why launching the glider was easier in a high wind than in a light wind. Help them see that the wind helped support the plane's weight and give it the necessary speed. Mention that the glider was probably hard to control in a really high wind.

Interact
with
Literature

Responding Activities

Let Go Ideas

✎ Personal Response

Let students respond in their own way to the selection, or let them write in their journals about what it would have felt like to pilot one of the Wright brothers' gliders.

Anthology Activities

Encourage students to choose an activity from their Anthologies.

Literature Discussion

What would you define as the turning point in this narrative non-fiction? Why?

Selection Connections

Ask students to complete the chart for *The Wright Brothers* on *Literacy Activity Book* pages 147–148.

Make a Graph

How Fast Is Fast?

Make a graph that shows the speed of various things in miles per hour. For example, how fast can the average person walk? Run? How fast did the Wright Brothers' gliders move? How fast does a cheetah run? A race car? A train? A sailboat? How fast is the wind on a windy day? In a tornado or hurricane? How fast do airplanes fly? Jets? How fast does the earth spin?

Write About Brothers

Wilbur and Orville

What kind of relationship did the Wright brothers have? Competitive or cooperative? Close or distant? Were their personalities alike or different? Look for evidence in the words and photos of this selection. Then write a paragraph that makes a judgment about the brothers and gives examples to support it. Share your paragraph with another reader and see if he or she agrees.

418

Informal Assessment

Students should understand that the process of invention is imaginative, disciplined, and thoughtful.

Additional Support:

- Review Guided Reading questions.
- Have students reread confusing passages and summarize them in their journals.

Quick**REFERENCE**

Home Connection

Students can share books about different planes with family members. Have them compare the Wright brothers' gliders with later planes and explain how Wilbur and Orville contributed to aviation.

🧑‍🏫 Students Acquiring English

MEETING INDIVIDUAL NEEDS

Encourage students to choose activities occasionally that offer an alternative to writing. They may prefer working with a partner, drawing, or creating bulletin boards.

RESPONDING

Fly!

Bulletin Board Display

Write a Description

The Wonder of Flight

Now that you've read this chapter about the Wright Brothers' glider, observe a plane or a bird in flight and write about what you see, hear, and experience. Take notes as you watch. Try to include some words from this selection. Turn your notes into a descriptive paragraph or a poem that you share with your classmates.

The Imagination at Work

Think about the old saying, "If at first you don't succeed, try, try again." As a class or group, make a bulletin board with the saying as its headline. With words and pictures, show how various people and characters from this theme are good examples of this piece of advice. Feel free to include people and characters from other themes in this book, too. Let them inspire you to try, try again when you use *your* imagination.

419

Comprehension Check

To check student comprehension, use these questions and/or *Literacy Activity Book* page 184.

1. How did the Wright brothers use their imagination at work? Explain. (Answers should show an understanding of the connection between creative thinking and invention.)

2. Why was the addition of a rudder on the tail of the aircraft so important? (It enabled them to steer the plane in flight.)

3. What do you think the history of aviation would have been without the Wright brothers? (Allow students to speculate within reason.)

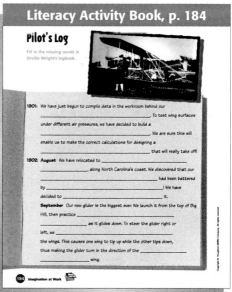

Literacy Activity Book, p. 184

Pilot's Log

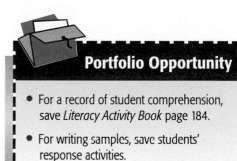

Portfolio Opportunity

- For a record of student comprehension, save *Literacy Activity Book* page 184.

- For writing samples, save students' response activities.

Instruct *and* Integrate

Comprehension

Literacy Activity Book, p. 185

Don't Just Wing It!

What were three problems and solutions that the author presented to organize information about the Wright brothers? Each cloud gives you a clue.

Calculations
Problem: _____
Solution: _____

Airfoil
Problem: _____
Solution: _____

Tailspin
Problem: _____
Solution: _____

Imagination at Work **185**

Transparency 4–20

Text Organization

The Wright Way to Solve a Problem

Problem: "We saw that the calculations upon which all flying machines had been based were unreliable."

Steps Taken:

1. _____

2. _____

3. _____

4. _____

Solution: _____

TRANSPARENCY 4–20
TEACHER'S BOOK: PAGE 419A

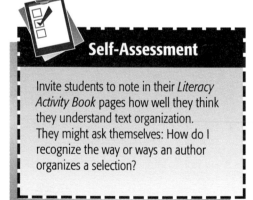

Self-Assessment

Invite students to note in their *Literacy Activity Book* pages how well they think they understand text organization. They might ask themselves: How do I recognize the way or ways an author organizes a selection?

TESTED SKILL

Text Organization

LAB, p. 185

Teach/Model

Ask students how they organize their time in the morning before school, for the rest of the day after leaving school, and on a weekend day. Discuss what would happen if no one organized their lives or gave some sort of structure to their day. Bring out the idea that organization helps us to make the best use of our time and our energy. Ask students why text organization is as important for writers as it is for readers.

Writers use text organization to
• present information so that it makes sense
• convey a message in a way that is meaningful
• help the reader learn new information

Readers rely on text organization to
• recognize the main ideas in a selection
• identify relationships between ideas
• understand the author's message

Have students recall how they recognized that the selection was organized by time sequence. (by noting words and phrases that referred to time)

Display Transparency 4–20. Have students reread pages 406–407 and identify the problem and the steps the brothers took to solve it. Help students recognize the author's text organization

- presents the problem
- details problem-solving steps

Practice/Apply
- Have students complete *Literacy Activity Book* page 185.

- Students can also choose one other nonfiction selection from this theme and identify how the author organizes the selection.

SKILL FINDER

Reteaching, p. 419B

Minilessons, pp. 373, 411; Themes 3, 6

Reteaching

Reteaching **Text Organization**

Point out the picture of the wind tunnel replica on page 407.

Have students locate the text that describes the wind tunnel. (last paragraph on page 406) Then have students identify the text that is related to each of the other pictures in the selection. Help students see how the author uses pictures to organize the text.

Portfolio Opportunity

Save *Literacy Activity Book* page 185 to record students' understanding of Text Organization.

Instruct *and* Integrate

Writing Skills and Activities

Literacy Activity Book, p. 186

Getting Organized

Question: How did Wilbur and Orville's experiments with the wind tunnel show that they were creative, patient, and curious?

How are you going to answer the essay question? Organize your ideas by filling in the planning chart. Then write your answer on a separate sheet of paper.

Opening Statement

Details to Support the Opening Statement

Closing Statement

186 Imagination at Work

Informal Assessment

Review each answer for organization, clarity, and focus.

INTERACTIVE LEARNING

Answering an Essay Question

LAB, p. 186

Teach/Model

Ask students how answering an essay question is different from answering other kinds of test questions. (It requires writing a paragraph; other kinds of test questions might involve choosing an answer, as in multiple choice, or writing a one-word answer or one or two sentences in response.) To help students meet the challenge of answering essay questions, present this three-point strategy:

---

1. **Read** the essay question.
2. **Determine** what the question is asking.
3. **Plan** the answer. Be sure to answer the question that is asked and to answer it completely. Organize the information.
   - **Write a topic sentence** for the paragraph by turning around the essay question and stating it as a main idea.
   - **Explain your answer** by providing examples or supporting details.
   - **Sum up your main point** in the last sentence.

Display Transparency 4–21, and read aloud the essay question. Ask students to tell what the question is asking. Then have students read the paragraphs to answer the essay question.

Ask students to consider these three questions:

- Do the paragraphs really answer the essay question?
- Do they answer the question completely?
- Is each paragraph well organized, with a topic sentence, supporting details, and a closing statement?

Practice/Apply

Assign the activity Write On! Remind students to follow the guidelines for answering an essay question.

Writing Activities

Write On!
Cooperative Learning

Distribute slips of paper and ask students to write an essay question about the Wright brothers or about another topic the class is studying. Urge students to be specific when wording their questions so that they will get a clear and direct response. Place all the slips in a paper bag and then have everyone draw an essay question to answer. Have students work in small groups of mixed abilities to share, discuss, and evaluate their answers to the essay questions. Students may want to use primary sources to answer some essay questions that require research. *(See Writer's Craft Minilesson on page 409.)*

Figure It Out

Have students write a paragraph about how they figured out a solution to a mechanical or a personal problem.

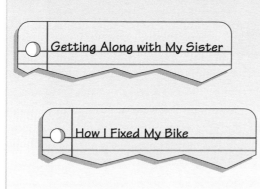

Getting Along with My Sister

How I Fixed My Bike

Shared Writing: Write a Song

 Let students work in small groups, as if each were in a recording studio, to write a song about the Wright brothers and their exploits. Students can always adapt their favorite tunes by taking music from popular songs and adding their own lyrics about Wilbur and Orville and their flying machines. Or, they can create an original soundtrack to a made-up movie about the Wright brothers, for example, one titled *Kitty Hawk*.

Students Acquiring English
Encourage students to write and perform in their primary language and to include music from their culture.

You better look out, they're going to fly
Without a doubt they're making a try
Orville and Wilbur Wright will succeed!

Students can use the **Student Writing Center** software for all of their writing activities.

Portfolio Opportunity

- Save *Literacy Activity Book* page 186 to record students' understanding of answering an essay question.
- Save responses to activities on this page for writing samples.

Instruct *and* Integrate

Word Skills and Strategies

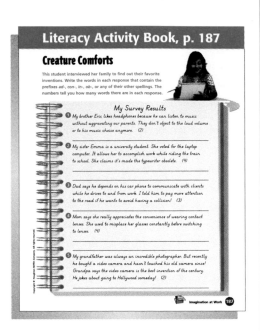
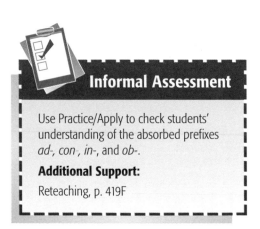

INTERACTIVE LEARNING

Structural Analysis
Absorbed Prefixes

LAB, p. 187

Teach/Model

Make a chart like the one below. Label each square with one of the prefixes *ad-, con-, in-,* or *ob-*. Then ask students to skim through *The Wright Brothers* to find words that include these prefixes.

ad-	con-	in-	ob-
means "toward or to"	means "together or with"	means "in or within" or "not"	means "opposite or against"
advance	controlled	investigate, insensible	obstruct

Explain that some prefixes change their spellings to match the first letter of the base word or word root that follows. Explain that the *as* and *ac* in words like *assembled* and *accomplished* are variants on the *ad-* prefix and have the same meaning. Other words with absorbed prefixes include *compile, improve,* and *opposite.* These words all contain variations of the *con-, in-,* and *ob-* prefixes.

Practice/Apply

Cooperative Learning List the following words on the chalkboard. Ask students to work in pairs or small groups to identify the prefix in each word and discuss the way the meaning of the prefix is related to the meaning of the word.

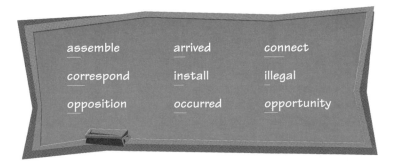

assemble	arrived	connect
correspond	install	illegal
opposition	occurred	opportunity

Reteaching

Absorbed Prefixes

Explain that a prefix that changes its spelling when it is added to certain words is called an absorbed prefix. Tell students that these changes usually occur because the new spelling is easier to pronounce. Ask students which group of words is easier to say: *comlected, comrect,* and *comfused* or *collected, correct,* and *confused.*

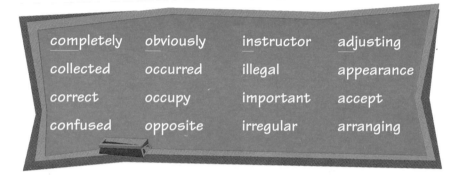

completely	obviously	instructor	adjusting
collected	occurred	illegal	appearance
correct	occupy	important	accept
confused	opposite	irregular	arranging

Write the lists of words above on the board and have students work in small groups to identify the prefixes in each of these lists of words.

M I N I L E S S O N

Think About Words

Teach/Model

Review the Think About Words strategy with students. Direct students to find this excerpt from *The Wright Brothers.*

> **Page 407** For several weeks they were absorbed in painstaking and systematic lab work—testing, measuring, and calculating as they tried to unlock the secrets of an aircraft wing. The work was tedious. It was repetitious. Yet they would look back on that winter as a time of great excitement. . . .

> **Think Aloud** The word *repetitious* might be important because it describes the type of work the Wright brothers did. The context gives a clue, because the work is also described as tedious, or dull. Keeping that in mind, I can see that *repetitious* looks like *repeat,* so I bet it means repeating the same thing over and over.

Practice/Apply

Cooperative Learning Have students work in pairs to find and discuss any unfamiliar words in *The Wright Brothers.* Then have the class compare their decisions about those words. Was the word important? What clues to meaning did they find in the word or in the text around it?

Think About Words Strategy

Ask yourself this question: Is this word important to your understanding of what you are reading?

If the answer is yes, follow these steps:
- Try to pronounce the word.
- Look for context clues.
- Think of other words that remind you of this one.
- Look for familiar prefixes, base words, roots, or suffixes.
- Use a dictionary.

Portfolio Opportunity

Save *Literacy Activity Book* page 187 to record students' understanding of absorbed prefixes.

3

Instruct *and* Integrate

Building Vocabulary

Vocabulary Activities

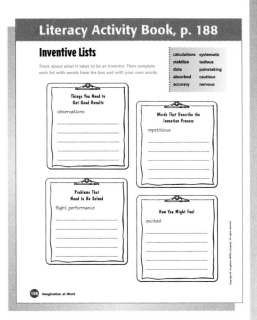

Literacy Activity Book, p. 188

Use this page to review Selection Vocabulary.

Aviation Terms

Draw a web chart like the one below on the chalkboard. Write *Aviation Terms* in the center of the chart. Then ask students to skim the selection from *The Wright Brothers* to find aviation terms. As students offer terms they find, write them on the board in the chart.

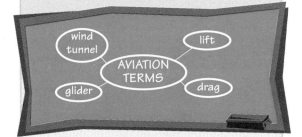

Possible responses: *glider, airfoil, wind tunnel, lift, drag, warping wires, elevator, stabilizer, angle of descent, banked turn, ailerons.*

Word History: *atmosphere*

Share this word history.

Tell students that the literal meaning of *atmosphere* is "a ball of air." The word part *atmo* comes from a Greek word meaning "breath or vapor." The *sphere* comes from Latin and Greek words for a sphere, or ball. Remind students that atmosphere means the layer of gases surrounding Earth or another planet, but it also means the mood or effect of a place: *The atmosphere in the room was tense.*

Word Root *vert/vers*

Write the selection word *vertical* on the board and circle the root *vert*. Explain that this root, also spelled *vers*, comes from a Latin word meaning "to turn." Show students the word family with *convert* below, and discuss meanings. Then have them use a dictionary to build families with the additional words *revert, advert, divert* and *invert.*

convert	converse	conversion
conversant	conversation	convertible

- **revert** (reverse, reversal, reversion, reversible)

- **advert** (adverse, adversary, advertise, advertisement, inadvertent)

- **divert** (diverse, diversion) • **invert** (inverse, inversion)

Spelling

MINILESSON

Spelling Words

*prepare *propose
*process persist
*perform preview
*problem profession
*perfect prehistoric

Challenge Words

*propel
precaution
perception
prosecute
persecute

*Starred words or forms of the words appear in *The Wright Brothers.*

TESTED SKILL

Prefixes *per-*, *pre-*, and *pro-*

LAB, pp. 189–190

- Write *perform, prepare,* and *propose* on the board. Underline the prefixes *per-, pre-,* and *pro-.*

- Remind students that knowing the meanings of prefixes and other word parts can help them figure out the meanings of words they don't know. For example, the word *propose* is a combination of the prefix *pro-,* meaning "to accept or be in favor of," and the base word *pose,* meaning "to present or put forward." *Propose* means "putting something forward for acceptance."

- Write the Spelling Words on the board. Tell students that each Spelling Word contains the prefix *per-, pre-,* or *pro-.* Say the words and have students repeat them.

Literacy Activity Book, p. 189

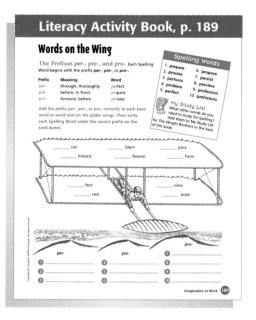

Literacy Activity Book, p. 190

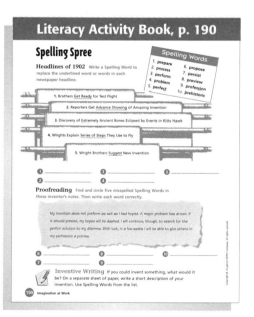

Spelling Assessment

Pretest

Say each underlined word, read the sentence, and then repeat the word. Have students write only the underlined words.

1. It is time to <u>prepare</u> for the trip to Kitty Hawk.
2. Building a flying machine is a hard <u>process</u>.
3. Our machine will <u>perform</u> well.
4. The first test glide was no <u>problem</u> at all.
5. The new glider gave a <u>perfect</u> performance.
6. We'll <u>propose</u> building a motorized glider.
7. We will <u>persist</u> until we are successful.
8. Friends came to <u>preview</u> the glider.
9. The shopkeepers changed their <u>profession</u>.
10. Their designs looked like <u>prehistoric</u> animals!

Test

Spelling Words Use the Pretest sentences.

Challenge Words

11. They used wind to <u>propel</u> the glider.
12. As a <u>precaution</u>, don't fly in poor weather.
13. His <u>perception</u> of the problem is different.
14. The judge decided to <u>prosecute</u> the law-breakers.
15. Don't <u>persecute</u> someone just because she's different.

SKILL FINDER

Daily Language Practice, p. 419J

Reading-Writing Workshop, p. 399E

MEETING INDIVIDUAL NEEDS

Challenge

Challenge Words Practice Have students use the Challenge Words to write quotes from the diary of an inventor who has created something unpopular.

Instruct *and* Integrate

Grammar

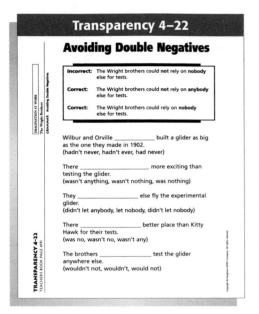

Transparency 4–22

Avoiding Double Negatives

Incorrect:	The Wright brothers could **not** rely on **nobody** else for tests.
Correct:	The Wright brothers could **not** rely on **anybody** else for tests.
Correct:	The Wright brothers could rely on **nobody** else for tests.

Wilbur and Orville _____ built a glider as big as the one they made in 1902.
(hadn't never, hadn't ever, had never)

There _____ more exciting than testing the glider.
(wasn't anything, wasn't nothing, was nothing)

They _____ else fly the experimental glider.
(didn't let anybody, let nobody, didn't let nobody)

There _____ better place than Kitty Hawk for their tests.
(was no, wasn't no, wasn't any)

The brothers _____ test the glider anywhere else.
(wouldn't not, wouldn't, would not)

TRANSPARENCY 4–22
TEACHER'S BOOK PAGE 419I

Literacy Activity Book, p. 192

The Airplane–An Unlikely Idea?

Literacy Activity Book, p. 191

Negative Notes

Incorrect: The Wright brothers **didn't never** stop with the success of their glider.
Correct: The Wright brothers **didn't** stop with the success of their glider.

Avoiding Double Negatives A reporter wrote these sentences about the Wright brothers' first successful airplane flight on December 17, 1903. Rewrite the sentences, correcting the double negatives.

❶ The brothers would not let no fear hold them back.
_____

❷ Weather conditions weren't no good that windy day.
_____

❸ The Wright brothers didn't hardly postpone the flight.
_____

❹ Orville could not barely hear the cheering people.
_____

❺ There hasn't never been anything like this historic flight!
_____

Imagination at Work **191**

Informal Assessment

Responses to the activities should indicate a general understanding of the correct use of negatives in sentences.

Additional Support:

Reteaching, p. 419J

TESTED SKILL

Avoiding Double Negatives

LAB, pp. 191–192

> • A **negative** is a word that means "no." It reverses the meaning of a sentence.
> • Avoid using a **double negative,** two negative words in the same sentence.

Teach/Model   Write the following sentences on the chalkboard:

We have school today.

We have no school today.

Ask a volunteer what the difference is in meaning. (Sample: The word *no* reverses the meaning.) Then write a list of negative words such as *no, not, nothing, nobody, nowhere, isn't.* Ask students what the words have in common. (All are negative words.) Invite students to add to the list, reminding them that contractions formed with negatives are also negative words. Introduce the term *negative.*

Then write this sentence:

The Wright brothers didn't have no experience at first.

Ask students what is wrong with the sentence. (Sample: It has two negative words.) Help students correct the sentence in two ways on the chalkboard. (The Wright Brothers **didn't have any/had no** experience at first.) Introduce the term *double negative.*

Students Acquiring English Ask students how many negatives are used in sentences in their native languages. Remind students to use only one negative in a sentence in English.

SKILL FINDER   Reading-Writing Workshop, p. 399E

INTERACTIVE LEARNING *(continued)*

Teach/Model Display Transparency 4–22. Discuss the example sentences, noting the double-negative error and the ways of correcting it. Have students correct the remaining sentences and read the corrected sentences aloud. Make sure students use both possible corrections. Have them take turns writing them on the transparency. Be sure students realize that one of the three choices is incorrect because it is a double negative.

Practice/Apply ***Literacy Activity Book*** Refer students to the Handbook at the back of the *Literacy Activity Book* for a list of negative words.

***Cooperative Learning:* Negative Sentences** Write ten or more different double-negative phrases on the chalkboard. Divide the class into two teams. Have a student from each team correct the same double negative at the same time, writing a sentence on the chalkboard. Let teammates decide on corrections. The team with the most correct sentences wins. Continue the activity until all students have written a sentence. If both teams correct a double negative in the same way, offer a bonus point for the team that first corrects the error differently.

 Writing Application: Trying Something New Ask students to think of an activity they have learned to do well. Suggest that they write a paragraph of advice to someone new at the activity, giving tips to help the person not get discouraged while learning.

Students' Writing Encourage students to check their writing in process to make sure they have not used double negatives.

Reteaching

Avoiding Double Negatives

Draw one or more ticktacktoe grids on butcher paper, and write a different double negative (*isn't no, can't hardly,* etc.) in each space. Write a correction of each double negative (*isn't any, can't,* etc.) on a separate card, and give one to each student. Then write a double negative in a sentence to review with students what a double negative is and how to correct it. Review what a negative word is also. Help students identify corrections for the double negatives. Have students one at a time paste their correction cards over the corresponding double negatives and use the correction in a sentence.

Daily Language Practice

Focus Skills

Grammar: Avoiding Double Negatives

Spelling: The Prefixes *per-, pre-,* and *pro-*

Each day write one sentence on the chalkboard. Have each student write the sentence correctly on a sheet of paper. Tell students to check for double negatives and for misspelled words. Have students correct their own paper as a volunteer corrects the sentence on the chalkboard.

1. At first the Wrights couldn't find nothing to perpose for the problem of flight.
At first the Wrights **couldn't find anything/could find nothing** to **propose** for the problem of flight.

2. They didn't have no idea how their glider would really pcform until they flew it.
They **didn't have any/had no** idea how their glider would really **perform** until they flew it.

3. They couldn't perfact no design without trial and error.
They **couldn't perfect any/could perfect no** design without trial and error.

4. Wilbur and Orville weren't hardly ever alone when they went to perpare for trial flights.
Wilbur and Orville **were hardly ever/weren't ever** alone when they went to **prepare** for trial flights.

5. They didn't never stop their porcess of discovery.
They **didn't ever stop/never stopped** their **process** of discovery.

3

Instruct
and
Integrate

Communication Activities

Listening and Speaking

Invention Exposition
Cooperative Learning

The stories behind other inventions, such as the telephone, the electric light, and the computer, are just as exciting as the story of the invention of the airplane. Have students work in small groups to prepare an oral report about an invention. Suggest that students divide the work as follows:

• Present a brief biography of the chief inventor or inventors.

• Describe how the invention was developed and tested.

• Explain how the invention works, using a diagram or model if desired.

Adventure in Air

Students Acquiring English Play the audio cassette recording of "The Twenty-One Balloons" by William Pène du Bois. After students listen to the tape, have them illustrate what they heard.

Breaking the News

Have students re-create a news broadcast of a historic moment in aviation, for example, the first flight in a hot-air balloon, breaking the sound barrier, flying to the highest altitude, flying solo around the world.

Viewing

Model Planes

Interested students might enjoy building models of the Wright brothers' first plane or other planes from different periods. One book they might consult is Frank Ross, Jr., *Historic Plane Models: Their Stories and How to Make Them* (Lothrop, Lee, and Shepard, 1973), which includes directions for making a model of the Wright brothers' first powered plane.

Video View

Extra Support Watch a video about flying. Ask students how viewing the video contributed to what they learned in the selection.

- FLYING, Media Basics Video
  This is a 30-minute, PBS, 3-2-1 Contact Series video. It covers kites, sailplanes, balloons, and blimps. Includes try-at-home activities that illustrate the basics of flight.

- THE AGE OF FLIGHT: Kitty Hawk, Media Basics Video
  This is one volume in a series of twelve, each lasting 60 minutes. This volume contains "breathtaking aerial footage and rare archival film" from the early days of aviation.

Pictures and Information About Early Flight

The Education Service Center of the Smithsonian Institution's National Air and Space Museum has several illustrated pamphlets about flight that are available to interested classes. Students can write to:

National Air and Space Museum
Education Service Center
P-700 MRC 305
Sixth and Independence Avenues SW
Washington, D.C. 20560

Cross-Curricular Activities

Book List

Science

The Smithsonian Book of Flight for Young People
by Walter J. Boyne

Before the Wright Brothers
by Don Berliner

Flight: Fliers and Flying
by David Jefferis

Social Studies

Inventions That Changed Modern Life
by Lois Markham

The Picture History of Great Inventors
by Gillian Clements

Experimenting with Inventions
by Robert Gardner

Outward Dreams: Black Inventors and Their Inventions
by James Haskins

Science

On Wings

Students can construct and fly paper airplanes with a variety of different wing sizes and shapes. Which fly fastest? Which glide for the longest distances? Which are best for aerobatics?

A bird's wing is curved in such a way that the air pressure is higher underneath the wing than above it.

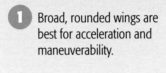

1 Broad, rounded wings are best for acceleration and maneuverability.

2 Slender, pointed wings are best for speed and endurance, and for gliding and hovering.

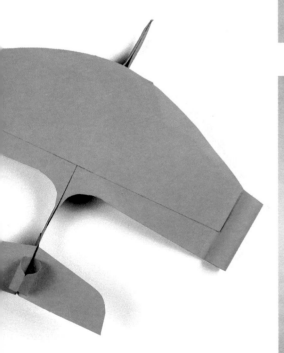

Choices for Social Studies

The First Flights

While most people who fly today use engine-powered aircraft, there are many flying enthusiasts who soar without the aid of machines or engines. Students will enjoy researching and reporting on recent events and records in hang-gliding, sailplaning, and hot-air ballooning. The first humans to fly were not the Wright brothers. In Paris, in 1783, the Marquis d'Arlandes and Pilatre de Rozier flew for several miles in a balloon designed by the Montgolfier brothers. The first to fly a heavier-than-air craft was a German, Otto Lilienthal, who designed and flew a hang glider in 1891.

Choices for Social Studies *(continued)*

The Turn of the Century

The first decade of the twentieth century saw the introduction of a number of items that we now take for granted as part of our everyday lives. Display a chart similar to the one shown here. List student predictions for innovations and inventions that they would like to see introduced during the years 2000–2010.

Items First Introduced in the Years 1900–1910

Household	Personal Care	Food, etc.	Misc.
vacuum cleaner	safety razor	ice-cream cone	paper cup
air conditioner	hair dye	decaf coffee	paper clip
washing machine	permanent wave solution	bubble gum	Teddy bear
			coffee filter
			collapsible stroller

Great Inventions

Do students ever wonder who invented the zipper, the ice-cream cone, or television? Challenge students to research the story behind an invention; for example, the printing press (Johann Gutenberg), the mechanical calculator (Blaise Pascal), the microscope (Anton Leeuwenhoek), smallpox vaccine (Edward Jenner), the telephone (Alexander Graham Bell), and the incandescent light bulb (Thomas A. Edison). Ask them to explain how the invention has affected our lives.

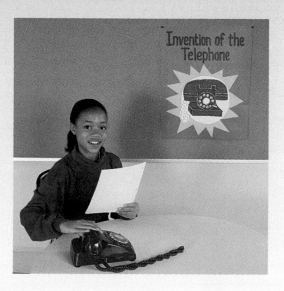

Invention of the Telephone

M I N I L E S S O N

Study Skill

Almanac

Teach/Model

Ask students what printed sources they use to find factual information.

- reference books, nonfiction articles in magazines, dictionaries, encyclopedias, atlases, newspapers, and almanacs

Ask volunteers to define or describe an almanac.

- An almanac is a book of facts published yearly. Almanacs contain short articles, lists, and tables and charts providing information and facts on a whole range of subjects. Some almanacs are specialized, like the *Farmer's Almanac*—which includes calendars, weather forecasts, tide charts, and astronomical information—or a sports almanac.

Practice/Apply

Students can use almanacs to find out more about inventions and the history of aviation.

 SKILL FINDER Full lesson, p. H4

Building Background

Have students complete this sentence stem in their journals:

My mind is like a _____.

(Samples: layer cake, elevator, train, chalkboard)

Encourage students to think about

- how they develop an idea and think it through
- what their mind does to absorb new information
- what kind of picture they might draw to show their mind at work

Be sure students understand what compost is: a mixture of decaying organic matter (leaves, manure, food scraps) used as fertilizer.

About the Poet

Born and raised in the American West, Gary Snyder began his career in the 1950s as a Beat poet. Since then, his poetry has combined details of nature with insight received through the practice of Zen Buddhism. Snyder won the Pulitzer Prize in 1975 for *Turtle Island.*

ON TOP *by Gary Snyder*

All this new stuff goes on top
turn it over   turn it over
wait   and water down.
From the dark bottom
turn it inside out
let it spread through, sift down,
even.
Watch it sprout.

A mind like compost.

Encourage students to read the poem silently and then listen as a volunteer reads it aloud. Let them respond freely, or offer prompts such as these:

- How exactly is a mind like compost?
- What is the *new stuff* that goes on top?
- Do you like this poem? Why or why not?
- Write a poem in which you compare your mind to something.

DAVID MACAULAY

THE WAY THINGS WORK

FROM LEVERS TO LASERS, CARS TO COMPUTERS—A VISUAL GUIDE TO THE WORLD OF MACHINES

David Macaulay invites you to have serious fun as he uses the Great Wooly Mammoth to explain the principles behind inventions and how things work.

421

Introduce the Literature

Activating Prior Knowledge

Have students who have flown kites describe what it's like. Ask them:

- What does it feel like to try to control a kite once it's aloft? (It takes strength; you have to tug; there is a great deal of tension in the kite string from the wind force.)

Ask volunteers to explain the forces that keep a kite aloft. Encourage students to draw on the chalkboard to make their explanations clearer.

Continue by asking students to consider what would happen if

- the kite string were cut while the kite was in the air (The kite might be blown about briefly by the wind, but it would soon plummet to earth.)

- the wind died down (It would fall to earth.)

- an elephant were tied to the kite (Well, nothing would happen to the elephant!)

Introduce the Literature

MEETING INDIVIDUAL NEEDS Students Acquiring English

Vocabulary List the following words from "Flying": *mammoth, chanced upon, awning, tethered, startled, premises, launch, vertical take-off aircraft, deflects, exerts, spiral, novel, lift, thrust, drag.* Have students work together to help each other define the words they know. Encourage them to use context clues and dictionaries to make sense of words they don't know. Invite them to find synonyms for or pantomime all the words.

FLYING

ON THE ADVENT OF AIRFREIGHT

*O*ne day I chanced upon a delivery mammoth from a local awning manufacturer sighing under the weight of a large wooden frame over which was stretched a piece of canvas. Apparently waiting for its driver, the mammoth was tethered to a tree with the awning firmly secured to its back. Suddenly the wind picked up, lifting the startled beast dramatically into the sky. I noticed that as long as the wind blew and the rope between tree and mammoth held, the creature remained airborne. . .

. . .but when the wind abruptly died, the mammoth returned to the ground without ceremony, destroying not only the awning but also the manufacturer's entire premises.

HEAVIER-THAN-AIR-FLIGHT

In the struggle to overcome its not inconsiderable weight and launch itself into the air, the mammoth becomes in turn a kite, a glider and finally a powered aircraft. These are three quite different ways by which an object that is heavier than air can be made to fly.

Like balloons and airships, heavier-than-air machines achieve flight by generating a force that over comes their weight and which supports them in the air. But because they cannot float in air, they work in different ways to balloons.

Kites employ the power of the wind to keep them aloft, while all winged aircraft, including gliders and helicopters, make use of the airfoil and its power of lift. Vertical take-off aircraft direct the power of their jet engines downward and heave themselves off the ground by brute force.

The two principles that govern heavier-than-air flight are the same as those that propel powered vessels — action and reaction, and suction. When applied to flight, suction is known as lift.

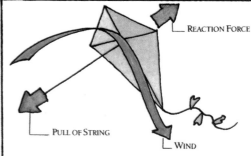

KITE

A kite flies only in a wind, and it is held by its string so that it deflects the wind downward. The wind provides the force for flight. It exerts a reaction force that equals the pull of the string and supports the kite in the air.

Discussion

- Do you think Macaulay's use of a mammoth to represent a heavier-than-air craft is a good choice? Why or why not?

- Why did the mammoth crash back to the ground?

- Why do you think that the efforts to make the mammoth fly by itself, without the aid of machines, were unsuccessful?

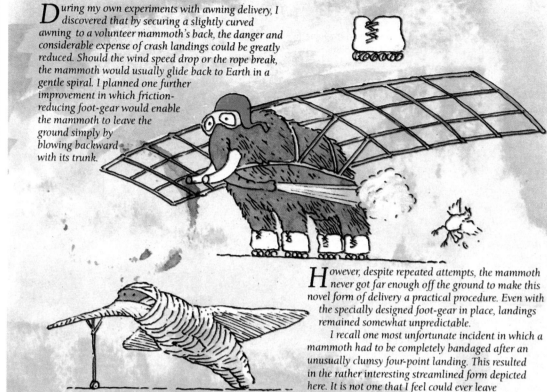

*D*uring my own experiments with awning delivery, I discovered that by securing a slightly curved awning to a volunteer mammoth's back, the danger and considerable expense of crash landings could be greatly reduced. Should the wind speed drop or the rope break, the mammoth would usually glide back to Earth in a gentle spiral. I planned one further improvement in which friction-reducing foot-gear would enable the mammoth to leave the ground simply by blowing backward with its trunk.

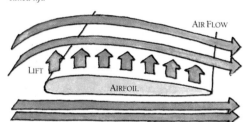

*H*owever, despite repeated attempts, the mammoth never got far enough off the ground to make this novel form of delivery a practical procedure. Even with the specially designed foot-gear in place, landings remained somewhat unpredictable.

I recall one most unfortunate incident in which a mammoth had to be completely bandaged after an unusually clumsy four-point landing. This resulted in the rather interesting streamlined form depicted here. It is not one that I feel could ever leave the ground.

AIRFOIL

The cross-section of a wing has a shape called an airfoil. As the wing moves through the air, the air divides to pass around the wing. The airfoil is curved so that air passing above the wing moves faster than air passing beneath. Fast-moving air has a lower pressure than slow-moving air. The pressure of the air is therefore greater beneath the wing than above it. This difference in air pressure forces the wing upward. The force is called lift.

GLIDER

A glider is the simplest kind of winged aircraft. It is first pulled along the ground until it is moving fast enough for the lift generated by the wings to exceed its weight. The glider then rises into the air and flies. After release, the glider continues to move forward as it drops slowly, pulled by a thrust force due to gravity. Friction with the air produces a force called drag that acts to hold the glider back. These two pairs of opposing forces — lift and weight, thrust and drag — act on all aircraft.

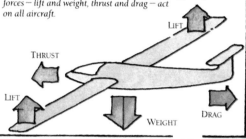

423

Instruct and Integrate **MINILESSON**

Study Skill
Using Diagrams

Teach/Model

Focus students' attention on the boxed text and diagrams on page 423. Review that a *diagram* is a drawing of something with labels identifying its parts and explaining how it works. Stress that diagrams are graphic aids that often clarify information presented in the text. Have students discuss how the diagrams of the glider and the airfoil help them understand the information in the text.

Practice/Apply

Have students work in small groups to create captioned diagrams of mechanical objects, such as a skateboard, pogo stick, or can opener. Groups can trade their work to see if their captions and diagrams make sense.

SKILL FINDER Full lesson, p. H5; Themes 2, 3, 6

Background: FYI

The *control column* might resemble a stick shift in a car, but it works more like a steering wheel.

Students Acquiring English

Vocabulary List the following words from "The Airplane": *dispenses, govern, propeller, fuselage, generated, swivel*. Have students work together to help each other understand the definitions of these words. Encourage them to use context, picture clues, and the dictionary if necessary. Invite them to find synonyms and pantomime meanings for fun and reinforcement.

THE AIRPLANE

Adding an engine to a flying machine gives it the power to dispense with winds and air currents that govern the flight of unpowered craft such as balloons and gliders. In order to steer an airplane, a system of flaps is used. These act just like the rudder of a boat. They deflect the air flow and turn or tilt the airplane so that it rotates around its center of gravity, which in all airplanes lies between the wings.

Airplanes usually have one pair of wings to provide lift, and the wings and tail have flaps that turn or tilt the aircraft in flight. Power is provided by a propeller mounted on the nose, or by several propellers on the wings, or by jet engines mounted on the wings, tail, or inside the fuselage.

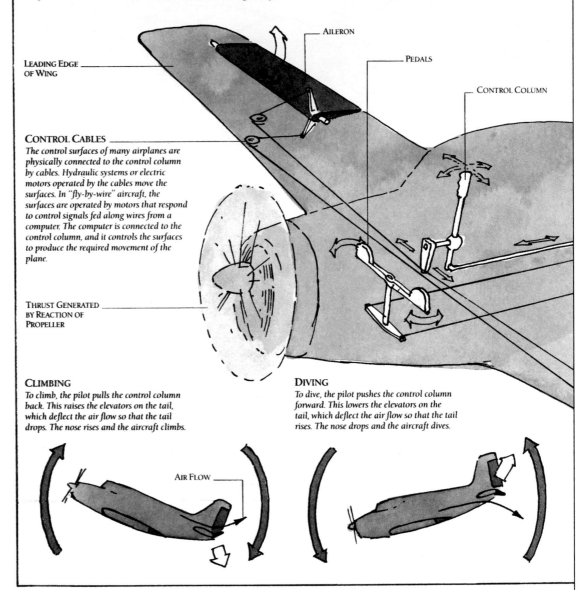

LEADING EDGE OF WING

AILERON

PEDALS

CONTROL COLUMN

CONTROL CABLES
The control surfaces of many airplanes are physically connected to the control column by cables. Hydraulic systems or electric motors operated by the cables move the surfaces. In "fly-by-wire" aircraft, the surfaces are operated by motors that respond to control signals fed along wires from a computer. The computer is connected to the control column, and it controls the surfaces to produce the required movement of the plane.

THRUST GENERATED BY REACTION OF PROPELLER

CLIMBING
To climb, the pilot pulls the control column back. This raises the elevators on the tail, which deflect the air flow so that the tail drops. The nose rises and the aircraft climbs.

DIVING
To dive, the pilot pushes the control column forward. This lowers the elevators on the tail, which deflect the air flow so that the tail rises. The nose drops and the aircraft dives.

AIR FLOW

Discussion

- Why don't airplanes need wind and air currents in order to fly?

- How does an airplane climb? Dive? How is an airplane steered and turned? Explain, using the diagrams.

- If there were no diagrams, would you have understood the information as well? Why or why not? What did you learn that surprised you?

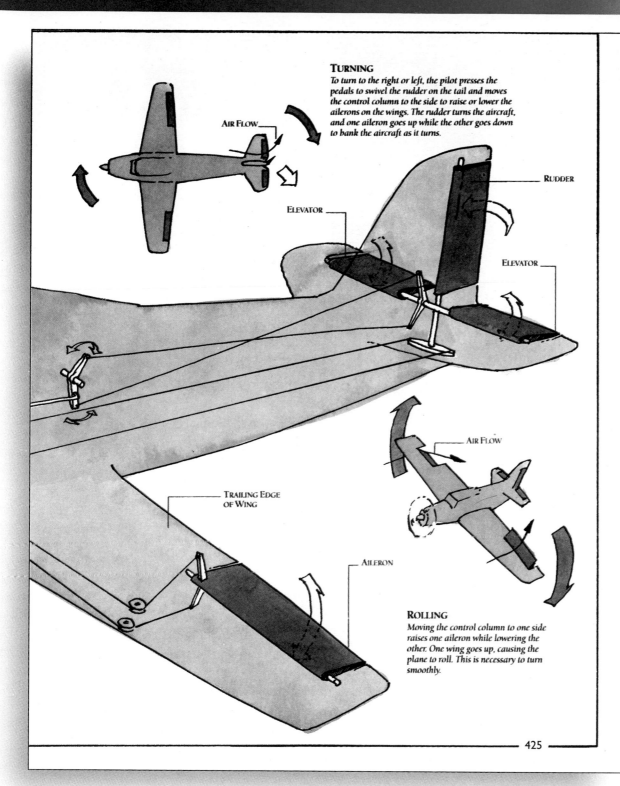

TURNING

To turn to the right or left, the pilot presses the pedals to swivel the rudder on the tail and moves the control column to the side to raise or lower the ailerons on the wings. The rudder turns the aircraft, and one aileron goes up while the other goes down to bank the aircraft as it turns.

AIR FLOW

RUDDER

ELEVATOR

ELEVATOR

AIR FLOW

TRAILING EDGE
OF WING

AILERON

ROLLING

Moving the control column to one side raises one aileron while lowering the other. One wing goes up, causing the plane to roll. This is necessary to turn smoothly.

425

Instruct and Integrate

Science

Challenge Have students research a particular heavier-than-air craft such as a satellite, the space shuttle, a helicopter, or a hot-air balloon. Invite them to prepare and present "How It Works" reports, complete with diagrams.

Social Studies

Cooperative Learning

Students can work together to collect aerial photographs, such as images of Earth taken from satellites, or post cards showing the bird's-eye view of a city. Encourage students to explain some of the uses for aerial photographs.

Music

Audio Collage What's uplifting in music? Students can collect samples of sounds of flight, or music that sends them soaring. Ask them to include anything from pieces of a symphony to sound bites recorded during a rocket launching.

Art

Model Making Have students follow the diagram of the airplane to create a three-dimensional or kinetic model of how it works.

Background: FYI

Since the beginning of film and television, animation has been a favorite fantasy medium. Many animation artists now use computers and videos to enhance their craft by combining computer graphics with the movements and facial expressions of mimes and puppeteers.

Vocabulary

Animation and *animated* come from *anima*, the Latin word for soul. Ask volunteers to define *animated*.

(lively; designed to appear alive and move in a lifelike fashion)

426

Feature Animation

"Ever since I was six years old I wanted to get into animation," Maurice Hunt explains. "I saw a clip of *Sleeping Beauty* (1959) and wanted to know how it was done."

His parents took him down to the local library where, after being given a quick lesson on the card catalogue, he devoured every book on the subject. Hunt's efforts have paid off considerably as he finds himself relaxing in his office at Turner Feature Animation, fresh off co-directing his first feature, *The Pagemaster*, for Turner Pictures Inc., in association with Twentieth Century Fox.

427

 Students Acquiring English

Vocabulary *Feature* here means a motion picture production, the kind of film that would be the main presentation at a movie theater.

Point out the idiom *fresh off*; some students may be more familiar with the term *fresh from*. Ask students what this means to them. (having just completed or just come from something)

Vocabulary

Have volunteers define or explain these words. Does anyone know where these words come from?

- **slew:** a large amount or number (first written down in American English in 1840; from the Irish Gaelic word *sluagh*, meaning *multitude*)

- **kaleidoscope:** a viewing tube in which mirrors reflect light from loose bits of colored glass contained at one end, causing them to appear as changing symmetrical designs when the tube is rotated (first written down in 1817 in modern English; from the Greek: *kalos*, beautiful, + *eidos*, form, + *scope*, to see)

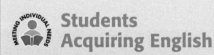

Students Acquiring English

Idiom What do students think Maurice Hunt means when he says "I want to stretch myself *to the max*. . ."(*max* is short for *maximum*, "the greatest possible degree")

The Pagemaster is the story of a young boy's journey from reality into imagination when he takes refuge in an empty library one stormy evening and is literally swept into the books and a world of fantasy.

With animation screen time clocking in at 55 minutes, compared to 16

minutes of live action, Hunt had his hands full bringing to life an animated world that had the young boy Richard, played by Macaulay Culkin, wandering through a slew of classic literary scenes ranging from *Moby Dick* to *Dr. Jekyll and Mr. Hyde*. It was the transitions from live action to animation and back that presented some of the greatest challenges for Hunt.

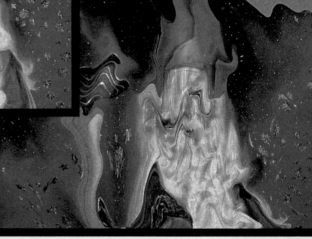

428

Background: FYI

Animation screen time refers to the part of the film that features animation only, whereas *live action* refers to the film sequences that are not animated.

"The Wave"

Young Richard has wandered into an enormous room in which a colorful mural, containing a drawing of *The Pagemaster* (played by Christopher Lloyd) and several of the other animated characters he is soon to meet, is painted on the ceiling. Paint from the mural drips down onto the unsuspecting Richard, slowly at first and then in torrents. The kaleidoscope of puddles on the floor gather to form a giant, raging wave of paint that chases Richard through the aisles of bookshelves, turning everything that it splashes against into animation — including Richard who, upon the discovery of his new state, promptly declares in half wonder, half disgust, "I'm a cartoon!"

"I want to stretch myself
    to the max, each and
every time I put pencil
    or pen
    or paintbrush to paper..."
he says with a laugh,
    ". . . or to computer!"

unt encourages young animators to obtain a command of the basics of traditional animation and a thorough understanding of the principles of creating a personality out of a human or an inanimate object.

"Personality is what appeals to people," he explains. Then one can move on to computers and combine knowledge of both worlds with limitless results.

by James Gates

429

Instruct and Integrate

Technology

Encourage students to research and report on state-of-the-art animation techniques that Maurice Hunt might have used to produce *The Pagemaster*.

Science

Holography Have students find out more about holography and virtual reality. How could these scientific discoveries contribute to animation?

✏️ Drama

Cooperative Learning

Have students work as a team to produce an animated adaptation of a scene from literature. Some students can write the dialogue, while others can work on creating the animation.

Art

Invite students to make their own kaleidoscopes.

Interact with Literature

 Home Connection

Students and members of their families may enjoy watching an animation feature on video together.

Theme Assessment Wrap-Up

Time: About 1 hour

Evaluates:

1 **Theme Concept:** Imagination makes art and technology possible.

2 **Skills:** Text Organization, Fantasy/Realism

This is a brief, informal performance assessment activity. For a more extended reading-writing performance assessment, see the Integrated Theme Test.

PERFORMANCE ASSESSMENT

Planning an Invention
LAB, p. 193

Introducing

Invite students to invent a machine. Have them use *Literacy Activity Book* page 193 to plan their project, following steps like these:

1 Plan the invention.

2 Draw and label the parts of the invention on a diagram.

3 Present the invention.

Materials
- drawing paper
- crayons
- pencils

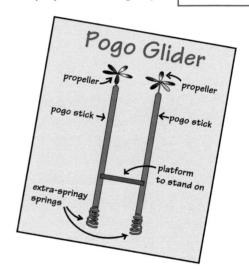

Evaluating

Students should explain whether their invention is plausible. They should address how they met the criteria on the *Literacy Activity Book* page 193 Checklist. Evaluate using the scoring rubric.

Literacy Activity Book, p. 193

Planning an Invention

Scoring Rubric

Criterion	1	2	3	4
Invents a machine to solve a problem	Concept of machine is vague or unclear	Invention is not useful or carefully planned	Invention is useful and complete	Invention is useful, creative, and carefully planned
Organizes text and diagram clearly	Text and diagram are poorly organized	Text and illustrations are partly organized	Text and illustrations are generally organized	Text and illustrations are clear and easy to follow
Distinguishes fantasy from reality	Does not distinguish fantasy/reality	Inconsistently distinguishes fantasy/reality	Generally distinguishes fantasy/reality	Gives convincing explanation of whether invention is realistic

Portfolio Opportunity

- *Literacy Activity Book* page 193
- Save students' inventions.

Choices for Assessment

Informal Assessment

Review the Informal Assessment Checklist and observation notes to determine:

- How well did students apply reading strategies?
- How well did students understand comprehension skills in the theme?
- Which selections interested students most?

Formal Assessment

Select formal tests that meet your classroom needs:

- Integrated Theme Test for Imagination at Work
- Theme Skills Test for Imagination at Work
- Benchmark Progress Test

See the *Teacher's Assessment Handbook* for guidelines on administering tests and using answer keys, scoring rubrics, and student sample papers.

Portfolio Assessment

Helping Students Make Selections for the Portfolio

Here are some ways to guide students through the selection process:

- Help students learn how to look through their work by modeling the process of portfolio selection. Make a list of reasons for choosing an item for a portfolio, such as one's best work, a favorite, or a piece that emphasizes a certain skill or type of work. Then model how to go through a work folder by selecting one or two items as candidates for the portfolio and thinking aloud about the reasons for making a selection.

- In the beginning, you may want to give your reasons for selecting a specific item. Then have students talk about their choices and reasons. Later, you might have open selection, with students completing entry slips telling why they selected certain items.

Evaluating Oral Language

To evaluate students' progress, observe their behavior at different times:

- During class discussion or small-group work, focus on one or two students. Watch for willingness to participate, ability to express ideas, clear articulation, and vocabulary development. Note your observations on the Oral Language Checklist.

- Provide structured opportunities, such as oral book reports, sharing time, or Performance Assessment presentations, when students will communicate with larger groups. Use these opportunities to help students evaluate their own oral language abilities.

- Role-playing or dramatizing a story will give students acquiring English an opportunity for interaction as they practice, and an opportunity for evaluation as they perform.

Managing Assessment

Evaluating Writing

Question: How can I evaluate students' writing?

Answer: Try these tips for evaluating writing processes, informal writing, and formal writing.

- Use the Writing Process Checklist to record observations of students as they engage in the stages of the writing process. Discuss the process with students, as needed.

- Use first drafts and journal writing to evaluate writing fluency. Encourage students to get their ideas on paper and not to worry about spelling, grammar, or sentence structure at this time.

- For more formal writing assessment, use the rubrics in the *Teacher's Assessment Handbook* for criteria for different types of writing. Most writing can be evaluated using categories such as purpose, organization, presentation of content, and conventions.

- When evaluating writing, identify one area of concern and concentrate on this area. Periodically collect representative samples to use in checking for growth in a general area, such as sentence clarity, word choices, ability to communicate by writing, sentence structure, or logical flow of thoughts. In this way, you will not be involved in too many different things at one time.

- As students learn usage and mechanics skills, have them keep a list of the skills. Ask them to become responsible for using these skills by referring to their checklists when they are writing for an audience.

For more information on this and other topics, see the *Teacher's Assessment Handbook*.

Celebrating the Theme

Choices for Celebrating

Write a Resolution

Have students write one-to-four-paragraph resolutions about how they will better use their imaginations. Suggest ideas such as these:

- "exercising" my imagination
- ways to use my imagination
- things I wish I could do
- myself as an artist

Mind Shots

Gary Snyder pictures it as compost; Norton Juster pictures it as a fantasy highway full of surprises. Have students make visual representations of their imaginations, complete perhaps with labels of the various parts. An attic? A roller coaster? A barn? An ocean? The possibilities are limitless. Let them have fun.

See the **Teacher's Resource Disk** for theme-related **Teacher Support Material**.

Self-Assessment

Have students meet in small groups to compare and discuss their Selection Connections charts (*Literacy Activity Book,* pp. 147–148). Ask groups to discuss questions such as the following:

- What did you learn about imagination, invention, and art in this theme?
- What questions do you still have about imagination and creativity?
- How has this theme helped you better understand and appreciate the power of your own imagination?

Inventors' Day

Have students plan and present a three-part celebration of the Spirit of Invention. It can include:

- presentations about famous inventors such as Thomas Edison, Igor Sikorsky, or Gertrude Rogallo
- displays of their own inventions, such as the original toys from the activity on page 332H
- any relevant products from the activities throughout this theme

Suggest that they invite another class or parents and relatives to share in the celebration.

Gertrude Rogallo perfected the hang glider in 1948

Thomas Edison invented 1093 patents; more than any other individual

Igor Sikorsky invented the helicopter

Glossary

Some of the words in this book may have pronunciations or meanings you do not know. This glossary can help you by telling you how to pronounce those words and by telling you the meanings with which those words are used in this book.

You can find out the correct pronunciation of any glossary word by using the special spelling after the word and the pronunciation key that runs across the bottom of the glossary pages.

The full pronunciation key opposite shows how to pronounce each consonant and vowel in a special spelling. The pronunciation key at the bottom of the glossary pages is a shortened form of the full key.

Full Pronunciation Key

Consonant Sounds

b	bib	l	lid, needle	th	thin
ch	church	m	mum	th	this
d	deed, milled	n	no, sudden	v	valve
f	fife, phase, rough	ng	thing	w	with
g	gag	p	pop	y	yes
h	hat	r	roar	z	zebra, xylem
hw	whoop	s	sauce	zh	vision, pleasure,
j	judge	sh	ship, dish		garage
k	kick, cat, pique	t	tight, stopped		

Vowel Sounds

ă	pat	îr	dear, deer, pier	ŭ	cut
ā	pay	ŏ	pot	ûr	urge, term,
âr	care	ō	toe		firm, word,
ä	father	ô	caught, paw, for		heard
ĕ	pet	oi	noise	ə	about, item,
ē	bee	ŏŏ	took		edible, gallop,
ĭ	pit	ōō	boot		circus
ī	pie, by	ou	out	ər	butter

Stress Marks

Primary Stress ′   Secondary Stress ′

bi•ol•o•gy [bī ŏl′ ə jē]   bi•o•log•i•cal [bī′ə lŏj′ ĭ kəl]

Pronunciation key © 1994 by Houghton Mifflin Company. Adapted and reprinted by permission from *The American Heritage Student Dictionary*.

A

amputate
The word *amputate* comes from the Latin word *amputāre*, meaning *"to cut around."* The word is derived from the Latin *ambi-*, *"around"* + *putāre*, *"to cut."*

ab•sent•ly (**ăb′**sənt lē) *adv.* As if lost in thought or not paying attention: *The director stared* **absently** *out the window during the performance.*

ab•sorbed (ab **sôrbd′** or ab **zôrbd′**) *adj.* Completely interested in; taken up by: *The scientist was* **absorbed** *in her work, finding little time to eat or sleep.*

anxiously
Derived from *anxious*, which comes from the Latin *ānxius*, from the verb *angere*, *"to torment."* Tormenting people will cause them to behave anxiously.

ab•stract (ăb **străkt′** or **ăb′**străkt′) *adj.* **1.** In art, concerned with designs or shapes that do not show a person or thing realistically: *The* **abstract** *painting uses bold colors and irregular shapes to express feelings of love.* **2.** Hard to understand: *The speaker's topic was so* **abstract** *that the students could not follow his arguments.*

ac•cu•ra•cy (**ăk′** yər ə sē) *n.* Exactness; precision: *The new computer allows for much greater* **accuracy** *in our test results.*

amateur

autopsy
The word *autopsy* developed from the Greek word *autopsia*, which means *"seeing for oneself."*

am•a•teur (**ăm′** ə tûr or **ăm′** ə chŏŏr′ or **ăm′** ə tyŏŏr′) *n.* A person who does something without professional training or skill: *The leaky roof had been put on by* **amateurs.**

am•pu•tate (**ăm′**pyŏŏ tāt′) *v.* **am•pu•tat•ed, am•pu•tat•ing, am•pu•tates.** To cut off a part of the body, especially by surgery: *The man's foot was badly infected and had to be* **amputated.**

anx•ious•ly (**ăngk′**shəs lē or **ăng′**shəs lē) *adv.* **1.** In an uneasy or worried way. **2.** In an eager and earnest way: *We waited* **anxiously** *for the recess bell to ring.*

ar•chae•ol•o•gist or **ar•che•ol•o•gist** (är′kē **ŏl′**ə jĭst) *n.* A person who studies the remains of past human activities: *For years, the* **archaeologist** *had sifted through the ruins of the ancient city.*

ar•ti•fact (**är′**tə făkt′) *n.* A handcrafted object of archaeological interest: *Pottery, jewelry, and other* **artifacts** *were exhibited in the museum.*

au•top•sy (**ô′**tŏp′ sē) *n., pl.* **au•top•sies.** A medical examination of a dead body to determine the cause of death: ***Autopsies*** *were performed on the disaster victims.*

B

bound•a•ry (**boun′**də rē or **boun′**drē) *n.* A border or limit; a dividing line that marks the area of a place: *The stone wall marks the northern* **boundary** *of their property.*

boy•cott (**boi′**kŏt′) *v.* **boy•cott•ed, boy•cott•ing, boy•cotts.** To join together to refuse to buy or use something, usually as part of a protest: *By* **boycotting** *tuna fish, students helped bring about dolphin-safe tuna fishing.*

C

cal•cu•la•tion (kăl′kyə **lā′**shən) *n.* The result of using mathematics to determine an answer: *Our* **calculations** *enabled us to improve the design of the aircraft.*

cam•paign (kăm **pān′**) *n.* Activity organized to reach a certain social, political, or commercial goal: *The group organized a* **campaign** *to save the lives of dolphins.*

can•yon also **ca•ñon** (**kăn′**yən) *n.* A steep and narrow valley cut into the earth by running water: *The walls of the* **canyon** *rose high above the river banks.*

chafe (chāf) *v.* **chafed, chaf•ing, chafes.** To irritate or make sore by rubbing: *The constant* **chafing** *of his poorly darned sock had caused a blister.*

chron•ic (**krŏn′** ĭk) *adj.* Lasting for a long time or recurring frequently: *A* **chronic** *infection kept him indoors for most of the winter.*

claim (klām) *v.* **claimed, claim•ing, claims.** To state to be true: *Dan* **claimed** *that he had found the gold necklace in the locker room.*

claus•tro•pho•bic (klô′ strə **fō′** bĭk) *adj.* Suffering from claustrophobia; uncomfortably confined or hemmed in: *Working in the crawlspace, the plumber began to feel* **claustrophobic.**

cleft (klĕft) *n.* A crack or crevice: *My compass fell into a* **cleft** *in the rock.*

com•po•si•tion (kŏm′pə **zĭsh′**ən) *n.* The arrangement of parts forming a whole, as in an artistic work: *The artist rearranged the objects on the table to form a more pleasing* **composition.**

boycott
Charles Boycott was an English land agent in Ireland. When Boycott refused to lower rents on his properties, his tenants refused to work for or trade with him. Their action came to be known as **boycotting.**

calculations
The ancient Romans used small pebbles to help them add and subtract. From the Latin word for pebble, calculus, we get **calculate** *and* **calculations.**

claustrophobic
Claustrophobic *is derived from the word claustrophobia, which developed from the Latin word claustrum, meaning "enclosed place," plus the Greek word phobos, meaning "fear."*

cleft

condensed

contamination

data

con•dense (kan děns′) v.
**con•densed, con•dens•ing,
con•dens•es.** To change from a gas
to a liquid or solid: *Water vapor in
the air* **condenses** *and falls as rain.*

con•fi•dent (kŏn′fĭ dant) adj.
Feeling or showing confidence; being
sure of oneself: *Since I have studied
all weekend, I am* **confident** *that I
will pass the test.*

con•sol•i•date (kan sŏl′ĭ dāt′) v.
**con•sol•i•dat•ed,
con•sol•i•dat•ing,
con•sol•i•dates.** To combine into
one; unite: *We can* **consolidate** *the
various study groups into one research team.*

con•tam•i•nate (kan tăm′a nāt′)
v. **con•tam•i•nat•ed,
con•tam•i•nat•ing,
con•tam•i•nates.** To pollute or
make unclean by contact or mixture:
The spilled oil **contaminated** *the sea-
water, killing animal and plant life.*

con•vey (kan vā′) v. **con•veyed,
con•vey•ing, con•veys.** To express
or communicate; to make known:
My images and stories **convey** *my
feelings about my family.*

corpse (kôrps) n. A dead body:
*The police photographer took pic-
tures of the* **corpse** *before the'
ambulance arrived.*

cringe (krĭnj) v. **cringed,
cring•ing, cring•es.** To shrink back
in apprehension or fear: *The old dog*
cringed *when the child reached out
to pet it.*

cul•ture (kŭl′char) n. The arts,
beliefs, customs, and institutions of a
people at a particular time: *Many*
cultures *were represented in the
festival.*

cur•rent (kûr′ant or kŭr′ant) n.
1. A mass of liquid or gas that
moves: *Ocean* **currents** *are like
giant rivers flowing through the sea.*
2. A flow of electricity through a
wire: *When a tree fell across the
wires, the maintenance crew had to
turn off the current to make the repairs.*

D

da•ta (dā′ta or dăt′a) pl. n.
Information used as the basis for a
decision: *Scientists are collecting and
analyzing* **data** *on the effects of the
new safety procedures.*

de•ceit•ful (dĭ sēt′fal) adj.
Deceptive; intentionally misleading:
The company was fined for using
deceitful *claims in their
advertisements.*

ă pat / ā pay / âr care / ä father / ĕ pet / ē be / ĭ pit / ī pie / îr pier / ŏ pot / ō toe

630

---

de•com•pose (dē′kam pōz′) v.
**de•com•posed, de•com•pos•ing,
de•com•pos•es.** To decay, rot,
or break down: *The leaves had*
decomposed *and were ready to
be used for compost.*

ded•i•cate (dĕd′ĭ kāt′) v.
**ded•i•cat•ed, ded•i•cat•ing,
ded•i•cates.** To devote oneself
fully to something: *Our team was*
dedicated *to baseball; we did all we
could to improve our game.*

de•fi•ant•ly (dĭ fī′ant lē) adv.
Boldly resistant; in open opposition:
The crew **defiantly** *ignored the cap-
tain's orders.*

de•ject•ed•ly (dĭ jĕk′tĭd lē)
adv. In a depressed or low-spirited
way: *After losing the tennis match,
the boy walked home* **dejectedly.**

des•o•late (dĕs′a lĭt) adj.
1. Having few if any inhabitants; de-
serted: *The* **desolate** *island has few
visitors.* **2.** Having little if any vegeta-
tion; barren: *They passed through a*
desolate *stretch of desert.* **3.** Dreary
or dismal: *Rain and fog made this a*
desolate *day.*

de•spair (dĭ spâr′) v. **de•spaired,
de•spair•ing, de•spairs.** To lose
all hope: *Delayed by the storm, we*
despaired *of arriving before the
program ended.*

des•per•ate (dĕs′par ĭt) adj.
Driven by a great need for something: *My paper was due, and I was*
desperate *for a good idea.*

dig•ni•ty (dĭg′nĭ tē) n. Poise and
self-respect: *Although she had been
falsely accused, she responded with*
dignity.

di•men•sion (dĭ mĕn′shan or
dī mĕn′shan) n. **1.** The measure-
ment of a length, width, or thick-
ness: *The dimensions of the window
are 2 feet by 4 feet.* **2.** Aspect; ele-
ment: *The old photographs in the
book add a human* **dimension** *to
the historical narrative.*

dis•may (dĭs mā′) n . A sudden loss
of confidence or courage: *The child
was filled with* **dismay** *when he realized he was lost.*

dis•per•sion (dĭ spûr′zhan or dĭ
spûr′shan) n. The process of scat-
tering in different directions: *Wind
and waves cause the* **dispersion** *of
spilled oil into an ever-wider area.*

dis•tinc•tive (dĭ stĭngk′tĭv)
adj. Serving to identify or set apart
from others: *We recognized the
whale by her* **distinctive** *white
stripe.*

ô paw / oi boy / ou out / ŏŏ took / ōō boot / ŭ cut / ûr urge / th thin / th this /
hw whoop / zh vision / a about

631

---

distract
The word distract *was first spelled in
Middle English as* dis-
tracten. *It comes from
the Latin word* distra-
here, *meaning "to
pull away."*

drift

evidence
Evidence *developed
from the Latin*
ēvidēns, *which means
"obvious." The word
passed through the
Late Latin, Old
French, and Middle
English languages be-
fore becoming part of
modern English.*

dis•tract (dĭ străkt′) v.
**dis•tract•ed, dis•tract•ing,
dis•tracts.** To draw the attention
away from something: *The driver
lost control of the car when he was*
distracted *by a wasp.*

dis•trust (dĭs trŭst′) v.
**dis•trust•ed, dis•trust•ing,
dis•trusts.** To doubt or lack confidence in; suspect: *Though we had
helped him many times, he still*
distrusted *our motives.*

drift (drĭft) v. **drift•ed, drift•ing,
drifts. 1.** To be carried about on a
current of water or air: *The canoe*
drifted *downstream as we rested.*
2. To move slowly and aimlessly:
She **drifted** *from one task to
another.*

E

em•balm•er (ĕm bäm′ar) n. A
person who treats a dead body with
preservatives in order to prevent
decay: *The good condition of
the mummy is the result of skilled*
embalmers.

es•sen•tial (ĭ sĕn′shal) adj. Of
the greatest importance; necessary:
In basketball, teamwork is **essential.**

es•ti•mate (ĕs′ta māt′) v.
**es•ti•mat•ed, es•ti•mat•ing,
es•ti•mates.** To calculate roughly or
approximately: *I* **estimate** *that the
meeting will last for about an hour.*

et•i•quette (ĕt′ĭ kĕt′ or ĕt′ĭ kĭt) n.
Rules or customs of proper or formal
behavior: *Good* **etiquette** *requires
you to thank someone for a gift or a
favor.*

e•vap•o•rate (ĭ văp′a rāt′) v.
**e•vap•o•rat•ed, e•vap•o•rat•ing,
e•vap•o•rates.** To change from a
liquid into a vapor or gas: *In the hot
sun, the water* **evaporates** *and the
pavement dries.*

evi•i•dence (ĕv′ĭ dans) n. Thing or
things that help one make a judgment or come to a conclusion:
Stone axes and arrowheads were
evidence *that hunters had used the
cave in ancient times.*

ex•e•cute (ĕk′sĭ kyōōt′) v.
**ex•e•cut•ed, ex•e•cut•ing,
ex•e•cutes. 1.** Perform: *The dancer*
executed *the move gracefully.* **2.** To
put (usually a criminal) to death: *The
prisoners had been told that they
would be* **executed,** *but they were
rescued.*

ă pat / ā pay / âr care / ä father / ĕ pet / ē be / ĭ pit / ī pie / îr pier / ŏ pot / ō toe

632

---

ex•pec•ta•tion (ĕk′spĕk tā′shan) n.
1. The act of expecting. **2.** Anticipation: *The profits from
the bake sale exceeded our*
expectations.

ex•po•sure (ĭk spŏ′zhar) n. Being
subjected to a situation, condition, or
influence: *The campers'* **exposure**
*to the wilderness helped them ap-
preciate the hardships of pioneer life.*

F

fa•tal (fāt′l) adj. **1.** Capable of
causing death: *Many* **fatal** *accidents
occur on our highways.* **2.** Causing
ruin or destruction; disastrous: *The
player's lack of attention proved to
be* **fatal** *to the team.*

G

gla•cier (glā′shar) n. A large mass
of ice that accumulates over many
years and moves very slowly down
mountains and through valleys:
Glaciers *can be thought of as huge
rivers of ice.*

grav•i•ta•tion•al (grăv′ĭ tā′shan
al) adj. Having to do with the force
that attracts and tends to draw together any two objects in the uni-
verse: *The* **gravitational** *pull of the
moon causes ocean tides.*

H

her•i•tage (hĕr′ĭ tĭj) n. Something
other than property that is passed
down from one generation to the
next: *An interest in quilts and quilt-
making was part of the family's*
heritage.

hes•i•tate (hĕz′ĭ tāt) v.
**hes•i•tat•ed, hes•i•tat•ing,
hes•i•tates.** To pause or wait briefly
due to uncertainty: *Jake* **hesitated,**
*trying to decide how to answer the
question.*

hu•mil•i•ate (hyōō mĭl′ē āt′) v.
**hu•mil•i•at•ed, hu•mil•i•at•ing,
hu•mil•i•ates.** To lower the pride,
dignity, or self-respect of a person:
I was **humiliated** *by their rude
laughter.*

glacier

ô paw / oi boy / ou out / ŏŏ took / ōō boot / ŭ cut / ûr urge / th thin / th this /
hw whoop / zh vision / a about

633

manuscript
The original meaning of manuscript was "a book written by hand." The word comes from two Latin words: manus, "hand," and scriptūs, "written."

I

im•age (**ĭm'ĭj**) *n.* The concept of a person or thing that is held by the public, especially as a result of advertising or publicity: *The ads create the **image** of a company that cares about the environment.*

im•pul•sive•ly (ĭm pŭl'sĭv lē) *adv.* In a sudden or wishful manner: *A few minutes after meeting the Smiths, we **impulsively** invited them to dinner.*

in•stinct (ĭn'stĭngkt') *n.* **1.** An inborn pattern of behavior that is characteristic of a given species: *Birds' **instincts** determine their migration patterns.* **2.** A powerful impulse: *We didn't know what made the noise, but our **instincts** told us to run at once.*

in•te•grate (ĭn'tĭ grāt') *v.* **in•te•grat•ed, in•te•grat•ing, in•te•grates.** To bring all the parts together to form a whole: *The scientists will **integrate** the separate findings into one report.*

L

leg•a•cy (lĕg' ə sē) *n., pl.* **leg•a•cies.** Something handed down to those who come later; heritage: *The great writers and artists of the past have left us a rich cultural **legacy**.*

M

man•u•script (măn'yə skrĭpt') *n.* The form of a book, paper, or article as it is submitted for publication: *I had sent **manuscripts** to several magazines before one was finally published.*

med•i•ta•tion (mĕd'ĭ tā'shən) *n.* The process of thinking deeply and quietly: *A few moments of quiet **meditation** will help you relax before a game.*

me•di•um (mē'dē əm) *n., pl.* **me•di•a** (mē'dē ə) or **me•di•ums. 1.** A technique, material, or means of expression used by an artist: *Although his paintings were famous, sculpture was his favorite **medium**.* **2.** A substance in which scientists grow bacteria or other microorganisms: *The researcher learned that some organisms grow best when the **medium** is kept evenly moist.*

å pat / ā pay / âr care / ä father / ĕ pet / ē be / ĭ pit / ī pie / îr pier / ŏ pot / ō toe

634

---

mi•crobe (mī'krōb') *n.* A disease-causing organism so small that it can only be seen under a microscope; a bacterium: *Microbes living in the sea slowly break down spilled oil.*

mim•ic (mĭm'ĭk) *v.* **mim•icked, mim•ick•ing, mim•ics. 1.** To copy or imitate another's speech, expression, or gesture: *The monkey **mimicked** the trainer's gestures.* **2.** To imitate in order to ridicule or mock: *He **mimicked** his brother's whining tone of voice.*

mis•treat (mĭs trēt') *v.* **mis•treat•ed, mis•treat•ing, mis•treats.** To treat badly or inconsiderately; to abuse: *We should never **mistreat** animals.*

mod•er•ate (mŏd'ə rāt') *v.* **mod•er•at•ed, mod•er•at•ing, mod•er•ates.** To make less extreme: *The warm Gulf Stream **moderates** our climate in winter.*

mum•my (mŭm'ē) *n., pl.* **mum•mies.** The body of a person or animal embalmed after death: *Inside the ancient coffin was a **mummy**.*

N

non•cha•lant•ly (nŏn'shə länt'lē) *adv.* In an unconcerned or carefree way: *Not wanting to seem embarrassed, I strolled **nonchalantly** down the street.*

O

o•blige (ə blīj') *v.* **o•bliged, o•blig•ing, o•blig•es.** To make indebted or grateful: *I am **obliged** to you for your hospitality.*

P

pa•tient•ly (pā'shənt lē) *adv.* Enduring trouble, hardship, annoyance, or delay in a calm and uncomplaining manner: *For over three hours, I waited **patiently**.*

per•sist (pər sĭst') *v.* **per•sist•ed, per•sist•ing, per•sists.** To insist or repeat stubbornly: *Although I wouldn't answer her question, she **persisted** in asking it.*

Phar•aoh also **phar•aoh** (fâr'ō or fā'rō) *n.* A king of ancient Egypt: *The **pharaoh** was seated on a throne of gold.*

microbes

microbes
Microbes are tiny life forms. The word comes from the Greek: mikro-, "small" and bios "life."

mimic
The word mimic has retained its basic meaning through the centuries. It comes from the Greek words mimikos and mimos, meaning "imitator" or "mime."

patiently
The Latin verb form patiēns meant "enduring." So if you are patient, you endure pain, boredom, or other difficulty without complaining.

ô paw / oi boy / ou out / ŏŏ took / ōō boot / ŭ cut / ûr urge / th thin / th this / hw whoop / zh vision / ə about

635

---

prehistoric

procrastinate
The Latin word for "tomorrow" is cras. The prefix pro- means "forward." When it comes to doing some jobs, lots of us pro-crastinate — put something forward until another day.

rapids

prac•ti•tion•er (prăk tĭsh'ə nər) *n.* A person who practices an occupation, sport, or other activity: *Several **practitioners** of judo were working out in the gym.*

pre•his•tor•ic (prē'hĭ stôr'ĭk or prē hĭ stôr'ĭk) *adj.* Of or belonging to a time before things or events were recorded in writing: *Scientists have discovered the remains of many **pre-historic** animals, such as dinosaurs.*

pres•en•ta•tion (prĕz'ən tā'shən or prē'zan tā'shən) *n.* Something presented to an audience, such as a lecture, demonstration, or performance: *In my **presentation** to the class, I explained several causes of water pollution.*

pre•serve (prĭ zûrv') *v.* **pre•served, pre•serv•ing, pre•serves.** To keep in perfect or unchanged condition or form; to maintain intact: *The museum specimens were **preserved** in climate-controlled rooms.*

prim•i•tive (prĭm'ĭ tĭv) *adj.* Basic, simple, or crude: *The child drew several **primitive** stick figures to represent his family.*

pri•va•cy (prī'və sē) *n.* Seclusion; freedom from the presence or view of others: *I wrote my journal entry in the **privacy** of my room.*

pro•cras•ti•nate (prə krăs'tə nāt') *v.* **pro•cras•ti•nat•ed, pro•cras•ti•nat•ing, pro•cras•ti•nates.** To put things off until later; to delay: *Because of her constant **procrastinating**, the job was never finished.*

pros•pect (prŏs'pĕkt') *n.* Something expected or foreseen: *I was encouraged by the **prospect** of warm weather and good company.*

pro•test (pra tĕst' or prō'tĕst') *v.* **pro•test•ed, pro•test•ing, pro•tests.** To express strong objections to (something), as in a formal statement or public demonstration: *People **protested** the killing of dolphins by tuna boats.*

public relations (pŭb'lĭk rĭ lā'shanz) *pl. n.* (used with a singular verb). The art or science of establishing and promoting a favorable relationship with the public: *To improve **public relations**, the company invited the townspeople to tour the new plant.*

R

rap•id (răp'ĭd) *n.* A part of a river where water flows swiftly over a steep descent in the riverbed. Usually used in the plural: *The hikers de-*

å pat / ā pay / âr care / ä father / ĕ pet / ē be / ĭ pit / ī pie / îr pier / ŏ pot / ō toe

636

---

*cided not to cross the river because of the dangerous **rapids**.*

rav•en•ous•ly (răv'ə nas lē) *adv.* Greedily; in an extremely hungry manner: *The crew ate **ravenously** at the end of the long shift.*

re•as•sur•ance (rē' ə shōōr'ans) *n.* The act of restoring confidence: *My teacher's positive words gave me the **reassurance** that I needed to finish the story.*

re•lieve (rĭ lēv') *v.* **re•lieved, re•liev•ing, re•lieves.** To free from pain, worry, or distress: *The medicine will **relieve** her discomfort.*

re•sign (rĭ zīn') *v.* **re•signed, re•sign•ing, re•signs.** To give up or quit one's job or position: *The officer will **resign** from duty next week.*

re•sort (rĭ zôrt') *v.* **re•sort•ed, re•sort•ing, re•sorts.** To have recourse; to turn on or to for help: *I could not reach him by telephone, so I had to **resort** to writing a letter.*

re•vi•sion (rĭ vĭzh'ən) *n.* A new or edited version of a piece of writing: *After many **revisions**, the author was finally satisfied with her story.*

rid•i•cule (rĭd'ĭ kyōōl') *n.* Words or actions intended to cause laughter at or scorn of a person or thing: *His silly antics earned the **ridicule** of his classmates.*

ro•tate (rō'tāt) *v.* **ro•tat•ed, ro•tat•ing, ro•tates.** To turn on or around an axis or center: *The earth **rotates** once every 24 hours.*

ru•in (rōō'ĭn) *n.* The remains of something that has been destroyed or has fallen apart from age. Often used in the plural: *The explorers discovered the **ruins** of an ancient city.*

S

sa•cred (sā'krĭd) *adj.* Revered as a religious symbol, object, or place: *Archaeologists study **sacred** objects to learn about ancient religions.*

sar•coph•a•gus (sär kŏf'ə gas) *n. pl.* **sar•coph•a•gi** (sär kŏf'ə jī') or **sar•coph•a•gus•es.** A stone coffin, often inscribed with words or ornamented with sculpture: *The ancient **sarcophagus** found at the burial site weighed several tons.*

ravenously
The word raven-ously comes from the French raviner, meaning "to take by force." This French word came from the Latin rapina, meaning "plunder."

ridicule
Ridicule comes from the Latin words ridiculum, meaning "joke," and ridiculus, meaning "laughable." The Latin word was used by the French before becoming part of English.

ruin

ô paw / oi boy / ou out / ŏŏ took / ōō boot / ŭ cut / ûr urge / th thin / th this / hw whoop / zh vision / ə about

637

sheer

seep (sēp) v. **seeped, seep•ing, seeps.** To pass slowly through a small opening; to leak: *Cold air was seeping in under the door.*

sheer (shîr) adj. Extremely steep; almost perpendicular: *We had to climb down a sheer cliff to reach the river.*

shroud (shroud) n. The cloth used to wrap a body for burial: *The king's body had been wrapped in a shroud of fine linen.*

sig•nif•i•cance (sĭg nĭf′ĭ kans) n. **1.** Importance: *We understood the significance of the court's decision.* **2.** Implied meaning: *Although she said nothing, we grasped the signif-icance of her frown.*

stabilize
This came from the Latin word stabilis, "firm," which traveled through Old French to become the English stable and stabilize. The Latin stabulum, "standing place," is the source of the other English mean-ing of stable: "the place where domestic animals stand."

site (sīt) n. The place where some-thing was, is, or will be located: *This was the site of the original court-house.*

skirt (skûrt) v. **skirt•ed, skirt•ing, skirts.** To pass around something rather than across or through it: *The runners skirted the large puddle in the path.*

slink

slink (slĭngk) v. **slunk** or **slinked, slink•ing, slinks.** To move in a quiet and stealthy way: *I saw the cat slinking toward the birds that were hopping about under the tree.*

som•ber•ly (sŏm′bar lē) adv. **1.** In a melancholy manner: *"I really miss my old home," he said somberly.* **2.** Seriously; gravely: *The honor guard filed somberly onto the stage, carrying their flags.*

sta•bi•lize (stā′ba līz′) v. **sta•bi•lized, sta•bi•liz•ing, sta•bi•liz•es.** To hold steady; to make stable or firm: *The new tail helped stabilize the glider during turns.*

sup•press (sa prĕs′) v. **sup•pressed, sup•press•ing, sup•press•es.** To hold back or keep in: *The student suppressed his re-lief when the bell rang just as the teacher called on him to answer.*

sur•vey (sar vā′ or sûr′vā′) v. **sur•veyed, sur•vey•ing, sur•veys.** To inspect or study carefully: *Scientists are surveying the harbor to see how many different types of fish live there.* —n. (sûr′vā′). A de-tailed study or investigation: *The survey lists every type of fish in the bay.*

sus•pi•cion (sa spĭsh′an) n. The act of suspecting something on little evidence or without proof: *Her sus-picions were aroused when she saw that the dog would not look at her directly.*

à pat / ā pay / âr care / ä father / ĕ pet / ē be / ĭ pit / ī pie / îr pier / ŏ pot / ō toe

638

---

sys•tem•at•ic (sĭs′ta măt′ĭk) adj. Done in an orderly, step-by-step way: *A systematic check of every wire led the electricians to the problem.*

tar•get•ed (tär′gĭt ĭd) adj. Identified as the person or group in-tended to be influenced by an action or event: *The targeted group was young women, and the ads were aimed at them.*

tech•nique (tĕk nēk′) n. An estab-lished method or procedure for ac-complishing a task: *Researchers are working to develop new 'tech-niques' for preventing disease.*

te•di•ous (tē′dē as) adj. Tiresome because slow, dull, or long; boring: *Computers are now used to carry out complicated and tedious mathe-matical calculations.*

tomb (tōōm) n. **1.** A place of bur-ial; a grave. **2.** A chamber or vault for the burial of the dead: *Many beauti-ful objects were buried with the king in his tomb.*

tomb

tour•na•ment (tōōr′na mant or tûr′na mant) n. A contest in which players compete in a series of games or matches: *I won two of my three matches in the karate tournament.*

tra•di•tion (tra dĭsh′an) n. A set of customs or practices handed down from generation to genera-tion: *We follow our family tradition and attend a reunion each summer.*

trail•head (trāl′hĕd′) n. The place where a trail or path begins: *The hikers gathered at the trailhead to form teams and distribute supplies.*

tournament
In the Middle Ages, French knights en-joyed torneiement, a sport in which they used swords and lances to knock each other off their horses. Fortunately, most tournaments today aren't so rough!

un•ex•pect•ed•ly (ŭn′ĭk spĕk′tĭd lē) adv. In a way that is not expected; without warning; suddenly: *The answer to my question came unexpectedly in a dream.*

tradition
The word tradition comes from the Latin tradere, which means "to hand over, deliver, or entrust."

veer (vîr) v. **veered, veer•ing, veers.** To swerve or change course or direction: *She veered sharply to avoid running into the bicycle.*

trailhead

ô paw / oi boy / ou out / ŏŏ took / ōŏ boot / ŭ cut / ûr urge / th thin / th this / hw whoop / zh vision / a about

639

---

wilderness

wil•der•ness (wĭl′dar nĭs) n. An area left in its natural condition; un-settled and uncultivated land: *The campers checked their supplies be-fore setting out to explore the wilderness.*

wist•ful•ly (wĭst′fal lē) adv. In a way full of wishful longing: *The hungry dog looked wistfully at the refrigerator door.*

wrong•do•ing (rŏng′dōō′ĭng or rŏng′doo ĭng) n. An act that is con-sidered to be unethical or immoral: *He had never cheated, and was sur-prised when the referee accused him of wrongdoing.*

à pat / ā pay / âr care / ä father / ĕ pet / ē be / ĭ pit / ī pie / îr pier / ŏ pot / ō toe

640

ACKNOWLEDGMENTS

For each of the selections listed below, grateful acknowledgment is made for permission to excerpt and/or reprint original or copyrighted material as follows:

Selections

"After the Spill," from *Oil Spills*, by Laurence Pringle. Copyright © 1993 by Laurence Pringle. Reprinted by permission of Morrow Junior Books, a division of William Morrow & Company, Inc.
"Anne of Green Gables," by Lucy M. Montgomery, adapted by Jamie Turner, from April 1987 *Plays: The Drama Magazine for Young People*. Copyright © 1987 by Plays, Inc. Reprinted by permission of *Plays: The Drama Magazine for Young People*.
From *Beardance*, by Will Hobbs. Copyright © 1989 by Will Hobbs. Reprinted by permission of Atheneum Books for Young Readers, an imprint of Simon & Schuster Children's Publishing Division.
From *Betsy Byars The Moon And I*, by Betsy Byars. Copyright © 1991 by Betsy Byars. Reprinted by permission of Julian Messner, a division of Simon & Schuster.
"Coming Here, Going There," by Katie Monagle, from *Scholastic Update*. Copyright © 1991 by Scholastic Inc. Reprinted by permission.
From *Dig This! How Archaeologists Uncover Our Past*, by Michael Avi-Yonah. Copyright © 1993 by Runestone Press, a division of Lerner Publications Company. Reprinted by permission.
Selections from *Extremely Weird Sea Creatures*, by Sarah Lovett. Copyright © 1992 by John Muir Publications. Reprinted by permission.
From *Faith Ringgold*, by Robyn Montana Turner. Copyright © 1993 by Robyn Montana Turner. Reprinted by permission of Little, Brown and Company.
"How Old Is It?" by Alison S. Brooks from *Faces* magazine. Copyright © 1991 by Cobblestone Publishing, Inc. Reprinted by permission.
"Hypothermia," by Franklyn M. Branley from February 1993 *Cricket* magazine. Copyright © 1984 by Franklyn M. Branley. Reprinted by permission of the author. Cover copyright © 1993 by Leo and Diane Dillon. Reprinted by permission of the artists.
The Iceman, by Don Lessem. Copyright © 1994 by Don Lessem. Reprinted by permission of Crown Publishers, Inc.
From *Into the Mummy's Tomb*, by Nicholas Reeves. Copyright © 1992 by Nicholas Reeves and The Madison Press Limited. Reprinted by permission of The Madison Press Limited.
From *Island of the Blue Dolphins*, by Scott O'Dell. Copyright © 1960 by Scott O'Dell. Reprinted by permission of Houghton Mifflin Company. All rights reserved.

"Joel Rubin," from *It's Our World, Too! Stories of Young People Who Are Making a Difference*, by Phillip Hoose. Copyright © 1993 by Phillip Hoose. Reprinted by permission of Little, Brown and Company.
"Joey, age fourteen," from *How It Feels to Be Adopted*, by Jill Krementz. Copyright © 1982 by Jill Krementz. Reprinted by permission of Alfred A. Knopf, Inc.
From *Last Summer with Maizon*, by Jacqueline Woodson. Copyright © 1990 by Jacqueline Woodson. Reprinted by permission of Bantam Doubleday Books for Young Readers.
From *Maniac Magee*, by Jerry Spinelli. Copyright © 1990 by Jerry Spinelli. Reprinted by permission of Little, Brown and Company, Inc.
"Meet . . . George Lucas: Setting the Scene for Adventure," from October 1992 *National Geographic World*. Copyright © 1992 by *National Geographic World*. *World* is the official magazine for Junior Members of the National Geographic Society. Reprinted by permission.
"Mummy Making: The Why and the How," from *National Geographic World*. Copyright © June 1990 by National Geographic Society. Reprinted by permission of *National Geographic World*.
"The New Wave in Feature Animation," by James Gates, from January 1995 *Animation Magazine*. Copyright © 1994 by *Animation Magazine*. Reprinted by permission.
"The No-Guitar Blues," from *Baseball in April and Other Stories*, by Gary Soto. Copyright © 1990 by Gary Soto. Reprinted by permission of Harcourt Brace & Company.
Oceans, by Seymour Simon. Copyright © 1990 by Seymour Simon. Reprinted by permission of Morrow Junior Books, a division of William Morrow & Company, Inc.
From *Pacific Crossing*, by Gary Soto. Copyright © 1992 by Gary Soto. Reprinted by permission of Harcourt Brace & Company.
From *The Phantom Tollbooth*, by Norton Juster. Copyright © 1961,1989 by Norton Juster. Reprinted by permission of Random House, Inc.
From *The Pinballs*, by Betsy Byars. Copyright © 1977 by Betsy Byars. Reprinted by permission of HarperCollins Publishers.
The Pyramids of Egypt, edited by Stella Sands, from premier issue 1992 of *Kids Discover* magazine. Copyright © 1991 by *Kids Discover* magazine. Reprinted by permission.
Quotes by di Suvero, Grooms, Oldenburg, from *The Sculptor's Eye*, by Jan Greenberg and Sandra Jordan. Delacorte, 1993.
"Rain at the Koster Dig," by Gerry Armstrong from November 1990 *Cricket* magazine. Copyright © 1990 by Gerry Armstrong. Reprinted by permission of the author.

641

CREDITS

Teacher's Handbook

TABLE OF CONTENTS

 Index

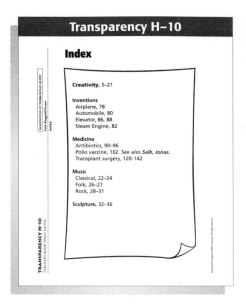

Index

Creativity, 5–21

Inventions
Airplane, 78
Automobile, 80
Elevator, 86, 88
Steam Engine, 82

Medicine
Antibiotics, 90–96
Polio vaccine, 102. *See also Salk, Jonas.*
Transplant surgery, 120–142

Music
Classical, 22–24
Folk, 26–27
Rock, 28–31

Sculpture, 32–36

INTERACTIVE LEARNING

Teach/Model

Have students share what they know about an index.

- An index is located at the end of a book.

- It lists alphabetically all the topics covered in the book.

- It gives the exact pages on which to find specific information.

Display Transparency H–10 to model using an index for students. Tell students that the transparency shows an index from a text on imagination.

Use the following Think Aloud to show students how to use an index.

Think Aloud

I want to find information about the invention of the elevator. I will look under the topic *Inventions* and scan until I find *Elevator.* I see that it is covered on page 86. A comma is between 86 and 88. Because there is no hyphen, I know that some information is on page 86 and more is on page 88, but none is on page 87. When I try to locate information about rock music, I see that information begins on page 28 and goes through 31. To find information about the polio vaccine, I check under *Medicine* first and see that it is found on page 102. The index also tells me that there is more information under the topic of *Salk, Jonas.* This makes sense; he invented the polio vaccine.

Practice/Apply

Have students locate the indexes in either their science or social studies texts. Have them work in pairs and ask each other questions about index entries for the text they have selected. Point out to students that being able to use an index will help them locate specific information about a topic without having to read the entire source carefully.

SKILL FINDER Minilesson, p. 385N

Study Skills
K-W-L

INTERACTIVE LEARNING

Teach/Model

Remind students that the K-W-L strategy will help them to better understand, organize, and remember what they read. Create the following chart on the chalkboard, leaving space for responses.

K-W-L STRATEGY		
WHAT I **K**NOW	WHAT I **W**ANT TO FIND OUT	WHAT DID I **L**EARN?

Use this chart to model the K-W-L strategy for reading an article about the Wright brothers. Fill in the chart as you go along.

Think Aloud

K– What do I know? I know that the Wright brothers made the first successful airplane, and I know that they both flew the plane on December 17, 1903.

W– What do I want to find out? I want to find out how they learned how to build an airplane. Now I know what I will look for when I read the article. Listen as I read:

The Wright brothers, Orville and Wilbur, were always fascinated by anything mechanical. Even though Orville started a printing business and Wilbur was the editor of a newspaper, they played with machines. They opened a bicycle shop where they repaired and rented bicycles, and eventually they began to build them. They became interested in flying and began putting together kites, then gliders. Their mechanical ability and their interest in flying led them to build the first airplane.

L– What did I learn? I learned that Orville and Wilbur were mechanically inclined, and even manufactured their own bicycles. What do I still want to know? The article mentions gliders and kites. Now I want to know more about how they first became interested in flying.

Practice/Apply

Have students create a K-W-L chart. Ask them to select a passage from a science or social studies text to read. Before they begin, have them fill out their charts for WHAT I KNOW and WHAT I WANT TO FIND OUT. After they read, have them complete the chart.

SKILL FINDER ▸ Minilesson, p. 405

Study Skills
Almanac

Teach/Model

An almanac is a book published once a year containing lists, charts, tables, and other information covering many different fields.

Write the following topics on the board:

- Taxes
- Astronomy and Calendar
- Entertainers
- U.S. Memorable Dates
- World History
- Area Codes and ZIP Codes
- States
- Nations
- Olympic Games

Think Aloud

If I wanted to find out how much the rate of federal income tax changed in 1993, I would find an almanac after that year and look up the topic of taxes. I would see the rate of taxation for 1993 and the two previous years. If I wanted to find out who won a gold medal in diving at the 1988 Summer Olympics, I would find an almanac after that year and look up the topic of Olympic Games.

Practice/Apply

Have students name the topics they would use to find the following information:

- the month in which there were the most meteor showers (Astronomy)
- the ZIP code for Hartford, Connecticut (ZIP Codes)
- the state bird for Louisiana (States)
- who won an Oscar for Best Supporting Actress (Entertainers)
- who ruled France in 1830 (World History)
- the main industries in Israel (Nations)

SKILL FINDER — Minilesson, p. 419N

Study Skills
Diagrams

INTERACTIVE LEARNING

Teach/Model

Tell students that a diagram is any specialized drawing, such as a cross section or a floor plan, that shows how something works or is put together. Demonstrate for students how to interpret a diagram, using a Think Aloud such as the one given.

Display Transparency H–4.

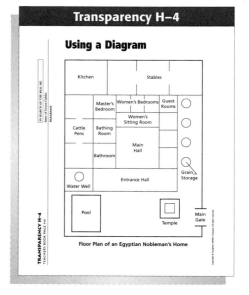

Transparency H–4

Using a Diagram

Floor Plan of an Egyptian Nobleman's Home

Think Aloud

I can see by the caption that this is a floor plan of an Egyptian nobleman's home. The cattle pens and stables were actually part of the grounds. Also included in the property were a pool, a well for water, and a temple. The outer wall was in the shape of a rectangle. I can read the labels to find out what each part of the house was.

Practice/Apply

Have students use the floor plan to answer questions similar to these:

- What do the labels tell about the diagram?

- Can you point out the main house inside the outer wall?

- What are some of the rooms inside the house?

- What is another feature of the property outside the house?

Have students point out different areas of the home and name them. Ask them to discuss the features that are outside the house itself but inside the outer wall.

Encourage students to find other diagrams in other textbooks or reference books. Have volunteers share their findings with the class and discuss the different kinds of information presented in each diagram.

SKILL FINDER Minilesson, p. 423

INFORMAL ASSESSMENT CHECKLIST

Record observations of student progress for those areas important to you.

- **– = Beginning Understanding**
- **✔ = Developing Understanding**
- **✔+ = Proficient**

Student Names

The Phantom Tollbooth

Reading									
Responding									
Comprehension: Fantasy/Realism									
Writing Skills: Writing Instructions									
Word Skills: Homophones									
Spelling: Plurals of Words Ending with *f*									
Grammar: Principal Parts of Regular/Irregular Verbs									
Listening and Speaking									

Faith Ringgold

Reading									
Responding									
Comprehension: Noting Details									
Writing: Writing a Biographical Sketch									
Word Skills: Word Roots *graph, ven*									
Spelling: Plurals of Words Ending with *o*									
Grammar: Adjectives									
Listening and Speaking									

The Moon and I

Reading									
Responding									
Comprehension: Author's Viewpoint									
Writing Skills: Elaborating with Adjectives									
Word Skills: Word Roots *scrib/script, port*									

INFORMAL ASSESSMENT CHECKLIST

Record observations of student progress for those areas important to you.

− = **Beginning Understanding**
✔ = **Developing Understanding**
✔+ = **Proficient**

Student Names

The Moon and I (continued)									
Spelling: The Prefixes *dis-, mis-, ex-*									
Grammar: Comparing with Adjectives									
Listening and Speaking									
Reading-Writing Workshop									
The Wright Brothers									
Reading									
Responding									
Comprehension: Text Organization									
Writing Skills: Answering an Essay Question									
Word Skills: Absorbed Prefixes									
Spelling: The Prefixes *per-, pre-, pro-*									
Grammar: Avoiding Double Negatives									
Listening and Speaking									
Performance Assessment									
General Observation									
Independent Reading									
Independent Writing									
Work Habits									
Self-Assessment									

Audio-Visual Resources

Adventure Productions
3404 Terry Lake Road
Ft. Collins, CO 80524

AIMS Media
9710 DeSoto Avenue
Chatsworth, CA
91311-4409
800-367-2467

Alfred Higgins Productions
6350 Laurel Canyon
Blvd.
N. Hollywood, CA
91606
800-766-5353

**American School
Publishers/SRA**
P.O. Box 543
Blacklick, OH
43004-0543
800-843-8855

Audio Bookshelf
R.R. #1, Box 706
Belfast, ME 04915
800-234-1713

Audio Editions
Box 6930
Auburn, CA 95604-6930
800-231-4261

Audio Partners, Inc.
Box 6930
Auburn, CA 95604-6930
800-231-4261

Bantam Doubleday Dell
1540 Broadway
New York, NY 10036
212-782-9652

Barr Films
12801 Schabarum Ave.
Irwindale, CA 97106
800-234-7878

Bullfrog Films
Box 149
Oley, PA 19547
800-543-3764

Churchill Films
12210 Nebraska Ave.
Los Angeles, CA 90025
800-334-7830

Clearvue/EAV
6465 Avondale Ave.
Chicago, IL 60631
800-253-2788

Coronet/MTI
108 Wilmot Road
Deerfield, IL 60015
800-777-8100

Creative Video Concepts
5758 SW Calusa Loop
Tualatin, OR 97062

**Dial Books for Young
Readers**
375 Hudson St.
New York, NY 10014
800-526-0275

Direct Cinema Ltd.
P.O. Box 10003
Santa Monica, CA 90410
800-525-0000

**Disney Educational
Production**
105 Terry Drive,
Suite 120
Newtown, PA 18940
800-295-5010

Encounter Video
2550 NW Usshur
Portland, OR 97210
800-677-7607

Filmic Archives
The Cinema Center
Botsford, CT 06404
800-366-1920

**Films for Humanities and
Science**
P.O. Box 2053
Princeton, NJ 08543
609-275-1400

Finley-Holiday
12607 E. Philadelphia St.
Whittier, CA 90601

Fulcrum Publishing
350 Indiana St.
Golden, CO 80401

G.K. Hall
Box 500, 100 Front St.
Riverside, NJ 08057

HarperAudio
10 East 53rd Street
New York, NY 10022
212-207-6901

Hi-Tops Video
2730 Wiltshire Blvd.
Suite 500
Santa Monica, CA 90403
213-216-7900

Houghton Mifflin/Clarion
Wayside Road
Burlington, MA 01803
800-225-3362

Idaho Public TV/Echo Films
1455 North Orchard
Boise, ID 83706
800-424-7963

Kidvidz
618 Centre St.
Newton, MA 02158
617-965-3345

L.D.M.I.
P.O. Box 1445,
St. Laurent
Quebec, Canada
H4L 4Z1

Let's Create
50 Cherry Hill Rd.
Parsippany, NJ 07054

Listening Library
One Park Avenue
Old Greenwich, CT
06870
800-243-4504

Live Oak Media
P.O. Box 652
Pine Plains, NY 12567
518-398-1010

Mazon Productions
3821 Medford Circle
Northbrook, IL 60062
708-272-2824

Media Basics
Lighthouse Square
705 Boston Post Road
Guilford, CT 06437
800-542-2505

MGM/UA Home Video
1000 W. Washington
Blvd.
Culver City, CA 90232
310-280-6000

Milestone Film and Video
275 W. 96th St.,
Suite 28C
New York, NY 10025

Miramar
200 Second Ave.
Seattle, WA 98119
800-245-6472

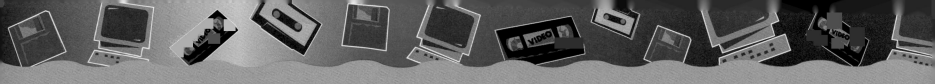

Audio-Visual Resources *(continued)*

National Geographic
Educational Services
Washington, DC 20036
800-548-9797

The Nature Company
P.O. Box 188
Florence, KY 41022
800-227-1114

Philomel
1 Grosset Drive
Kirkwood, NY 13795
800-847-5575

Premiere Home Video
755 N. Highland
Hollywood, CA 90038
213-934-8903

Puffin Books
375 Hudson St.
New York, NY 10014

Rabbit Ears
131 Rowayton Avenue
Rowayton, CT 06853
800-800-3277

Rainbow Educational Media
170 Keyland Court
Bohemia, NY 11716
800-331-4047

Random House Media
400 Hahn Road
Westminster, MD 21157
800-733-3000

Reading Adventure
7030 Huntley Road,
Unit B
Columbus, OH 43229

Recorded Books
270 Skipjack Road
Prince Frederick,
MD 20678
800-638-1304

SelectVideo
7200 E. Dry Creek Rd.
Englewood, CO 80112
800-742-1455

Silo/Alcazar
Box 429, Dept. 318
Waterbury, VT 05676

Spoken Arts
10100 SBF Drive
Pinellas Park, FL 34666
800-126-8090

SRA
P.O. Box 543
Blacklick, OH
43004-0543
800-843-8855

Strand/VCI
3350 Ocean Park Blvd.
Santa Monica, CA 90405
800-922-3827

Taliesin Productions
558 Grove St.
Newton, MA 02162
617-332-7397

Time-Life Education
P.O. Box 85026
Richmond, VA
23285-5026
800-449-2010

Video Project
5332 College Ave.
Oakland, CA 94618
800-475-2638

Warner Home Video
4000 Warner Blvd.
Burbank, CA 91522
818-243-5020

Weston Woods
Weston, CT 06883
800-243-5020

Wilderness Video
P.O. Box 2175
Redondo Beach, CA
90278
310-539-8573

BOOKS AVAILABLE IN SPANISH
Spanish editions of English titles referred to in the Bibliography are available from the following publishers or distributors.

Bilingual Educational Services, Inc.
2514 South Grand Ave.
Los Angeles, CA
90007-9979
800-448-6032

Charlesbridge
85 Main Street
Watertown, MA 02172
617-926-5720

Children's Book Press
6400 Hollis St., Suite 4
Emeryville, CA 94608
510-655-3395

Childrens Press
5440 N. Cumberland Ave.
Chicago, IL 60656-1469
800-621-1115

Econo-Clad Books
P.O. Box 1777
Topeka, KS 66601
800-628-2410

Farrar, Straus, & Giroux
9 Union Square
New York, NY 10003
212-741-6973

Harcourt Brace & Company
6277 Sea Harbor Drive
Orlando, FL 32887
800-225-5425

HarperCollins
10 E. 53rd Street
New York, NY 10022
717-941-1500

Holiday House
425 Madison Ave.
New York, NY 10017
212-688-0085

Kane/Miller
Box 310529
Brooklyn, NY
11231-0529
718-624-5120

Alfred A. Knopf
201 E. 50th St.
New York, NY 10022
800-638-6460

Lectorum
111 Eighth Ave.
New York, NY 10011
800-345-5946

Santillana
901 W. Walnut St.
Compton, CA 90220
800-245-8584

Simon and Schuster
866 Third Avenue
New York, NY 10022
800-223-2336

Viking
357 Hudson Street
New York, NY 10014
212-366-2000

Index

Boldface page references indicate formal strategy and skill instruction.

K

Knowledge, activating prior. *See* Background, building.

K-W-L Strategy, 405, H3

L

Language and usage
adjectives, 385I–385J, 396D, 396E
homophones, 345, 357E
language games, 355, 357F, 357J, 385J, 396K, 419J
spelling connection, 399E
See also Grammar and usage.

Language concepts and skills
casual language, 392
clue words/transition words, 411
colloquialisms, 352
descriptive language, 344, 396C
dialects, 385K
emotional words, 344, 349, 351
expressions, 393, 394, 412
idioms, 393, 394, 427, 428
negatives, 419I, 419J
nonverbal communication, 332F
primary language activities, 353, 356, 389C, 397, 419D
pun, 353
standard English, 385K
word play, 333C, 349, 353, 355, 356, 357, 357D, 414
word roots, 347, **357F**, 385E, 385F, 396F, 396G

Language mechanics. *See* Mechanics, language.

Learning styles, activities employing alternate modalities to meet individual, 333C, 333D, 336, 356, 356A, 363C–363D, 384, 385, 403C–403D, 418, 419. *See also* Individual needs, meeting; Reteaching.

Library, using, 338, 384, 396O, 418

Limited English proficient students. *See* Students acquiring English.

Linking literature
to art, 377
to health, 352, 374
to the media, 356, 374, 384, 416

to multicultural studies, 370, 376, 380, 382
to science, 344, 351, 368, 407, 408, 417
to social studies, 338, 348, 364, 369, 375, 376
to technology, 343
to visual literacy, 366, 368, 395, 404, 406
See also Cross-curricular activities.

Listening activities
content
to an audiotape, 332B, 356, 357, 363, 363B, 385K, 389B, 389C, 399E, 403B, 419K
to a debate, 357K
to dramatics, 357K
to interview questions, 361, 362, 389C, 396, 399B
to literature discussion, 356, 384, 418
to music, 363, 385K
to oral presentations, 332H, 357H, 370, 387, 396, 396L, 403, 419K
to oral reading, 344, 346, 351, 354, 357D, 378, 392, 396A, 396K, 396P, 399E, 414, 416. *See also* Rereading.
to a speech, 385N, 396L
in a writing conference, 395, 399B, 399D
guidelines
for listening to music, 385K
purpose
to analyze and evaluate, 340, 357K, 392, 399D
for enjoyment, 356, 357K, 363, 385K, 419K
to follow directions, 357C, 357D
to gain information, 357C, 385N
to generate questions, 357K
to recall information and details, 357K. *See also* Main idea and supporting details.
to reread, 343, 354, 357B, 383, 384, 418, 419A
for sharing, 333C, 357, 357L, 363, 363C, 368, 373, 381, 385A, 389C, 393

to think aloud, 336, 337, 343, 348, 366, 369, 376, 385A, 393, 414
to visualize, 333C, 339, 340, 385A, 385J, 385K

Literacy, expanding, 358–363, 386–389, 397–397A, 400–403, 420, 421–425, 426–429

Literary appreciation, 332G, 353, 356, 357, 382, 384, 396, 396A, 399, 418, 419. *See also* Interactive Learning; Literary devices; Literary genres; Literature, analyzing.

Literary devices
author's viewpoint, **393, 396B–396C,** 419C. *See also* Themes 5, 6.
author's voice, 392
descriptive language, 344, 396C
detail, use of, 396M. *See also* Main idea and supporting details.
dialogue, 429
exclamations, 392
humor, 353
imagery, 386
mood, 348
objectivity, 417
play on words, 333C, 349, **353,** 355, 356, 357, 357D, 414
poetic devices
language, 420
stanzas, 397, 397A
point of view, first-person, 393, 396B
repetition, 347
rhythm, 396C
similes, 393
symbols, 389C, 391, 396, 396M
tone, 399C

Literary genres
autobiography, 389A–396
biography, 363A–386
career profile, 426–429
fantasy, 333A–357
fine art, 386–389
interview, 358–363
nonfiction narrative, 403A–419
personal essay, 398–399
poetry, 397, 420
profile, 400–403
science article, 421–425

Speaking activities
form
creative dramatics, 349, 357E,
357K, 419K
description, 333C, 337, 353, 374,
385C, 389C, 417, 419K, 421,
424
discussion, 332G, 333C, 333D,
340, 352, 357, 357B, 357L,
357M, 358, 363C, 366, 376,
382, 385E, 385G, 386, 392,
393, 395, 399A, 413, 416,
419A, 422
interview, 361, 362, 389C, 396,
399B
oral presentation, 332H, 357H,
370, 387, 396, 396L, 403,
419K, 425, 429A, 429C
storytelling, 333C, 371
summary, 356, 364, 370, 376,
384, 396L, 399B, 406, 410,
416
guidelines
for presenting how-to writing
books, 396L
purpose
analyzing/evaluating literature,
357, 357B, 361
contributing information, 342,
343, 357M, 396, 406, 418,
419K, 425
explaining, 342, 343, 349, 356,
406, 418, 419N, 421, 425,
428, 429A
giving opinions, 368
making up sentences, 333D,
396K, 403D
reading with expression, 414
role-play, 344, 349, 357K, 396,
419K
self-expression, 356, 357, 384,
396, 418, 419
See also Creative dramatics;
Fluency, speaking; Modeling,
student writing; Oral,
reading.

Speech, parts of
adjectives
articles, **385I,** 385J, 399E
comparative, **396J–396K,** 399E
demonstrative, **385I,** 385J, 399E
superlative, **396J–396K,** 399E

using *more* and *most*,
396J–396K
verbs
linking, 385I
locating, 350
regular and irregular, **357I, 357J**
See also Grammar and usage;
Language and usage.

Spelling
assessment, 333D, 357H, 363D,
385H, 389D, 396I, 403D, 419H
dictionary, using, 385F
integrating grammar and spelling,
399E
integrating spelling and reading
inflected forms, 385F
plurals
of *f, ff, fe,* **357H,** 357J, 399E
of words ending with *o,*
385H, 385J, 399E
prefixes
dis-, mis-, ex-, **396I,** 396K,
399E
per-, pre-, pro-, 399E, **419H,**
419J
revising, 357J, 385J, 396K, 419J
See also Decoding skills.

Spelling, personal word lists for,
357H, 385H, 396I, 419H

Story elements/story structure
character, 339, 343, 354, 357B,
357E, 357K, 358
events, 336, 342, 343, 357A, 357B,
357K, 365
problem, 419A
setting, 336, 339, 342, 343, 348,
354, 379
solution, 419A
See also Graphic organizers, story
map; Literary devices.

Strategic reading. *See* Strategies,
reading; Vocabulary, during
reading.

Strategies, reading
Evaluate, **336, 342, 364, 374, 392,
394, 406, 410, 414**
Monitor, **392, 394**
Predict/Infer, **336, 346, 348, 364,
366**
Self-Question, **346**

Summarize, **364, 370, 376, 406,
410**
Think About Words, **336, 344, 350**

**Structural analysis, 385E–385F,
396F–396G, 419E–419F.** *See also*
Vocabulary, selection; Vocabulary,
extending.

Student self-assessment. *See*
Assessment, Self-assessment; Self-
assessment.

**Students acquiring English, activities
especially helpful for**
expressions/idioms, 352, 360, 393,
394, 427, 428
extended learning, 344, 347, 350,
360, 365
mentoring, 350, 356, 384
sharing, 371, 373, 377
vocabulary, 403C, 421, 424, 427
word meanings, 333C, 360, 363C,
412
written English, 336, 396, 397
See also Idioms.

Study skills
graphic sources
calendar, 396N
charts, 357M
diagrams, 395, 419K, **423,** 425,
H5
information skills
interviewing, 361, 362, 389C,
396
locating. *See* Study skills, reference sources.
questionnaire, writing, 389C
survey, conducting, 396
parts of a book
index, **385N, H2**
reference sources
almanac, 419N
atlas, 348
dictionary, 419N
encyclopedia, 419N
globe, 357N
magazines, reading, 384, 419N
maps, using, 357N
newspaper, reading, 384, 419N
on-line resources, 384
primary sources, **409,** 419D
reference books and pamphlets,
338, 419L, 419N